# THE PROPRIETARY STATE

## A CAPITALIST VISION *for* BETTER GOVERNANCE

ANDRIES KERPESTEIN

I have made this book free to read and distribute because I believe that the ideas in it are important to spread. Starting in the summer of 2022, writing this book has cost me more than a year during which I lived off my savings. From anyone who appreciates my work, I welcome any donation. The money would be used well, in the first place to undertake other important projects. If you would like to donate, please access the following link to transfer cryptocurrency to one of my addresses, or contact me directly.

andrieskerpestein.com/donate

Andries Kerpestein
23 August 2024

ISBN 979-8-9923807-0-5

Published by Free Cities Foundation, USA

*Market forces, not political majorities, will compel societies to reconfigure themselves in ways that public opinion will neither comprehend nor welcome.*

...

*The massed power of the nation-state is destined to be privatized and commercialized. Like all truly radical institutional change, the privatization and commercialization of sovereignty will involve a revolution in the "common sense" of the way the world is comprehended.*

— *William Rees-Mogg and James Dale Davidson, The Sovereign Individual*

# CONTENTS

## PART III PROPRIETARY DEMOCRACY

# PART I

# INTRODUCTION AND FOUNDATION

CHAPTER 1.

# INTRODUCTION

Over the centuries, political institutions have been modified to make political elites act more favourably to their subjects. In countries with the most developed institutions, this has enabled great improvements in human welfare. The economic success of Western countries, city-states like Hong Kong and Singapore, the United Arab Emirates, and other advanced jurisdictions is a testament to the power of these institutional innovations. The rule of law, well-defined and strictly enforced property rights, fair trials, the separation of powers and legal constraints on excessive government intervention in society have enabled many countries to reach new heights of prosperity. But many problems are still endemic in all systems despite these innovations, which should not be necessary. In particular the world's most prevalent political system, representative democracy, suffers from a number of afflictions regardless of who is elected with whatever goals and ideology. Inefficiency, corruption, fear-mongering and polarising demagoguery, as well as many other problems, can be found in considerable degrees in almost every representative system in the world. In recent decades, economists have shown that these 'public choice' problems are systemic.

But while the systemic problems of representative systems are well known, it is widely believed that there is simply no better alternative. In the words of Sir Winston Churchill, 'No one pretends that democracy is perfect or all-wise. Indeed it has been said that democracy is the worst form of government except for all those other forms that have been tried from time to time'.[1] In fact, it is also commonly believed that progress would invariably march in one direction – All hereditary monarchies and dictatorships would eventually be transformed into, or replaced by, representative systems.

In this book I will argue that there is in many respects a better alternative – the proprietary state. Unlike the representative system, the

1 Winston S. Churchill in a speech in parliament on 11 November 1947.

proprietary state does not suffer from the problems of public choice. If created with the right institutional arrangements, it will enable societies to achieve levels of prosperity that their representative systems currently prevent.

## THE PROPRIETARY GOVERNMENT

The central thesis of this book may seem quite radical to people who encounter it for the first time. It is that the role of the state can be fulfilled better, in many respects, by a government in the form of a profit-maximising private corporation. That is, privatising governments can lead to better governance, but only if the right institutional arrangements are made. Instead of voters with one voting right each, a government would then have shareholders with varying numbers of shares each. As certain shareholders will then naturally have significant numbers of shares in the *proprietary government*, it will not suffer from the problems of public choice – the systemic problems of representative democracy.

This book argues that this will result in the most efficient form of governance possible and, under the right conditions, in a governance more democratic than the representative system could ever provide. I believe it is appropriate to compare the potential impact of such governance by private entities, i.e. *proprietary governance*, with that of nuclear fusion.[2] In fact, it stands to have a more profound impact on the world than nuclear fusion will have. As with nuclear fusion, it will enable other changes in its wake, we are likely to see a successful pilot of it in the near future and it will require political approval. However, unlike nuclear fusion, proprietary governance can lift hundreds of millions, if not billions, out of poverty. It can bring greater harmony between different ethnic groups and greater political stability, and greatly reduce the institutional and cultural

2 Nuclear fusion, when feasible, is expected to safely provide limitless, clean and affordable energy to power entire metropoles. When it arrives, it is also expected to enable new innovations and technologies that are currently infeasible because of high energy prices.

decay that has stricken the developed world. Many people may find this difficult to imagine. Due to a widespread distrust of corporations and a dogmatic belief that representative democracy is the best and most moral form of government, it is bound to be met with suspicion and confusion. But the reader of this book will understand why such misgivings are misplaced.

## AN EMERGING MOVEMENT

In recent years, a real movement has emerged in favour of privatising jurisdictions. One variant of the proprietary jurisdiction is the so-called 'free private city', described by Titus Gebel in his book 'Free Private Cities: Making Governments Compete for You'.[3] Titus Gebel has been directly involved in setting up the most notable semi-proprietary jurisdiction to date, in Honduras.[4] The Free Cities Foundation, which he has founded, organises an annual conference that attracts hundreds of people involved in or simply enthusiastic about related initiatives, cryptocurrencies and other related themes. Meanwhile, many proponents keep in contact with each other over the internet. The rapid growth of this movement shows the momentum of the idea. If the first projects currently underway and those initiated in the coming years succeed, more governments may be persuaded to allow the establishment of proprietary jurisdictions in their territories. If the right steps are taken and fortune is on our side, this could be a pivotal moment in the history of government systems and economic development. Much care must therefore be taken to ensure that proprietary governments fulfil their potential. To this end, this book has been written not only as a positive economic text to contribute to the progress of ideas, but also to provide useful insights for those involved in the establishment and governance of proprietary jurisdictions.

3 See Gebel (2018)

4 What distinguishes the semi-proprietary jurisdiction will be explained in Section 12.1.

## AN ECONOMIC-POLITICAL THEORY

This book contains a praxeological economic theory that describes the unique features of a proprietary government, what its advantages are under the right conditions, how to ensure that these conditions are met, what its shortcomings are compared to the representative system, and how best to create it.

For the purposes of this book, it has been necessary to delve deeply into economic theory and to provide new perspectives on themes that have been addressed by economic theorists since the dawn of economics. The layman may therefore find it difficult to keep up with the book as it takes the reader along a somewhat winding road through economic theory.

Given the myriad conflicting answers to the question of what the best possible system of government would be, as given by many political figures and philosophers over the centuries, it seems unlikely that this book will prove all others wrong. I can only hope that this book will prove to be a revolutionary breakthrough for political philosophy, but I do not allow myself to believe something so unlikely. Nevertheless, if this book did not contain new ideas, I would not have written it. I believe that it contains significant innovations in political theory, and it is distinctive in that it is at its core purely positive and logical-deductive. I make no attempt to discern between right and wrong, only between true and false. Moreover, my conclusions are based on reasonable definitions and assumptions.

## SUBJECT AND PURPOSE

The main purpose of this book is to explain the feasibility and benefits of a profit-maximising, 'private' government. Above all, this book explains what happens, under certain conditions, when the state itself is a private enterprise.

If done properly, the privatisation of jurisdictions will result in the most adaptive and efficient form of government possible. It can solve many problems that affect most, if not all jurisdictions in the world. In particular the world's poorest countries, which could potentially benefit greatly from better government institutions. In this book, I explain how proprietary governance, under the conditions resulting in what in here will be called 'proprietary democracy', will deliver more value to the subjects of governments than representative governance ever could. I also describe what these conditions are, and how to ensure that they are met such that the benefits of proprietary democracy can be fully enjoyed by the masses. Furthermore, I explain the shortcomings of proprietary democracy and the relative strengths of the representative system, and explain how to get the benefits of both.

The conditions that are necessary for a proprietary government to deliver its benefits are explained, providing valuable lessons for policymakers, investors and entrepreneurs involved in the (re)emerging proprietary jurisdiction sector. The useful insights contained in this book are, among other things, how proprietary jurisdictions can be created and used for different purposes, what institutional arrangements must be made to do so and how proprietary governments can govern their jurisdictions most profitably.

The conclusions derived in this book relate to many important themes in economics and political science, including political systems and institutions, contract and property rights, entrepreneurship and consumer sovereignty and political history. As the book progresses to support its main claims, new perspectives will be cast on these old themes. I hope they will prove to be valuable contributions, whether small or large.

I believe this book will prove to be valuable to (political) economists, philosophers, historians, policymakers, investors and entrepreneurs. Together, the important conclusions in this book deliver a promising message about a form of government that can greatly improve human well-being in all corners of the world.

## STRUCTURE AND SCOPE

This book consists of four parts to be read in numerical order. Part I, consisting of Chapters 1 to 3, describes what the reader can expect to learn from this book, explains its methodology and lays a small theoretical foundation necessary for understanding the rest. In Part II, a theory is built from the ground up about cooperative action, contract, property rights and government. Starting from the notion of cooperation, it explains the functions of contract, rights and enforcement in order to explain both the inevitability and necessity of the state, as well as the possibility of consensual and voluntary subordination to a state. Building on this, it explains the defining features of the proprietary state and contains a critical review of the theory of proprietary administration developed by Spencer Heath and his grandson, Spencer Heath MacCallum.

Part III forms the core of the book. In Chapter 7, I explain the role of entrepreneurship in a cooperative society, to then explain the notion of *consumer sovereignty* and its limits. Consumer sovereignty refers to the democratic nature of a society with free cooperation, in which the consumers are the inexorable masters of the entrepreneurs. Under consumer sovereignty, entrepreneurs can only maximise profit by maximising the value they create for their customers. Placing the notion of consumer sovereignty in the context of the government-subject relationship, the notion of *proprietary democracy* is then explained as consumer sovereignty over governments – The condition under which governments can only maximise profits by satisfying the preferences of their subjects. Subsequently, several conditions required for proprietary democracy are explained in Chapter 8. Chapter 9 then addressed several benefits of proprietary democracy. Chapter 10 explains two ways in which institutional arrangements can maximise the extent to which the conditions described in Chapter 8 are satisfied, and thus maximise proprietary democracy. Chapter 11 first explains the limitations of proprietary democracy in maximising well-being and what shortcomings it has compared to representative democracy. It is subsequently explained why the 'hybrid system' introduced in Chapter 10 can deliver the 'best of both worlds' and therefore that every political system can be improved by introducing proprietary governance. Finally, the representative system is explained to be a 'governance cooperative' and why it as such suffers from the problems that would arise in any cooperative with many members: The problems of public choice. Cooperatives still have strengths over investor-owned companies in some circumstances, and this also applies to governance cooperatives relative to proprietary governments.

In contrast to the previous parts, Part IV will be partly empirical. Chapter 12 described some different variants of the proprietary jurisdiction and the hybrid system, which can be created for different contexts, and explains different ways to privatise jurisdictions as well as ways to find support for their privatisation. Chapter 13 gives an overview of historical proprietary governments and their jurisdictions. Chapter 14 explains where proprietary jurisdictions can prove themselves especially valuable today, as well as why their importance will probably grow in the future. Section 15.1, compares the proprietary government with related terminology and ideas. Section 15.2 explains why the ideas in this book refute some of the fundamental ideas in anarcho-capitalist and libertarian thought. Finally, the afterword is intended for people involved or looking to get involved with proprietary jurisdictions. In the afterword, I propose to combine our efforts to promote 'proprietarianism', while ensuring that jurisdictions are privatised properly such that proprietary democracy is maximised and the shortcomings of the proprietary system are avoided by incorporating it into hybrid systems.

As this book progresses and its main claims are supported, it also provides useful lessons along the way for proprietary governments themselves, explaining how they should approach certain aspects of their business to maximise profits.

CHAPTER 2.

# METHODOLOGY

## THE METHOD OF PRAXEOLOGY

The main method used to prove the claims in this book is the method *a priori*. The method a priori, also known as the abstract method or the 'method of praxeology', is what sets apart the Austrian School from other economic schools of thought. The Austrian School got its name in a 19th century polemic between a group of Austrian economists and the German Historical School – the *methodenstreit*, the battle of methods. The Austrian economists argued for a logical and deductive approach to economics, while the German Historical School favoured a more historical and inductive approach. In this book, the term 'Austrian School' refers to all economists who have supported its defining methodological approach since the Austrian School got its name. This definition does not depend on any other viewpoint. In some fields of economics, such as monopoly theory[5], there is no consensus among Austrian School economists. Nor is there any need for one. This book will contradict views that are today commonly held by 'the Austrians', especially relating to the state, as well as other themes about which they are divided.

The Austrian School's methodology is based on the idea that economic laws can only be proven by deriving them a priori from definitions and axioms. Carl Menger founded the Austrian School by taking this stance in the *methodenstreit*, although he was not the only or the first to do so.[6] Later, in the twentieth century, Ludwig von Mises considered economics as a part of praxeology, the abstract

5 Which this book covers in Chapter 7.

6 Mill (1844)

science of human action.[7] The method of praxeology was to be the method *a priori*, with the 'action axiom' as its general assumption. The appraisal of this method and its fundamental tenets is what binds the Austrian School together. In the words of Peter Boettke, professor of economics and philosophy at George Mason University:

> Austrian economics entails a set of methodological and analytical commitments, and these are often (but not always) correlated with certain ideological sensibilities. But not every paper or book written by an Austrian economist is Austrian economics, and many works written by those who would never identify as Austrian are actually contributions to Austrian economics in substance and style. ...[8]

Praxeology seeks an understanding of everything intrinsic to the various categories of human action. Its method is logical inference, to derive the laws of human action concerning its regularities, causes and inevitable consequences, from its intrinsic characteristics. It involves inferring one thing from another in the abstract. In a sense, praxeology relates to its subject, human action, like Euclidian geometry relates to physical objects.[9]

7 There seems to be some confusion about the term praxeology, because some use it to refer to the method while originally, and in my view correctly, it is to refer to the field of study. But the method is inextricably linked to the field of study. In the words of Roderick T. Long, "The definition [of praxeology] I've offered is the one that I think is implicit in both Mises and Rothbard: praxeology is the study of those aspects of action that can be grasped a priori. Thus the method is constitutive of the field." (Long, 2008)

8 In a tweet posted by him on Twitter on 28 November 2022. Retrieved on the same day.

9 In one instance of the methodenstreit, Carl Menger compared the empirical testing of economic laws to 'correcting the principles of geometry by measuring real objects' (Menger, 1985 [1883]), p. 70.

The praxeological method relies on a single, simple axiom – the action axiom. The action axiom can be stated as follows.

> Human beings engage in purposive behaviour—i.e. they choose which scarce means are to be more fruitfully (or economically, or rationally) employed in order to satisfy their most preferred ends. This behaviour—stemming from human free will—is what we call *action*. As long as means are scarce and wants are not fully satisfied, human beings will keep on intentionally (or purposefully) acting.[10]

While few praxeological investigations use this axiom explicitly and many use additional assumptions, all require the action axiom. It is the abstract inquiry into human action while relying on the action axiom that defines praxeology.

The reader must know that empirical methods are not rejected here. The abstract method is only assigned its rightful place as the foremost method in economics and, above all, the only method by which its laws can be discovered with certainty. This book is not fully praxeological, since it also goes into the history of the proprietary government. But praxeological conclusions will be relied on when interpreting history and speculating about the future. Most economists of the Austrian School, including myself, value the use of empirical data to show where the application of praxeology can be most fruitful, to ascertain the magnitude of phenomena and praxeologically proven relationships, and to obtain insights without certainty. Where the abstract method of praxeology does not provide answers in the social sciences, empirical methods can still be useful. In the land of the blind, one-eyed man is king.

## METHODOLOGICAL INDIVIDUALISM

The abstract method of praxeology is inextricably linked to the idea of methodological individualism. Methodological individualism is the principle that the laws of human action can only be proved in reference

[10] In the words of Fabrizio Ferrari (Ferrari, 2021).

to the individual, his actions, characteristics, circumstances, preferences and so on.[11] It follows from ontological individualism, according to which social phenomena always consist of phenomena present at the level of individuals.[12] Decisions made by groups, for example, are according to ontological individualism always exclusively made by the individuals groups consist of. Methodological individualism then follows from this, since it implies that the laws of human action are laws of individual action and therefore must be proven at the level of the individual.

The importance of methodological individualism, while today widely recognised in economics, is in political theory often overlooked. The state is often treated as a unitary actor. The purpose of this book requires focusing on the incentives of individuals, so methodological individual is important to address even if only briefly.

Many arguments have been made for and against methodological individualism, a discussion of which is beyond the scope of this book. At this point, all the reader needs to understand about methodological individualism is that I will strictly adhere to it throughout this book. I may write about groups of individuals in singular terms, such as 'the government', but not without defining this group according to the common characteristic(s) of the individuals it consists of. No group is in this book actually treated as a singular agent. A group may consist of individuals sharing preferences and acting in coordination with each other, but only individuals act. What class of individuals a group consists of will be made clear in each case. I may write in terms of groups whenever I aim to prove or explain something relating to the individuals in them, because writing in terms of the individual may be unnecessarily tedious, confusing and complicating. The meaning of what is written in this book is not in the least affected by this.

[11] In the words of Kaushik Basu: 'Methodological individualism holds that a proper explanation of a social regularity or phenomenon is grounded in individual motivations and behaviour.' (Basu, 2018).

[12] In the words of Steven M. Lukes: 'Ontological individualism is the thesis that social or historical groups, processes, and events are nothing more than complexes of individuals and individual actions.' (Lukes, n.d.).

CHAPTER 3.

# A SHORT FOUNDATION

## CHOICE AND PREFERENCE

Throughout our lives we have to make choices. Action, the choice between different ends and between different means to achieve those ends, is intrinsic to our existence. When we act, we always aim to avoid or bring about certain future states of affairs. Our species has evolved to a great degree for the purpose of action. Our bodies and mental capacities have evolved enable us to affect the world to our advantage. Some humans are in a vegetative state, coma, or still in the womb, but most of us can act. For most, life is a continuous series of situations in which we act, based on our preferences.

The ends of our actions necessarily lie in the future, because the past and the present are beyond our control and action takes time. We therefore act to affect the future – Action involves choosing one future state of affairs over another. If the future were already certain or people would not prefer one possible future state of affairs over another, they would not act. Hence, people only act when they believe to be able to affect the future and prefer one possible future state of affairs over another. They have no reason to act if these conditions are not both satisfied.

When people trade, for example, they choose to exchange goods they own for goods owned by the people they trade with. People only do this if they prefer to have some goods of another over the goods they give them in return. For example, when someone buys coffee, the seller prefers the money received, and the buyer prefers the coffee. Both value the other's good over their own.

People sometimes mistakenly conclude from this that everyone involved in a voluntary exchange benefits from it. However, people sometimes make choices that they later regret. They may prefer to engage in exchanges that will turn out to harm them. In fact, they may not even perceive to benefit. They may perceive it to be to their own detriment, but still choose to engage in the exchange for ideological reasons or to help someone else. A person's consciousness may tell them that a particular choice will be bad for them, but they may not be able to resist the urge to make that choice. All we can say is that when someone acts, he prefers to take that action and the outcome he expects to any other he thinks he can bring about. So when two people cooperate, they prefer to do so.

By the definition of preference, people would not act to bring about one state of affairs over another if they did not value that state of affairs more. Action implies preference, i.e. value.

## VALUE

Economists often use the term 'value', but they have not always agreed on its proper definition. Different theories of value have been popular. The classical economists viewed the value of a good as objective and universal depending on its utility. The labour theory of value, popularised by Marx, considered the value of a good to result from the amount of labour used to produce it. But these theories have been disproven.

The modern theory of value has won the battle and is now dominant in economics. It holds that the value of something does not depend on its objective usefulness or the amount of labour used to produce it, but on the subjective value someone attributes to it as a means to an end. And because people choose means to achieve ends, their valuation of the means is derived from their valuation of the ends. Value is subjective and differs for each person, time and place. Because everyone has unique preferences, i.e. chooses unique ends and means based on different needs, beliefs and expectations, subjective value is not an objective quantity or magnitude. Every person and every state of affairs is unique, and so are the future states of affairs considered when making choices. For instance, to prefer coffee to tea today is to prefer a different end than to prefer coffee to tea tomorrow, however similar the days may be. The same person values the same means differently in different circumstances and at different times, and different people value the same means differently in the same circumstances.

There can therefore be no absolute, objective or measurable value. Value is ordinal, not cardinal. The most that can be said about value is that it is synonymous with preference. When someone chooses a means or an end, he values it over all the alternatives he considers to be within his reach.

Furthermore, it is impossible to know what alternatives someone considers when making a decision. He may not even be conscious of it himself. Some economists believe that preferences can be inferred from choices, but this is false. To infer preferences from actions, one needs to know all the alternatives that the agent considers within his reach, as well as the precise purpose of his action. That is, both the state(s) of affairs aimed for and those intentionally avoided must be known with certainty, and this is impossible. The theory of revealed preferences is therefore simply wrong. Only physical data about actions can be observed, not the values on which actions are based. Educated guesses may be possible – Human preferences are subjective but not random and may therefore be predicted with some accuracy. But the study of preferences is not within the scope of praxeology. Praxeology takes them as given. The origins of preferences belong to the domains of psychology, neurology, biology and other fields of study.

A comparison of the various theories of value is beyond the scope of this book. At this point, the reader only needs to know what is meant by 'value'. Economists now generally accept the modern theory of value, which is the only one used in this book. They may still disagree on its application, but the idea of value as subjective and ordinal is nowadays uncontroversial.

## PARETO EFFICIENCY AND PARETO SUPERIORITY

If a course of action is Pareto efficient, no deviation from it is possible such that someone is better off without anyone else being worse off. A deviation from a course of action is a Pareto improvement if it makes some people better off without making anyone else worse off.

To understand much of this book, the following is crucial to remember. Unless stated otherwise, in this book 'Pareto …' will refer to the preferences of people regarding actions and outcomes, not to actual outcomes. And, unless stated otherwise, it will refer to the preferences of the acting individuals. This does not necessarily include everyone affected by the cooperation.

## DEFINITIONS

To avoid confusion, it is important to define certain terms before presenting the theory in the rest of the book.

As will be explained in Chapter 4, the people considered to be a government are characterised by their rights of government, a bundle of rights held over a certain territory and varying according the roles the government fulfils. One right that is typically included is the right to superior force, which allows the government to provide enforcement of rights. The right to superior force gives a government the superior ability to direct the use of force in order to interfere with the actions of people in its jurisdiction. This typically includes the right to delegate the use of force to others and to restrict access to weapons. This right allows its holder to direct the use of force within certain bounds. These bounds are normally so restrictive that the right to superior force does not give its holder much discretion – The wanton use of force is forbidden and force can only be used in limited ways under some specific circumstances.

This definition of a government is at odds with common usage because it does not consider ministers and civil servants as part of a government, but as the agents of a government. Instead, the owners of the rights of government over a territory are identified as a government. By not referring to the government's agents, the government becomes a more definite group of people. If agents would be included, where should the line be drawn? Does the government include all civil servants? If so, does it also include temporary employees of the civil service? If so, what about freelancers and suppliers? The boundary between employee and non-employee is not easily drawn. This grey area is avoided by excluding all government agents, from ministers and parliamentarians to civil service interns and freelancers.

The *jurisdiction* of a government is the territory over which its rights of government are granted by other governments and by its subjects.

Its *rights of government* are the rights by which a government governs its jurisdiction. What is typically included in the rights of government is explained in Section 4.6.

The *subjects* of the government are the people present within its jurisdiction and thereby governed by it, i.e. subject to its rights of government. They are in *subordination* to their government.

Section 5.3 explains other crucial terms, including *proprietary governance*, *proprietary government*, and *proprietary jurisdiction*.

# PART II

# COOPERATION AND THE PROPRIETARY STATE

CHAPTER 4.

# CONTRACT, CONGRUITY AND THE ROLE OF GOVERNMENT

## 4.1 A PRAXEOLOGY OF CONTRACT

People seldom act alone. While many actions seem to be undertaken solitarily without any regard to the actions of others, human actions are usually cooperative. Cooperation is ubiquitous because there are many ends that require certain actions from others to be attained. We take many actions that, to result in the ends aimed for, require others to do or not to do certain things.[13] We therefore only take these actions under the expectation that others will or will not undertake certain actions, in particular the expectation that others will not interfere with ours.

Cooperative action, or simply 'cooperation', is defined here as the actions of multiple people conditional on actions they expect from each other, which they all need to take place to attain their own ends. People cooperate when they believe that they need certain actions from each other in order to attain their own ends. They therefore make their actions conditional on the actions they expect from the people they cooperate with. Cooperation enables people to achieve ends they prefer and that are otherwise impossible.[14] They believe that they can only

[13] Choosing not to do something is action as much as choosing to do something is. All choice is action. When someone requires another 'not to take certain actions', he therefore requires that person to take a certain action, namely the action of not doing certain things.

[14] One could also say that people have an interest in cooperating when this enables them to attain the same ends at a lower cost. But this is a distinct

achieve their desired outcomes if others take or refrain from certain actions. That is, they perceive the actions to be complementary means necessary for the ends they pursue, and prefer them to take place. The ends they seek require some limitations on the actions of each participant, eliminating one or more courses of action for each participant and often leaving only one for a participant to undertake.

As defined above, cooperation may appear to be a narrow category of action. Quite to the contrary, it is ubiquitous. More actions are cooperative than might seem. Obviously, all trade is a form of cooperation. When people exchange goods, they cooperate to bring about the state of affairs in which one has the good previously owned by the other and vice versa. Both only perform their action if they expect the other to do so as well and both prefer the actions to be performed. Economists typically focus on the exchange of definite quantities of goods, but cooperative actions are a much broader category. People cooperate not only when they undertake a venture together or spend time as friends, but even a simple thing such as walking down a street is cooperative. Someone does so with the expectation that others do not have the intention to bump into him or otherwise stop him from doing so. When using public spaces, people need the actions of all other users to be limited in some ways. This particular cooperative action relies on institutions, in the form of the social custom as well as the legal obligation to allow others to traverse the public domain. Cooperation requires such institutions.

The complementarity of means implies that people participate in cooperation conditional on the expectation that others will also do their part. Each cooperating participant requires some restrictions on the actions of all others – Achieving one's goal requires other participants to fulfil their parts to the cooperation. One's course of action thus depends on the expectation that others will fulfil their parts to the cooperation. If others do not fulfil their parts to it, there is no reason to fulfil one's own. These expectations are therefore necessary for participants to cooperate. Because the actions are complementary, the expectations that other participants will fulfil their parts to

outcome since it differs from the outcome wherein one incurs a higher cost. It is therefore itself a distinct preferred end.

the cooperation are crucial.[15] These expectations are often based on realistic general assumptions about the preferences of others, as well as on institutions such as social norms and customs. But not all actions can rely with much certainty on such expectations. The necessary expectations are not always present – They must often be created. Prior communication is then necessary. To elicit the actions they desire from others, the participants must convince each other that they themselves intend to fulfil their parts.

## THE NECESSITY OF CONTRACT

Cooperative action requires expectations about the future actions of others, whether distant or immediate. Future actions are directed by future preferences, so forming these expectations involves ascertaining whether one's future preferences conflict with those of other potential participants. That is, potential participants must find out whether all will prefer to cooperate rather than pursuing an alternative – Whether the ends are compatible. Besides that, they also need to know whether their desired outcomes depend on each other's actions, i.e. whether the individually chosen means are complementary. Otherwise their participation is unnecessary. All participants must prefer the cooperation to take place and all participants must need, for attaining their own ends, certain actions from other participants. Only under these circumstances does it make sense to cooperate.

15 These requirements follow from the definition of cooperation introduced in this book. Although I might perhaps be the first to prove the ideas in here to be logically inevitable, they are not entirely new. In the words of Friedrich Hayek: '… the plans of different individuals must in a special sense be compatible if it is to be even conceivable that they should be able to carry all of them out. Or, to put the same thing in different words, since some of the data on which any one person will base his plans will be the expectation that other people will act in a particular way, it is essential for the compatibility of the different plans that the plans of the one contain exactly those actions which form the data for the plans of the other.' (Hayek, Individualism and Economic Order, 1958 [1948]), p. 38.

Cooperative action can therefore require coordination through the prior communication of preferences. This coordination is called *contract*. Contract is the communication of intentions, whether true or false, to undertake courses of action as part of a cooperation. This includes courses of action specified in the negative – Promises can also be made to forego some course of action. One contracts to induce others into performing actions that one prefers them to. When engaging in contract, one specifies what he intends to do under certain circumstances. For instance, when two people cooperate to cook a meal together, they contract with each other to determine who will cut the vegetables, who will add the seasoning and who will clean the dishes afterwards. And before two businessmen engage in a venture together, they contract over who is to be responsible for what aspect of it, how they will make decisions over the factors of production they will own together and who will receive what benefit from the venture.

Many expectations necessary for cooperation are derived from sources other than contract, such as social norms and customs and general knowledge of human preferences. Contract is therefore not always necessary. There are many people from whom we need certain constraints on their actions but with whom we do not contract because we already expect what we need from them. So not all participants to a cooperation are necessarily involved in the contracting that precedes it.

## COMPLETE INFORMATION

In a world where this information, the present and future preferred actions of other (potential) participants, is not already known by all (potential) participants, prior communication is often a crucial requirement for cooperative action. Cooperation often requires contract. If everyone knew the actions to be taken by those with whom they interact, there would be no reason to coordinate their actions. That is, if everyone had *complete information*[16], i.e. that everyone knew

[16] The definition of complete information used here corresponds to its common use, even though the term is taken from game theory and in that context may differ in its exact description from its definition here.

each other's preferred actions, contract would not be necessary for cooperation to take place.

If all participants in a coördination of action possess complete information about each other, there is no reason for any individual participant to it to communicate any intended course of action. Whatever claims one makes about his preferences, others will already know. Whenever a participant then falsely claims to intend to take some course of action, other participants know that his claim is false. There is no reason to bluff, since it will not affect anyone's beliefs or actions anyway. And whenever the intended course of action is communicated, other participants will already know. Communicating any preferences to take some actions, whether true or false, will have no effect whatsoever. The courses of action of others are independent of whatever one claims about his own. Complete information renders contract useless.

In the real world, nobody ever has complete information, so cooperative action requires its prior coordination. Since the (potential) participants in cooperative action do not have complete information, contract can affect the information on which they base their courses of action.

In short, when people do not fully know what actions other (potential) participants in a cooperation prefer to take, i.e. when people have *incomplete information*, cooperative action may require coordination in the form of communicating one's intention to fulfil one's part to the cooperation. The actions of one can only lead to their intended end if others undertake certain actions. Without the expectation that others will do so, one does not expect to attain the end he pursues by fulfilling his own part, and therefore has no reason to do so.

## CONTRACT AS ACTION TO ELICIT ACTION

Expectations about the actions of others thus affect one's own actions. Importantly, under incomplete information these expectations can be influenced by those whose actions they are about. This allows others to affect one's own actions, as one's actions are conditional on these expectations. By communicating intentions to take certain actions, one can thus impel others to take actions that one desires.

Communication is itself a form of action and is thus intended to affect the future. Clearly, the communication of intended courses of action is itself intended to move or affect others. It is unlikely to satisfy any wants by itself. In principle, whenever someone claims to intend to undertake a certain course of action, he does so to change the course of action of others. In turn, this is then expected to lead to the satisfaction of some preference. In some circumstances, contract may seem to be intended to make someone feel in a certain way. One may tell one's grandmother that one intends to visit her soon simply to make her feel good, but this is not contract. This is a unilateral communication not intended to elicit any actions. In a world with incomplete information and wherein one's actions can affect another, people communicate to influence the actions of others, even though this may not be its only effect. Some bargaining may be done for pleasure, but this can be expected to be exceptional and will not result in any actual contract being established unless the contracting parties want the according actions to be taken. What is commonly understood as contract thus corresponds with what is here defined as such.

Contracting can be described as the mutual communication of intended courses of action, true or false, to make others undertake courses of action that one believes to be beneficial to oneself. Before engaging in contract, the participants come to believe that a certain set of actions to be taken by others can be beneficial to themselves, and that those others can be made to do so by communicating the intention to undertake certain actions.

Through and before contract, the participants are led to believe that some possible courses of action are mutually complementary. This belief often originates in a mutual exploration of mutually beneficial actions, but may also result from one participant initiating the process by trying to convince others into participating. But contract also requires people to interested in discovering the intentions of others. One side of the process is the communication of some intentions, while the other is the deliberate learning of those intentions by others. Both sides of the process require each other. Without someone engaging in the process to learn about the intentions of others, there is no reason for those communicating their intentions to do so. And without someone communicating his intentions, there is no prospect of learning about any.

Contract does not only contain credible preferences, nor does it always result in the desired courses of action. Not all contracts are adhered to and not all communicated preferences are true. People do not necessarily contract with the intention to fulfil their part to it. Nor does it imply that cooperative action always brings about the expected results. Action takes place in a world of uncertainty and people are fallible. It is only to say that contract serves to induce others into taking certain actions and that it is necessary for much human cooperation.

Contract is thus a coordination of actions – It is mutual process of inducing certain actions. It merely serves to induce others to take certain actions by communicating a true or false intention to take certain actions. It is the communication of the true or false preference to fulfil one's part to a cooperative course of action in order to elicit actions from others. People only contract when they expect the intended recipients to be unaware of those preferences if they are not communicated, i.e. when they think there is incomplete information. Otherwise, the intended recipients would not adjust their own actions in response.

## COMPLETE INFORMATION ON THE PART OF THE GOVERNMENT

What is colloquially called a contract is more accurately called a *proof of contract*. By signing a proof of contract, someone declares to other participants that he will act in accordance with it. This itself is an act of contract, but the main purpose of a physical proof of contract is different. It is a means of communicating one's intended course of action not only to other participants, but in particular to those who are to enforce this promise.

The government and its agents do not have complete information about its subjects. They do not know all terms to all contracts engaged in within its jurisdiction. If they had complete information with respect to its subjects, it would not need any proof of contract to enforce what has been contracted. Proofs of contract would be useless, because the government and its agents would already know everyone's intended course of action for all possible circumstances, which includes all actions to be taken after prior contracting. Because the government and its agents do not have complete information about the government's subjects, their actions depend on the proofs of contract they are presented. In a world with incomplete information, proof of contract thus serves to induce the government and its agents to enforce what has been contracted.

Consider an imaginary world in which non-governmental participants to cooperation possess complete information about each other. As a result, they do not contract among themselves. But their complete information does not imply that they will not make a *proof* of contract. If the government needs a proof of contract to enforce the contract, contract without proof cannot rely on communicated preferences that are conditional on government enforcement. For instance, a company may promise to make a payment after a certain amount of goods has been delivered. But this communicated intention is more credible and possibly only credible if the government is expected to enforce the contract if necessary. If enforcement is not to be expected, the promise made is not credible and this coordination of action does not happen in the first place. The government's communicated intention to enforce its subjects' communicated intentions give the latter credibility. The government thereby enables mutually beneficial cooperative actions that would otherwise not take place. So even if the parties to a contract possess complete information but the government does not, proof of contract is necessary to enable certain cooperative actions.

Compare this to an imaginary world wherein the government has complete information about its subjects. In this world it precisely knows the terms of all cooperations as it knows the intentions of all its subjects. There is therefore no need for any proof of contract. Any proof of contract would be inconsequential.

## CONTRACTING WITH THE GOVERNMENT

Not all coordination happens between subjects. Governments also engage in coordination with each other and their subjects. Their laws and policies contain their communicated intended actions. Laws and policies are the terms of the contract between the government and its subjects. They are unilaterally communicated intentions to take certain actions. When the law specifies that doing something is illegal and government policy is to enforce this law, the government through this law and policy makes a commitment to punishing those who break it. In a world where everyone had complete information about the government, any false government intention communicated would be ineffectual and all true government intentions would already be known. Any publication of law or policy would not affect anybody's expectations and thus actions towards the government or each other. There would be no reason to publish any law or policy.

Obviously, a government that communicates its laws and policies believes, first, that the subjects and non-subjects (including other governments) to whom these commitments are addressed have incomplete information about it. Second, it expects to thereby affect the actions of others, and therefore expects them to find these commitments credible. By making its laws and policies known to the public, a government communicates what actions it will punish for and what it will reward. If such threats and promises are not credible, there is no reason to account for them nor to communicate them. Nor is there any reason to do so if the actions committed to are already expected. Contract, including the communication of laws and policies, only makes sense if what is communicated is credible to the intended recipient, otherwise unknown to him, and expected to affect his course of action.

In short, the same applies to everyone, including those in the role of government. Laws and policies are simply a government's terms to a contract between itself and those it cooperates with.

## SUMMARY

One person's actions often depend on those he expects from others, who can influence these expectations. Threats, promises, bargaining, and negotiation all serve this purpose.

Cooperation is a category of action characterized by the condition that every participant to it perceives to need certain actions from other participants to attain his own ends. The participants can only achieve their desired outcomes if the others fulfil their parts in the cooperation. A participant will thus only fulfil his part if he expects others to fulfil theirs too. Since we live in a world of incomplete information, cooperation often requires that such expectations are first created through contract – The mutual communication of true or false intentions to take certain actions. Other institutions such as social customs can also create the necessary expectations. But this is not always the case, which is why contract is often required for cooperation to take place.

Contract serves to convey information about one's intended courses of action to influence the actions of others. There would be no contract if there was complete information. Rights and obligations, proofs of contract colloquially called 'contracts', laws and policies are only features of a world in which people do not fully know each other's preferences and prefer to cooperate. They are tools used to induce cooperation in a world with incomplete information.

Contract is an act of communication by which people create expectations about their own actions by making claims about what they would do under certain circumstances. It only serves to induce others to take certain actions. Contracts, including laws and policies, are thus 'incentive systems' consisting of communications. By communicating to prefer to take certain actions, actions can be elicited from others. That is not to say such communication fully determines human action, but it plays a crucial role in enabling much cooperation in a world wherein people have incomplete information.

## 4.2 RIGHTS

As defined here, *rights* are the terms that contracts consist of. The process of contract establishes rights. Right are communicated preference to act in a certain way. They are constraints we put on our actions. By granting a right, someone promises to take or not to take certain actions. Often, such actions are simply to keep from interfering with certain actions to be taken by the recipient.

A right is a restriction of the actions of one or more people in a way that the holder of the right usually values. For example, a right can specify that people are not to interfere in certain actions of its holder, or that they are to do things he wants them to. By this definition, the category of rights includes all possible kinds of rights, such as property rights, use rights, economic rights and legal rights.[17]

[17] Economists use various definitions of property rights, because their proper definition is still contested. With the definition of rights used in this book, no position is taken regarding the proper definition of property rights because rights as defined in this book include all property rights according to all common definitions. This also applies to all other kinds of rights, such as legal and economic rights. All such categorisations are

Lastly, rights refer to actions. They only refer to goods when goods are involved in action, which is not necessarily the case.

### OWNERSHIP

In this book, ownership is defined as holding residual control rights, the definition originally conceived by Sanford Grossman and Oliver Hart.[18] One can own objects but also people, as they have been in most of history and still are in some places today. Nowadays, self-ownership is the norm, i.e. people own the residual control right over themselves. This allows them to decide on the use of their bodies within the bounds left by the rights of others. Like any sort of ownership, self-ownership is necessarily limited by the rights of others. We are for example not allowed to use our bodies to harm others without their consent.

### NATURAL AND INALIENABLE RIGHTS

Many ethicists have claimed that humans have 'natural' or 'inalienable' rights.[19] These claims are either normative in one way or another, referring to what rights humans ought to have according to the ethicist, or supposedly has been ordained by a god. In any case, it

---

avoided here. In my view, distinctions between different kinds of rights, such as between economic rights and legal rights or between property rights and use rights, are all arbitrary, useless and confusing.

18 Introduced in their foundational 1986 article, Grossman & Hart (1986).

19 Most notably John Locke in his Second Treatise of Government from 1689. Also, which may be relevant since I attack some ideas commonly held by anarcho-capitalists, the anarchist philosopher Lysander Spooner in his book Natural Law, from 1882. For a refutation of some ideas underpinning anarchism and a comparison of these ideas with the ideas defended in this book, see Section 15.2.

lies outside the scope of praxeology as it does not refer to anything necessarily intrinsic to any kind of human action. In this book, all rights are considered to be rights referring to actions of real human beings, not moral principles of any kind. The definition of rights used here follows from the definition of contract used in this chapter, which follows from the definition of cooperation given at the beginning. Where mutually profitable cooperation is possible and information is incomplete, the cooperating parties often need to establish rights as they are defined here.[20]

## ALIENABILITY

Rights are usually *alienable*, i.e. their owners can transfer them to others. The communicated intentions initially referring to their initial owner are then made to refer to their recipients. If they remain alienable, these recipients can then transfer them on to other people. Advanced societies, which are based on extensive cooperation, cannot function without the alienability of rights. When rights are inalienable, the scope of trade is drastically limited. Only the initial recipients of rights would be allowed to perform the actions which these rights permit, such as using the goods over which rights are established. When they find others with whom an exchange of these goods would be mutually beneficial, the inalienability of rights renders it impossible. Alienability is therefore indispensable for the allocation of resources to their most preferred ends – Without the alienability of rights, many cooperations are kept from taking place. Alienability is also crucial for people to assume the role for which they are most suited. When someone transfers rights to another, which requires alienability, the recipient thereby gains the capacity to take the actions enabled by those rights instead of the original

[20] The definition of property rights given in this book is also broad enough to include the most common definitions, such as those that refer to 'goods' or 'assets' instead of actions. What is in this book explained to apply to property rights thus also applies to property rights as commonly defined otherwise.

owner. Acquiring rights is thus what enables people to take certain actions in society, including entrepreneurial actions. People cannot become entrepreneurs without the alienability of rights. The alienability of rights is crucial if decisions, such as entrepreneurial decisions, is to be made by those most capable at it.

## EXCHANGE AS A TRANSFER OF RIGHTS

Some economists have explained trade not as the exchange of goods but of the rights established over goods.[21] But mutually beneficial trade does not only require the transfer of rights over a good, it also needs action in accordance with it. When people cooperate, they value each other's actions as these can enable or preclude the ends they pursue. Exchange is the cooperation that takes place, and the granting of rights is the contracting that precedes and enables it. Not only the granting of rights itself is valued, but also the actions that the rights serve to elicit. For instance, when someone promises to deliver goods in exchange for money, this promise itself is merely the communication that necessarily precedes the action that is valued. Making promises is itself only a valued action if it keeps those who do so from breaking them. Otherwise, people would not contract at all because it would be ineffectual. A right is not valuable by itself, it is the expected results of the according actions that people value. Certainly, exchange is a form of cooperation that as such relies on its characteristic communication – It relies on the mutual granting of rights. But it is the goods exchanged those rights refer to and if these goods were not valued, the rights over them would not be either. Communications alone are not sufficient for achieving the desired ends.

If an exchange involves illegal goods, such as drugs, it is not recognized by any government and therefore no government-granted rights are exchanged. The only rights involved are those granted by the individuals participating in the exchange. Illicit trade involves cooperation without transferring government-granted rights and vi-

[21] Such as North (2003).

olates promises made to the government not to break the law. Therefore, defining exchange as the transfer of government-granted rights cannot account for illegal cooperation or legal cooperative actions made without any promise of enforcement. Exchange does not necessarily involve government-granted rights, because some people are willing to pay for stolen or illegal goods. Exchange must account more than government-granted rights, because criminals also coordinate their actions among themselves.

People are willing to pay for goods because of their subjective use value. The ability to use them is what holds value and drives exchange. A government affects the value of a good because the ability to use it partly depends on government recognition and enforcement of rights over it, but it does not determine this value completely. Nor do rights granted by the individual parties fully determine it. It is the according acts that are the principal subject of exchange.

The value of a right comes from the ability it gives its owner to achieve an end he pursues, often involving the use of some good. This ability is greatly affected by those enforcing it. The more certain one can be that the government will effectively enforce a right, the more valuable recognized property and the rights over it become, and the less valuable illegal and stolen goods are. If two goods are identical in every respect but over only one the rights are government-recognised and effectively enforced, they will not be of equal value. The difference in value between these goods stems from the government's actions regarding it. Such a pair of goods does not exist, so the precise value stemming from the enforcement of rights can never be known. The value of enforcement can also vary over time and according to place. Sophisticated modern locks and alarms may have made enforcement less necessary and less costly, and there is not much property to protect in places where natural constraints keep people poor.

## 4.3 CONGRUITY AND MUTUALLY PREFERRED COOPERATION

In this book, the actions of someone that accord with the rights he has granted are called *congruous* and those that violate these rights are called *violative.* The requirement of congruity ensures that all contracting participants prefer the resulting actions that are specified in the contract.[22]

When people contract, they can also communicate untrue intentions. For instance, if someone agrees to supply a tonne of sugar for an upfront payment in currency, he may plan to renege after receiving the payment. This turns what was supposed to be a mutually beneficial exchange into one that benefits only one party. If the reneging participant had communicated his true intentions when the participants were contracting, the other would not have agreed. If compliance with an agreement is enforced or otherwise unavoidable, people do not express false preferences for a course of action because they would be forced to take it. Only cooperative actions that are preferred by all contracting parties are then contracted and performed. This relationship holds not only when violative action is impossible – The more costly it is to act violatively, the less reason there is to communicate false intentions when contracting.

Congruous action is thus action in accordance with what has been contracted. When action resulting from contract is congruous, it is preferred by all contracting participants. Ensuring congruity is therefore crucial for cooperation to be mutually preferred by all participants – Congruity ensures that a cooperative action is a Pareto improvement with respect to the preferences of the contracting parties. The congruity of cooperative action is necessary for an allocation of resources to their most valued ends.

Violative action, as considered here, is the exact opposite – interaction without congruity. It is the violation of rights. It lacks the explicit or tacit consent of everyone involved. When congruity is neither imposed nor inevitable, cooperation can involve actions that not all contracting participants prefer. If the risk of violative action is too high, people may refrain from cooperating at all even though cooperation is possible and everyone would prefer to do so.

22 When actions are congruous with rights, the expected outcome of a change in actions induced by contracting is a Pareto improvement for all the contracting parties. This does not refer to actual outcomes. Participants all prefer the new course of action in expectation of their imagined outcomes, but may not necessarily be satisfied with its actual consequences.

## THE NOTION OF CONGRUITY VERSUS THE NOTION OF VOLUNTARINESS

In this book, a distinction is made between violative action and congruous action. The terms 'voluntary' and 'coercive' are deliberately avoided. The Merriam-Webster Dictionary defines voluntary as 'proceeding from the will or from one's own choice or consent' and 'unconstrained by interference' and defines the verb 'coerce' as 'to compel to an act or choice' and 'to achieve by force or threat'.[23] Every enforcement of contract is thus an act of coercion and every violation of it a voluntary act. And if the use of force in a way that keeps people from acting according to their will is supposed to be coercive, then is not much more coercive than is commonly considered to be? For example, if someone wants to cross a red light while other drivers are making it impossible by crossing the road, are the other drivers not interfering with his actions by force? And what should be considered force? For instance, if one shopper buys the last of some product right before another shopper can, does he not use physical force in taking the product and preventing the other to achieve his desired end, i.e. buying the product himself?

It is inevitable that in many cases the will of one person will conflict with the will of another. One person's will may for instance be that his favourite shop gives him goods for free, but it is the shopkeeper's will that his customers pay for the goods. Voluntariness is therefore impossible to achieve completely, whether or not rights are upheld. Not everyone can get what he wants. Moreover, the idea of voluntariness in human interaction leads to problems when we consider voluntary contracts. People voluntarily bind themselves to contracts, even though they may not want to uphold these contracts later. Voluntary breaches of contract are therefore in conflict with what was voluntarily contracted. One's present voluntary actions may violate one's past will.

Coercion, the use of force to make someone do something they do not want to do[24], is inevitable even in a society where rights are fully

[23] 'Voluntary.' Merriam-Webster.com Dictionary.
'Coerce.' Merriam-Webster.com Dictionary.

[24] In the words of the Cambridge Dictionary, referred to in the reference section.

upheld. For instance, when one person tries to stab another, he coerces the other into allowing himself to be stabbed. If the other defends himself, he coerces the assailant by forcing the assailant not to stab him, against the assailant's will. In both cases, according the common definition of coercion, coercion takes place. Clearly, one would be considered justified while the other would not.

For mutually preferred cooperation to be ensured, it is inevitable that the wills of people are sometimes violated. One person's will conflicts with another's and someone's will at one time may conflict with the rights he has granted. Not only is coercion inevitable, but it is even necessary to enforce rights. The purpose of enforcing rights is therefore not to ensure that all action is voluntary. It is to ensure that it does not violate rights, i.e. that action is congruous.

Nevertheless, the notion of voluntariness has widespread appeal, especially among libertarians. But ensuring voluntariness is not only impossible, it is incompatible with upholding rights. Liberals and libertarians wrongly associate voluntariness with freedom and coercion with oppression. By the very definition of coercion, no one wants to be coerced, so voluntarism has emotional appeal. However, scrutiny of the idea shows that it is both impossible and irreconcilable with a society based on upheld rights.

Coercion is inevitable and, for a society in which cooperative actions are preferred by all participants, it is sometimes necessary. What matters is that action is congruous, not violative. That is, that it does not conflict with anyone's rights.

## CONSENT

Without prior contracting, no action can be congruous. What is congruous must be established first – It requires consent, the prior granting of rights. Without consent or the denial of it, no rights are given or denied so no action can be congruous or violative. Congruity therefore requires consent, whether explicit or tacit.

For example, if a person assaults someone and has granted no rights to his victim that he would not do so, this is not a violative action. But for interactions to be preferred by all participants, it is not enough for action to be non-violative – It must be congruous. Rights must first be granted to allow an action, i.e. consent must be given. Otherwise, the action cannot be congruous with any rights.

In principle, anything is allowed through the institution of ownership, or residual control rights, within explicit limitations. Ownership, including self-ownership, is limited insofar contracting parties wish to limit it. It therefore rare that an action is neither congruous nor violative, as it is allowed in principle and forbidden if necessary. For example, one can own a knife, but the right to use it is restricted in many ways. Within the limits set by the law and other contracts, one is free to use one's knife as one wishes.

Mutually preferred cooperations can rely on the consent of all contracting participants and are then mutually preferred when consent is given, i.e., when contracting occurs. This consent can take various forms. Most common are express consent, which is given by explicit communication, and tacit consent, which is given by acting in a certain way. But consent may not be possible in some situations, in which it must then sometimes be presumed, such as when someone is incapacitated and needs immediate medical treatment. It is then common to rely on hypothetical consent. The conditions under which consent may be presumed can be specified in advance by law. When people consent to the law, they then give consent for actions in situations in which may not be able to give or deny it. It is then no longer purely hypothetical.

Different types of consent can be seen to be on a spectrum, a 'scale of consent', with express consent at one end and express unconsent, i.e. the explicit refusal of consent, at the other. When there is neither consent nor unconsent, there is non-consent. No willingness for certain actions take place is then communicated, but no preference for them not to take place is then communicated either.[25]

The idea of tacit consent will play an important role in this book, as will be seen in Chapter 8. In my view, tacit consent is given when someone's preference to cooperate in a certain way can be derived from his actions. In law, this definition is not uncommon.[26]

[25] See, for an explanation of the scale of consent, a treatment of the role of consent in cooperation and a treatment of consent as a justification of political coercion, Bell (2011).

[26] See American Law Institute, Restatement (Second) of Torts, § 10A. St. Paul, Minnesota, U.S.A.: American Law Institute Publishers, 1965.

The requirement of consent ensures that a cooperation is mutually preferred by the contracting parties if the person giving consent only does so when he prefers that cooperative course of action to happen. Any action that is only taken when a particular course of action is preferred thus qualifies as consent to that course of action. For instance, when someone can be presumed to join a members' club only when he intends to follow its rules, he consents to the rules by joining the members' club. This definition of consent is thus consistent with the definitions given in the Restatement (Second) of Torts referred to in footnote 25.

In my view, tacit consent and express consent are equally sufficient for mutually preferred cooperations, but the latter is easier to identify and to adjudicate. In the context of the government-subject relationship, the subject can be assumed to be at least aware of the existence of the government, its laws and their enforcement. If he chooses to stay while being free to leave unless he has given up the right to leave, he thus consents to his subordination. He then prefers to subordinate himself to the government. For more on consent and congruity in the government-subject relationship, see Section 8.3.

## VIOLATIVE THREATS

Contracting can only be congruous if it is not done under the threat of violative action. Think, for example, of a contract agreed to at gunpoint. For congruity to fulfil its purpose, which is to ensure that cooperative courses of action are preferred by all contracting participants, not everything can be a term to contract.

If contracts are perfectly enforced and the contracting individuals know this, threats to violate rights are meaningless since rights cannot be violated. But if threats of violative action are credible, it becomes possible to successfully threaten someone with it. The threat is

"The word 'consent' … denote[s] willingness in fact that an act or invasion of an interest shall take place."; id. § 892(1) (1979) "Consent is willingness in fact for conduct to occur. It may be manifested by action or inaction and need not be communicated to the actor."

only made because the threatening person expects it to influence the threatened person's actions. The threatening person thus thinks his threat is credible and that the threatened person prefers the action he seeks over the violative action he is threatening with.

The purpose of contracting is to change the intended actions of others. If contracting is congruous, i.e. if it does not involve making violative threats, it results in a reassignment of rights that all participants prefer over the original assignment. All contracting participants then prefer the deviation in actions they thereby expect to bring about. But if threats to violate rights are made and affect the actions of others, not all participants necessarily prefer the deviating actions over those intended before. People then agree to a reassignment of rights because they prefer the resulting actions to the violative action, not to the congruous actions they would expect if no threat was made. The violative action is one over which they prefer the initially expected congruous actions. Violative threats therefore do not necessarily result in a Pareto improvement for contracting participants, whereas congruous contracting does.

Someone makes violative threats because he considers it necessary to impel another to take actions he prefers the other to take. If the other would prefer these actions over those originally intended, he would not need to make the threat. He could simply propose a reassignment of rights without threatening with violative actions. The threatening person thus expects that the threatened person will not prefer to take the actions desired to taking those originally intended before contracting. Thus, people threaten others to induce cooperative actions that are not preferred by all participants. Threats to violate rights undermine the purpose of congruity, which is to ensure that contracting leads only to actions that are preferred by all contracting parties.

As explained earlier, congruity is crucial to any advanced society. The prosperity of a society depends on the mutual expectation that rights will not be violated. People will only save and accumulate capital if they trust that they can keep their resources. Only then will they be willing to make efforts to improve the value of resources, to accumulate capital and to produce for sale to others. Prosperity requires congruous contracting and action that is congruous with the resulting rights.

## THE FINAL ORIGINS OF RIGHTS

But to this view, which points to the importance of congruous contracting for the resulting rights and actions, there is a possible objection. For cooperative Pareto improvements, those who hold rights must have discretion over their use and their transfer, and contracting may not involve any threats to act violatively. But the ultimate origins of what can be contracted over always lie outside the domain of congruous contracting. Over all resources, some rights have once been first established. Before property over land is transferred, for example, it is always claimed. Many things have also been acquired by sheer luck. It is not congruous contracting that has given us our talents or determined whether we were born in favourable or unfavourable conditions. Nor is it congruous contracting that established the first rights over land. On reasonable grounds, one may therefore find the initial endowment of rights wholly immoral. Moreover, much of what is owned may originally have been obtained illegitimately in violation of rights. For example, if a grandfather leaves his watch to his grandson, that itself is a congruous transfer of rights, but he may have taken that watch from a soldier's corpse one day.

But whatever the initial assignment of rights, congruous contracting only ensures that further changes in their assignment, and thereby the resulting changes in courses of action, are preferred by all rights holders involved. It is not possible to reverse the course of history, and even if it were, it may not be justifiable from a utilitarian perspective. To ensure congruity is not to ensure a just distribution of rights or resources, but to ensure that all cooperation, and thus every change in the distribution of rights and resources, is preferred by all contracting participants to it.

## SUMMARY

If someone's actions accord with the rights he has granted, they are congruous. When they violate the rights he has granted, they are violative. The congruity of actions with rights is crucial for the actions resulting from contract to be preferred by all contracting participants. When congruity is imposed or otherwise inevitable, there is no reason for anyone to falsely commit to any action. Contracting is then done truthfully, and all resulting cooperations are then Pareto improvements with respect to the preferences of the contracting participants.

The voluntariness of actions, on the other hand, is both impossible and irreconcilable with congruous cooperation. The will of one can conflict with the will of another, and violative action must be prevented by coercion.

What actions are congruous depends on the rights that have been assigned. Congruity thus requires consent – It requires the assignment of rights to allow certain actions. For almost all possible actions, rights have been assigned that make that action either congruous or violative. If a planned action is Pareto inefficient, and some people can therefore contract to change the actions taken in a way that all contracting parties prefer, they can reassign rights. For the reassignment of rights and the resulting actions to then be preferred by the contracting parties, people may not be made to agree to it by the threat of violative action. Violative threats undermine the purpose of congruity.

Under congruous contracting, all the contracting parties prefer the resulting actions to be taken. They all prefer the outcomes they thereby expect over those they would otherwise expect. For some, the resulting actions may still be morally objectionable because the initial endowment of rights does not result from congruous contracting, but for example from luck or conquest. Congruous contracting only ensures, however, that any deviation from the initial endowment of rights and resources, and from any further endowment, is preferred by the contracting parties.

## 4.4 SOCIETY AND THE POWER TO VIOLATE RIGHTS

There are two ways for a cooperation to be a Pareto improvement for the contracting participants over another course of action. Either all participants prefer all of its actions, or some participants prefer some actions while others prefer other actions, but all participants prefer the cooperation overall. In the latter case, participants accept actions that they find less preferable to get other actions that they prefer. The preferable actions are then worth accepting the less preferable actions.

In the former case, one will prefer to fulfil his part to the cooperation given that the others do so as well, but not necessarily in the latter. If all participants prefer all the actions that make up a cooperation, the contract is self-enforcing because the expectation that other participants will act in accordance with it will make one prefer to do so as well. Action is naturally congruous with such a contract, with or without enforcement. But this is not necessarily the case for the other type of cooperation. If one prefers only some of the actions as part of a cooperation, the expectation that others will act in accordance with the contract does not necessarily make one do so as well. One may prefer to violate the contract given that others do not.

In the previous section, it was explained that when actions are congruous with rights, all contracting parties prefer the resulting courses of action. Whatever the initial endowment of rights, any rearrangement of rights is then preferred by the contracting parties. All cooperation resulting from contract is then a Pareto improvement for them. But if rights can be violated at little or no cost to the violator, society breaks down. Many cooperations, as well as actions directed to enable cooperation, such as investment, then do not take place. For example, if someone cannot trust that he will be able to keep the goods he has, why should he improve their use value or make the effort to create new goods from his resources? And if a seller cannot expect buyers to pay, or if the risk of theft is too high, why should people produce to sell? Such interaction does not encourage capital accumulation or productive behaviour. Many cooperations that are Pareto improvements for their participants, as well as the investments to enable those cooperations, are then kept from happening. The congruity of actions with rights is therefore crucial for prosperity.

But humans inevitably have the ability to violate rights. They can renege on prior agreements, steal, kill and so on. If this ability did not exist, people would be more prosperous as many mutually preferred cooperations would not be precluded. Resources could then be allocated to their most preferred ends, within the limits of human knowledge and abilities.

In a society where their access to goods and services is determined by their capacity to use force instead of the value of their actions to others, people have less reason to cooperate beneficially and more reason to violate rights. In such a society, people spend vast resources protecting their belongings instead of pursuing more pleasurable ends. And the ability to freely renege on prior agreements discourages people from contracting and cooperating. Such a society is unproductive and harsh, especially for the weak.

But if people were unable to act violatively, they could only get better terms to cooperation by offering terms to cooperation in return that others prefer. People would only be able to get valuable services and resources by providing valuable services and resources, not by threats and aggression. People would have no reason to spend resources on safety and protection, leaving more resources for more pleasurable uses. They would contract to cooperate toward common ends. The strongest might not be as prosperous as they would be if they had the superior capacity to use force, but everyone else would be better off to a greater extent. Overall, prosperity would be greater.

## SOCIETY WITHOUT THE POWER TO VIOLATE RIGHTS

Imagine a world where people could voluntarily limit their power over their own bodies. A sophisticated chip to be inserted into the brain allows people to give up their ability to act violatively. Anyone, including those who benefit from their own violative actions, can insert this chip into their own brains. If done without compensation, this would deliver great benefits to everyone except those who would be more prosperous if they could violate the rights of others. As explained above, they would benefit from their ability to act violatively, but only at a cost to others exceeding the value thereby conferred to themselves.

Total prosperity is greater if rights cannot be violated, so those who expect to be the victims of violative actions are willing to pay the potential violators, for inserting the chip into their brains, a price exceeding the value captured by acting violatively. There is some compensation that potential bandits can be given for giving up their ability to violate rights, one that would satisfy both the potential bandits and their potential victims. Therefore, everyone would give up the capacity to violate rights of they could do so at a sufficiently low cost, and some people would then be compensated for doing so. Someone's subsequent endowment of property would then partly depend on his capacity to violate rights. One might argue that this endowment would therefore be immoral, but the result would be preferred by all.

If the power to act violatively could be given up at a sufficiently low cost, including the cost of bargaining and of the technology used, everyone would do so. No enforcing agency would be necessary for rights to be upheld and society could prosper in *anarchy* – It would not have to be subject to anyone's coercive power. But this possibility does of course not exist in the real world. It is possible, however, to give one group of people the superior power to use force in return for enforcing rights.[27] This group can, of course, renege on its promise to enforce rights and abuse its power. It can choose to act exactly like the rights violators would do. But violating rights wantonly without enforcing rights makes people unproductive and hostile to each other, which is not in its interests.

## THE NECESSITY OF ENFORCEMENT

Imagine a society where a person or group has the superior capacity to use force. However, they refrain from stealing wantonly or reneging on prior agreements, because this would impel others to be less productive. Instead, they only choose to enforce rights and levy taxes. As a result, people in the territory they control are motivated to be more productive. This benefits these people, but also themselves. Those who use force to enforce rights can reap more in taxes than if they would use it to steal and shirk.[28]

The enforcement role of a government is necessitated by the ability to benefit from acting violatively and itself comes with this ability.

[27] It is not argued here that governments have always originated in this way. Most jurisdictions were acquired by conquest at some point. It is only argued that a relationship between people in which some have a right to superior force can be consensual and that such an assignment of rights can be efficient.

[28] The interest of an enforcement provider to create conditions conducive to prosperity is explained well in Chapter 1. The Logic of Power. The Stationary Bandit, in Olson (2000), pp. 30-36.
Alternatively, for a paper that also explains the origins of the state and its necessity in small-scale societies, the interests of the state as a stationary bandit, its different interests under pressure (e.g. outside threats) and the benefits of representative democracy, see Olson (1993).

The ability to violate rights cannot be given up, so some people must hold the superior power to use force to enable a prosperous society. People can only be kept from violating rights by those whose coercive power is greater than theirs.

Weapons are a crucial means of coercion if others have access to them as well. And even if enforcement providers have exclusive access to weapons, weapons make them more efficient at their task. Fewer policemen are needed if they are armed.

It is not without reason that every society has a government tasked with enforcing rights and that enforcement is done with the capacity to coerce. If people could not act violatively, enforcement would be a waste of resources. It would not make anyone more prosperous as it would not influence any anyone's actions. But it does influence people's actions in the real world. Enforcement encourages congruous actions, enabling mutually preferred cooperations and thereby the allocation of resources to their most valued ends.

Many cooperations thus require some people to have a superior power to coerce, because acting violatively is inevitable. Any effective enforcement provider relies on this power. Eliminating this power will have disastrous for the prosperity of a government's subjects. Instead, it must be ensured that those with the superior power to use force, or with the ability to direct it, do not use it to violate rights but to prevent violative actions. Chapter 10 will address the institutional arrangements that can be made to this end.

## 4.5 ENFORCEMENT

### ENFORCEMENT AS A TERRITORIALLY PROVIDED SERVICE

The ability to enforce rights requires the capacity to interfere with the actions of others. It thus requires the physical capacity to constrain others in the use of their bodies. This requires proximity to them and a capacity to use force superior to theirs. The ability to enforce rights therefore always exists over a territory. When one leaves the territory over which it is held, one is no longer subject to it. This is an important fact, because it implies that benefiting from enforcement requires one to be within a certain territory and that one does so when one is in that territory.

As explained in Section 4.1, the more costly it is to act violatively, the less reason there is to communicate false intentions when contracting. In the extreme, when violative action is impossible, there is no reason to communicate false intentions at all. Enforcing rights thus discourages false contracting, i.e. communicating false intentions regarding one's actions. This leads to truthful contracting and cooperative actions that all contracting participants prefer over their alternative courses of action.

Using the power to coerce to enforce rights efficiently make those subject to it more prosperous. Enforcement is therefore a valuable service. When an enforcement provider is effective and efficient, the land over which it provides enforcement appreciates because people are then both willing and able to pay more to live there. Efficient governments often attract immigrants seeking to enjoy the prosperity they foster. It is governance that has driven millions of Latin-Americans to migrate to the United States in recent decades. Their incomes multiply instantly upon arrival[29], but their own capabilities do not change nor is the land naturally more conducive to prosperity. The prosperity of the United States is enabled by the relative effectiveness

[29] When immigrants move to another country, nothing about them usually changes, only their institutional and economic context. Meanwhile, their wages jump significantly. These findings do not only show the effect of institutions, because the wages are in the end determined by capital accumulation, which is not only affected by institutions. Savings and investment also impact the capital stock, and while good institutions can encourage these activities, cultural values can also have an effect. See Richwine (2023).

Nonetheless, institutions do have a significant effect, as shown by the disparate performance of people of equal or similar culture, race, education and work experience in different institutional contexts. An example of how large the effect of better institutions could be: A Mexican with only a high school diploma would see his wages increase 2.5-fold by moving to the U.S. See Clemens, Montenegro & Pritchett (2016).

Migrants from Bangladesh to the United States have seen their wages jump from $3800 to $19,000, a fivefold increase (Pritchett, 2018). See also Clemens, Montenegro & Pritchett (2008).

and efficiency of their governance, which fosters capital accumulation, advanced specialisation, and advanced contracting and cooperation.

Enforcement can be very profitable to provide. It contributes to a government's tax base by making its subjects more productive and increasing what they are willing to pay in taxes. The worse other governments are at governing their territories and the better it governs its own, the more people are willing to pay for being present in its jurisdiction.

## THE RIGHTS OF THE ENFORCEMENT PROVIDER

To provide enforcement consensually, the enforcement provider needs the right to direct a superior ability to coerce its subjects, called here the *right to superior force*, together with the right to enforce rights. The right to superior force is crucial in any consensual relationship between people in which some are tasked with enforcing rights. The enforcement provider cannot fulfil its role without it – Other rights are useless, or at least worth much less, without the right and capacity to enforce them. Upholding the former requires the latter. It allows the enforcement provider to order the use of force over its territory to interfere in the actions of its subjects when these are violative. In fact, the right to superior force is typically accompanied by not only the right to enforce other rights, but also the obligation to. Every functional society with many cooperating members, and thus impersonal cooperation, requires a group of people who possess a right to superior force. To achieve congruity, repeated interaction, reputation mechanisms, and informal governance are not enough.[30]

[30] In some cases, repeated interaction, reputation mechanisms and other solutions have been observed to make people act congruously. But an enforcement provider can make a big difference in a large society in which many people cooperate without much repeated interaction, membership to the same community, reputation mechanisms and so on. This contradicts the claims of some anarchists and at least casts doubt on the value of the mechanisms they support. See, for example, those explained by Edward Stringham in his book Private Governance (Stringham, 2015).

The right to superior force is essential for enforcing other rights, but also limits them. Crucially, the right to superior force includes the right to forcefully keep the superior power to order the use of force. Specifically, it or its agents need a monopoly on the weapons used or vastly superior access to them.

## AN ANALYSIS OF THE RIGHT TO SUPERIOR FORCE

In a sufficiently small society, those who provide enforcement can hold the superior capacity to use force, in particular by a superior access to weapons. But in most societies, those who have this capacity are not those who decide how it is used or who has it. The enforcement provider does not need to hold the exclusive capacity to use force. For the use of force and wielding the arms, it hires agents such as a police force and a military.

In most societies, the right to superior force does not give the ability to use force, but to direct its use through an incentive system. It thus does not involve the exclusive ownership of weapons or the right to use them. The enforcement provider only needs the rights necessary to ensure force is used to enforce rights, including his own. If the right incentives are not in place, it risks losing its position, such as when a coup d'état takes place.

## CONGRUITY FROM THE ENFORCEMENT PROVIDER

The ability to enforce rights relies on the capacity to interfere with the actions of others. It thus requires the physical capacity to use force to constrain others in the use of their bodies. Thereby, the ability to enforce rights inevitably comes with the ability to violate them. When used for enforcement, it is only used to prevent violative actions by interference or punishment. However, an enforcement provider can also potentially benefit from using this power violatively. The position of the enforcement provider can allow him to violate the rights of his subjects without fearing retaliation, but this does not hold the other way around.

This creates a problem in the relationship between the enforcement provider and his subjects that does not typically exist in other cooperative relationships. Fortunately, there are institutional solutions to this problem. The rule of law can keep those with the right to superior force and accompanying rights from using their position to violate other rights.

## 4.6 THE ROLES AND RIGHTS OF A GOVERNMENT

Imagine an entrepreneur who seeks to undertake some profitable activity that produces negative externalities[31] exceeding the profits he makes and for which he is not charged. For example, he may plan to build and operate a factory that will harm nearby towns by emitting toxic gases. The townspeople value the absence of the factory at a value exceeding its profits, so they could perhaps benefit from bargaining with the entrepreneur to buy him out. But the costs of bargaining are prohibitively high. It would require them to bargain among themselves to determine each person's contribution to a sum used to buy out the entrepreneur. Someone must also bargain on their behalf with the entrepreneur to determine the sum. Since the bargaining costs are prohibitively high, multiple polluting factories are built over time near the village. As a result, the value of local properties drop because people are moving away. The property owners thus incur large costs from the negative externalities created by the factories. But then one property owner gets an idea. He can buy all the affected properties as well as the factories to close them down, and all nearby land to prevent new factories from being built. He will reap the net value thereby created, which is the magnitude of the negative externalities eliminated minus the costs of doing so. By bringing all properties in his ownership, his interest becomes to minimise the net negative externalities created, but also to invest in local infrastructure and other public goods to make his properties appreciate. His interest is to govern his properties and invest in their surroundings to maximise the total amount of money tenants are willing to pay, minus the costs of

31 A negative externality is a cost that confers on someone other than its creator without that person's consent. Noise and air pollution are common examples.

doing so. For example, he requires tenants who wish to organise loud events to buy permits from him at high prices. Thereby, he forbids events that are not valued above the negative externalities they create, such that events are only held when they create more value than costs.

But after acquiring all the properties in the town, his enterprise has grown beyond its optimal size. He can no longer manage all properties within his jurisdiction, so he decides to sell them again. But by doing this, he risks reintroducing the problems he first aimed to solve. Property owners prefer to be subject to a regime that maximises the value of their properties. So, they buy their properties from the entrepreneur on the condition that he continues to invest in infrastructure projects, regulate the jurisdiction, and carry out other activities as before. In return, the entrepreneur obtains the right to tax all property owners or those present in the jurisdiction at a certain percentage of property value or income. To be able to adapt his governance to changing preferences and conditions, he keeps the right to change his regulations. To be able to build infrastructure, he keeps purchasing options on all properties, i.e. the right to expropriate. This arrangement of rights induces him to govern the jurisdiction such that the total of all its property values and incomes, his tax base, minus his costs, is maximised. Both the entrepreneur and the townspeople expect to benefit – The government-subject relationship is in the interests of them all.

By governing his jurisdiction, regardless of whether he owns all properties in it, he increases the total net amount of money people are willing to pay for being there. By providing public goods and regulating the interaction of tenants, he increases the value of properties more than the cost of doing so. The difference is his profit. Let us for convenience group such endeavours together as *administrative entrepreneurship*.

This example shows that most present-day government endeavours are a form of congruous cooperation and that they can add value. Both a government and its subjects can benefit from governmental involvement beyond enforcement, and for this the government is then given the rights to do so and to levy taxes.

## THE ROLES OF A GOVERNMENT

What is commonly called a government typically engages in multiple things, such as providing enforcement, common goods, regulation and adjudication, but there is no single endeavour that makes people qualify as a government. In some societies, the national government provides enforcement, while in others municipal governments do. Some governments also engage in more extensive administrative entrepreneurship than others. Every society needs enforcement and administrative entrepreneurship to prosper, but governments vary in the extent to which they provide them.

In all these tasks of government, governments use a bundle of rights that allow them to interfere in the actions of their subjects. They communicate how they intend to govern by making public the laws and policies according to which they will do so. Remember that laws and policies are the rights granted and demanded by governments. They are the terms to the government-subject contract. Governments typically have the right to change the laws as they wish, but not to break them. They have to communicate their intended conduct in advance, which they do by making their laws and policies known. If an effective system of incentives impels the government and its agents to act in accordance with its laws, there is a *rule of law*.

When governments make laws, they thereby in effect forbid or require certain actions of their subjects or themselves. When done well, they can add much value to their jurisdictions, such as when they acquire the rights to limit the creation of negative externalities, ensure the quality of products and ensure entrepreneurial competitiveness. They also typically use purchasing rights on property in their jurisdictions, i.e. the right to expropriate, to add value by building infrastructure. This relationship may be experienced as coercive, but it is not violative and for good reason. Like members' clubs and restaurants, governments in principle get to change the rules whenever they wish. If the government does not violate any rights and its subjects have the right to leave unless consensually given up, this is a purely congruous relationship. Government activities typically include building infrastructure, regulating externalities, regulating or participating in 'natural monopolies' and restricting the freedom of consumers to protect them from harm.

Prosperous countries are characterised not only by effectively enforced rights, but also by the entrepreneurial governance of their governments. It plays a leading role in any contemporary government business model and relies on the government's far-reaching right to unilaterally make the laws by which it governs its jurisdiction. But its administrative-entrepreneurial functions are no different in nature from those of other non-governmental entities. There is only a difference of degree, one of scale. Administrative-entrepreneurial functions are performed in many sectors and at many scales. They are profitable because their value exceeds their cost and they are not violative because they are done with the right to do so. For example, private communities often regulate the behaviour of their members and private land developers also provide infrastructure. Members' clubs regulate the behaviour of their members, homeowners' associations provide public goods, shopping centres regulate the aesthetics of storefronts and so on. On a small scale, a restaurant owner may regulate the behaviour of his customers. On a larger scale, gated communities regulate the behaviour of people in common areas, prohibiting things like public nudity and littering.

Not only can administrative entrepreneurship, with its unpopular components such as antitrust, expropriation and the regulation of industries, add economic value and be congruous, it also would exist in a society without any violative action. In any society that upholds rights, people would freely constrain themselves to enjoy its benefits, as they do in many non-governmental sectors.

There are not only many contemporary but also historical examples of administrative entrepreneurship by governments, such as the setting of weights and measures, the issuance of national currencies, and the promotion of common languages.[32] In all these government functions, their policies have been conducive to economic prosperity. The roles of a government therefore include more than providing enforcement, and for good reason. And it can fulfil these roles based on the rights to do so – its *rights of government*.

## THE HOLD-UP PROBLEM AND THE IMPUTATION PROBLEM

Governments often fulfil many roles other than providing enforcement, and for good reason. The value of enforcement and the value of administrative entrepreneurship accrue to the same tax base because enforcement and administrative entrepreneurship are comple-

[32] See Spruyt (1994), pp. 158-159.

mentary to the same things. They enable the same actions together. Governance is to enable subjects to achieve some ends they prefer by administrative entrepreneurship and providing enforcement. For example, many trade relations require both enforcement and infrastructure. The value of administrative entrepreneurship and that of enforcement thus accrue to the value obtained through the same actions. Taxing the action of a subject, such as working or a selling something, therefore taxes away some of the value created by both. Besides, enforcement and other government goods and services are largely provided territorially and not charged for separately. Enforcement, public goods and services, regulations and so on are complementary to land. Some of this value therefore typically accrues to the value of being present in the jurisdiction and thereby to land values if they are not charged for otherwise.

The value created in these roles thus accrues to the same tax base. The synergy between large-scale administrative entrepreneurship and enforcement stems from a combination of two contracting problems that this complementarity leads to – the hold-up problem and the imputation problem.

Imagine a world in which the right to superior force, together with the right and obligation to enforce rights and to levy taxes, is in the hands of one group of people. The rights of administration, i.e. those used for administrative entrepreneurship, including for example the right to regulate human interaction and externalities and the right to expropriate, are in the hands of another group. To reap some of the value created by their endeavours, the administrative entrepreneurs also have the right to levy taxes.

Together, administrative entrepreneurship and providing enforcement enable the same actions of their subjects – Their endeavours are complementary to each other. Some of the value they create, such as by building infrastructure and public art and by increasing policing in some area, also accrues to land values as people must live near these things to enjoy them. This creates a hold-up problem – The enforcement provider and the administrative entrepreneurs, with the right to tax the same jurisdiction as they wish, can charge more than the value they add and thereby appropriate some or all of the value added by the other group. This can lead to conflicts of interest and discourage value-adding activities, which can only be resolved by contracting or aligning the interests. To perfectly align the interests, the two groups need to merge or one needs to acquire the relevant rights of the other in order to fulfil both the role of enforcement provider and of administrative entrepreneur.

Contracting could perhaps be a solution to this, but inevitably suffers from the 'imputation problem', which will be explained more extensively in Section 9.1. The imputation problem is that it is impossible to observe with any precision the value that each of them adds to the jurisdiction, while the value they create accrues to the same tax base. It is impossible to impute what part of the tax base is created by what role. This makes it impossible to tax only for performing one or some of those roles. One always taxes away some of the value created in the other roles. Because of the imputation problem, they cannot specify any rule or amount that results in them being commensurately compensated for their value-adding activities. Any amount of tax they would agree to levy individually would deviate, however slightly, from the value they add individually. If the taxes one group gets to levy are less than the value that they can create, there is no incentive for them to create any value above what they can tax for. If the taxes they get to levy exceed the value they can create, they can appropriate some of the value created by the others, which removes the financial incentive for the others to maximise the value they create. The same applies to determining a tax share after value has been created. Any share of the tax base does not entitle the holders to only the value they create, but to a share of the total value created. A share of tax revenues entitles a party to some of the value added by the other. The inevitable result is that only one or none of the parties has an incentive to maximise the value it adds.

The only way to align the interests is to integrate the two groups, i.e. to have the right to superior force along with its accompanying rights and obligations in the hands of the same people that have the rights to engage in large-scale administrative entrepreneurship. The rights of government, consisting of the right to superior force and rights of administration, must be held by the same group of people.

## THE STRICT LIMITATIONS AND OBLIGATIONS OF THE ENFORCEMENT PROVIDER

In a congruous government-subject relationship, the right to superior force is typically accompanied by an obligation on the part of the government to enforce the rights subjects grant to one another and to keep from violating them. The indiscriminate use of force is detrimental to prosperity and infringes on the rights of its subjects. The rights and obligations that come together with the right to superior force are important, because they leave the government, in its role of enforcement provider, little discretion and mainly obligations. For government-subject relations to be congruous, it can only choose to use its superior capacity to direct the use of force for the purpose of enforcement. It has rights specifically for its administrative-entrepreneurial role, but these are not intrinsic to its role of enforcement provider. Rights holders, including administrative entrepreneurs, determine whether their rights are to be enforced and what those rights are. The government's discretion given by its right to superior force is restricted by obligations it has to those who hold rights.

The government, itself holding rights in its administrative-entrepreneurial role, also typically has some discretion on how and when to enforce rights. In some cases, the cost of upholding rights may exceed the benefits. The net benefit of a cooperation may turn out to be negative when considering the cost of enforcement. Allowing some violations of rights can therefore be better than enforcing rights at all times and in all places. Because enforcement is costly and it is impossible to predict in what place, time and way it will be beneficial, governments typically have some discretion in matters of enforcement. If all actions would be either congruous or violative, i.e. if rights would be established regarding every possible action, and the government would have granted the unconditional right to enforcement, it would have no such discretion. But the subject's right to enforcement is not unconditional. A government can typically decide to some extent when to interfere, when to punish and how to punish, and can change its respective policies unilaterally. If complete contracting would be possible and costless, this discretion would not be necessary. When and how the government is to enforce would be established beforehand for all future situations. But these conditions are never satisfied, so some discretion on the part of government is necessary.

## THE RIGHTS OF GOVERNMENT

As explained before, there is nothing definite that makes people qualify as a government. However, there is a need for enforcement, regulation, public goods and services and so on. What is commonly considered a government typically provides many of these things. Accordingly, a government governs its territory based on a bundle of rights. This bundle, in this book called the *rights of government*, often include the right to superior force and some accompanying rights, as well as the rights it needs to engage in administrative entrepreneurship. Different governments have different rights of government, and in a consensual government-subject relationship a government can change these rights as it sees fit. It can give up some rights and claim others.

The rights of government can take many forms. A government may or may not have the right to expropriate, for example, or to interfere in the romantic lives of its subjects. It also does not necessarily have the right to unilaterally change its laws freely, i.e. to undertake any action if it communicates the intention to do so beforehand. When a government explicitly promises to never regulate beyond a certain limit, it cannot subsequently regulate beyond this limit without violating this right. It has then forever given up its right to do so. Conversely, if it passes a law that states that it cannot be repealed, it thereby also forever gives up the right to do so. In short, its conduct is not violative if it does not act in violation with prior contracting, including the laws in force.

The rights according to which a government governs, the rights of government, is a bundle of rights that varies over time and according to political context. Some governments have extensive rights to govern their subjects and much freedom to extend their rights further, whereas others are significantly limited by their constitutions and treaties. But in almost all government-subject relations in history and in the present, subjects are consensually subordinated and governments thereby have the rights of government.

A government is distinguished by its rights of government. This is a bundle of rights. As such, the rights of government can be used, transgressed, infringed on, inherited and, in theory, transferred to others. The ability to transfer rights, *alienability*, has important consequences for the conduct of people and the roles people have in society. Inalienability of the rights of government has pervasive effects and forms the core subject of the following chapter.

## CONSENSUAL SUBORDINATION

One could see the world as a 'governance market', in which governments provide a bundle of goods and services which subjects in most cases freely choose to consume. This freedom is not guaranteed, but governments today typically allow a subject to end his subordination by leaving their jurisdictions. By deciding not to leave, a subject thus chooses to receive their governance.

Any action from which a preference can be inferred counts as consent for what is preferred. If someone chooses to stay subordinated while being free to leave or has given up the right to leave, that counts as consent to the government-subject relationship as formulated in the government's laws and policies. The relationship between a government and its subjects, in which the latter are in subordination to the former, is therefore usually based on (tacit) consent.[33] Consent is thus only absent if a government prevents its subjects from leaving its jurisdiction without having the right to do so.

Remember that a right is simply a communicated intention to act in a way that the recipient prefers. If someone chooses to stay subordinated to a government while being free to end his subordination to it, he implicitly communicates the intention to obey its laws – He grants it the rights specified in the law. This tacit consent has analogies in many cooperative relationships between non-governmental persons. For example, when someone enters and stays at a hotel, he gives tacit consent to the guards to use force if he misbehaves. He agrees to follow the house rules and not to be a nuisance to other guests. Likewise, when someone decides to stay in a jurisdiction, he grants the government the right to govern him as specified in its laws.

By choosing to be subordinate to a government, one grants it rights of government over oneself. This bundle of rights can vary in the rights it contains. Some governments may have the right to limit the rights of others unilaterally. For example, if the law allows the government to expropriate land for large infrastructure projects, it in effect owns purchasing options on that land. When using the right

[33] For a description of different types of consent and what qualifies as consent, see 'Consent' in Section 4.3.

to expropriate, it does not violate any rights despite the fact that expropriation is widely disliked. A government is free to unilaterally alter the rights of its subjects insofar its right to do so is ordained by law. The government also makes its own laws and is usually allowed to change them unilaterally.

The law is simply a set of intended actions communicated by the government. It specifies rights of the government as well as rights of its subjects – The terms to their cooperation. One subjects oneself voluntarily to these laws, and thus commits to these terms. by choosing to be present in its jurisdiction. It only acts violatively when its actions conflict with the rights it has granted, including in its laws, policies and treaties. That it can change the law as it sees fit does not matter – It still communicates its intentions before carrying them out. The law is still a set of terms to a contract as defined in this book and a government's actions can still be congruous.

Despite the consensual nature of almost all government-subject relationships, many feel as if their subordination is neither consensual nor voluntary. After all, most governments are either dictatorships, oligarchies, hereditary monarchies, or very flawed and inefficient representative systems. As a result, governments rarely aim to maximise the value of their jurisdictions, leaving many needs and wants of people unfulfilled or fulfilled inefficiently. Governments also typically have a superior capacity to direct the use of force, with which they affect and sometimes aim to fully dictate their subjects' behaviour. Using this capacity is always in conflict with the will of some subject, making some interactions with the government involuntary. The large gap between the governance we receive and that which we prefer, combined with the forceful way in which governments exercise and maintain their rule, can easily make us believe that we are subordinated without our consent. But the above shows that this is in most cases a misunderstanding of the situation. Governments often frustrate us not because we do not consent to their authority, but because they provide poor governance at high tax rates and rely on force, sometimes excessively.

## GOVERNMENTAL DISCRETION AND STABILITY

A government typically needs some discretion in how it governs its jurisdiction and provides enforcement. This discretion is limited by the rights of its subjects and of other governments, but it can also withdraw some of the rights it has granted and claim new rights. It does so by introducing new laws and policies, withdrawing from international treaties, expropriating property owners and so on. One might think that a government can thus easily become totalitarian, because it only needs to pass new legislation shortly before doing something to make any of its actions congruous. But while this is technically possible, governments have little reason to.

When the government acts in accordance with its rights and does not frequently change them, its subjects can have realistic expectations about its conduct. This allows subjects to make informed decisions about whether to be subject to it. A government's rights are totalitarian if the law allows it to act without constraints and are easy to make totalitarian if it has the right to unilaterally change the law as it sees fit. But they are rights nonetheless, congruously contracted for and consented to, as long as its subjects are free to leave unless they have given up the right to leave. Totalitarian rights of government allow a government to freely interfere in the actions of its subjects. This may enable it to govern more efficiently, but is unlikely to be preferred by (potential) subjects. If its subjects additionally grant it an unconditional right to prevent them from leaving its jurisdiction, they thereby in effect sell themselves into slavery. But it stands to reason that not many would do this.

The law tells people what to expect from their government. When it is not changed to often, subjects can plan their actions more successfully, enabling them to better direct their investment activities. Legal stability is thus important for economic prosperity. It is not without reason that governments not only consider their rights of government as rights their subjects are obliged to respect, but also explicitly consider themselves obliged to uphold the rights of their subjects. A capricious and unreliable government is not one to which people want to be subordinated. To maximise profits, a proprietary government must offer legal stability.

Modern state-building involves assigning rights in such a way that they form an effective system of incentives keeping those with the rights of government, and their agents, from using their power violatively. Two ways for this will be explained in Chapter 10.

CHAPTER 5.

# THE PROPRIETARY GOVERNMENT

## 5.1 ALIENABILITY IN THE RIGHTS OF GOVERNMENT

Rights are usually *alienable*, i.e. the people who hold them can transfer them to others. When rights are transferred, the communicated intentions initially referring to their initial owners are made to refer to those who receive the rights. For instance, when one person sells a car to another, he in effect transfers to the recipient the conditional commitment of others not to interfere in his use of the car, as well as the commitment of the government to enforce his ability to use it if anyone were to interfere.

For many cooperations, the alienability of rights is crucial. When the right to perform some action is already granted, its alienability allows someone to obtain it without it having to be granted again. This is most visible in the exchange of goods. Without alienability, the scope of trade would be drastically limited – Only the initial recipients of rights would be allowed to use the goods over which their rights are granted. When people could benefit from an exchange of these goods, the inalienability of rights makes it impossible. The alienability of rights is therefore crucial for goods to be allocated to their most preferred ends.

This alienability can be restricted in various ways and to varying degrees. For instance, it can be limited to exclude certain classes of recipients or certain use purposes, such as when people donate art and want to prevent it from being sold on to private collectors. Alienability can also be conditional on the approval of others, such as when the sale of shares in a corporation requires the approval of other shareholders. Or, for example, when the original owner of a property sells it on the condition that the buyer only sells it to others after offering it for sale to the original owner himself. But there is no need to elaborate on the ways in which alienability can be limited. The possible limitations are numerous if not infinite. What is important to understand at this point is that people can agree to such limitations and can benefit from doing so. Limiting the alienability of rights can serve various purposes.

The rights at the centre of this book are the rights of government, the alienability of which can also be limited.

## A GOVERNMENT WITH INALIENABLE RIGHTS OF GOVERNMENT

Consider a government with rights of government of which the alienability is severely limited. The owners of the rights of government are called 'voters' and every owner can only have one share, i.e. one voting right.[34] Furthermore, let the owners of the government form a large part of its subjects – voting rights are widely distributed to the extent that a single vote is extremely unlikely to decisively affect an election outcome. Voting rights are inalienable, i.e. their owners cannot sell them and people therefore cannot accumulate them. Voters receive their voting rights when reaching adulthood. Voting rights cannot be inherited, but are bought back by the government without compensation when their owner dies.

The rights that these shares bestow on their owners are limited by design. Their owners do not vote on every matter themselves, but as in any other corporation delegate most decisions to an elected group. This is not an uncommon arrangement among shareholders in corporations. In non-governmental corporations this group is called the board of directors, who then appoint the executives for the daily management of the firm. In a government, the elected officials are known as the 'legislature' and the managers they appoint on behalf

[34] Voting rights can be regarded as (shares in) the rights of government as they are the residual control rights in a government hierarchy, analogous to shares in a corporation with which shareholders get to elect the board of directors. Shareholders are often called the owners of the company and are actually the company itself. Correspondingly, the electorate holding the voting rights in a representative system are themselves the government.

of the shareholders are commonly referred to as the 'cabinet' or 'administration'. Some governments elect their administrations directly, such as in presidential systems.

Such an arrangement of the rights of government is what representative systems are based on. The different types of representative democracy, i.e. presidential and parliamentary, differ only in how the legislature and executives are appointed, as well as the limitations to their authority. What they have in common is that those who hold the rights of government cannot transfer them at their own individual discretion. In the representative system, voters do not individually get to decide on the transfer of their voting rights.[35] The transfer of the rights of government is either forbidden altogether, or can only be done at the discretion of elected officials after lengthy and cumbersome procedures. Representatives cannot freely sell the rights of government on behalf of their voters. It typically requires approval by referendum, or constitutional amendments and thereby consecutive approvals by supermajorities, or both.

These are stringent limitations on the alienability of the rights of government. In effect, transfers of the rights of government are almost completely prevented. The rights of government are not strictly inalienable, since the representatives of voters can sell parts of the jurisdiction even though this may need a constitutional amendment first. However, the political procedures are too cumbersome, representatives have little to no incentive to initiate them and voting rights are inalienable. The inalienability of voting rights and the one-man one vote rule make it impossible to accumulate them. This is crucial, because otherwise someone could appropriate the state by accumulating a majority of all voting rights. A representative system thus requires this inalienability to keep its representative character.

Consequently, these limitations prevent society from allocating the rights of government into the hands of those who would put

[35] I am not the first to take this view. According to Alchian (1965), a key difference between public and private ownership is the inability of a public owner to sell his share of public ownership and secondarily the ability to acquire a share without the purchase of it, i.e. citizens are granted shares when they come of age.

them to their most valued use. Selling one's voting right to someone more learned and politically committed is made impossible.

## THE EFFECTS OF INALIENABILITY AND DISPERSION

What distinguishes a modern democratic government is that its rights of government take the form of inalienable voting rights, distributed according to the one-man-one-vote rule and widely dispersed over a great number of people. What sets apart representative democracies from direct democracies are the limitations to the discretion of their voters. Their voting rights only allow them to elect representatives who hold temporary custody of the rights of government on their behalf. The arrangement of rights that sets apart the modern democratic system results in several problems.[36]

First, since there is a cost to informing oneself of government matters that is for each voter independent of the amount of other voters, but the benefits of doing so decrease in the amount of other voters, the motive to become politically committed decreases in the size of the voting population. This encourages *rational ignorance*[37] and *rational irrationality*[38], providing a basis for the widespread abuse of principal-agent problems by government officials, i.e. corruption, and inadequate policy making toward irrational purposes. As voting rights are inalienable, they cannot be accumulated to form a stake significant enough in size such that their owners are committed to using them best. Even if they could use their voting rights best, voters would not have any interest in doing so.

36 For a more extensive exploration of the effects of inalienability, see Alchian (1965).

37 See Rational Ignorance, Wikipedia.org. Source included in the reference section.

38 See Caplan (2003) and Caplan (2001).

Second, the economic calculation problem emerges.[39] Since the rights of government are inalienable, they have no price that arises from free exchange – they have no 'market price'. If they did, the allocative process would move their price to the point where people believe it to reflect their value when used well. The price of the rights of government, whether as the price of voting rights accumulated or of the price paid to a government for relinquishing a part of its jurisdiction, would then be a factor on the balance sheet of their owners. This would allow them to include the opportunity cost of using the rights of government in the calculation of their profits. This nowhere being the case, the allocative function of exchange cannot compel governments to govern more efficiently and governments cannot know whether they do even if they aim to.

Third, there is the problem of incompetence. The vast majority of voters are barely competent in their roles. An accumulator of shares would typically be a group of professional investors employing teams of experienced consultants, economists and managers. The average voter does not have the capacity, nor any interest, to obtain such expertise. The inalienability of the rights of government keeps them from ending up in the hands of those who are most competent at fulfilling the roles that they bestow. The inalienability of rights stifles their efficient allocation, resulting in incompetent leaders, or 'irrational ignorance' and 'irrational irrationality'. Together with the incentive problems resulting from the wide dispersion of voting rights, this results in a combination of irrational ignorance, irrational irrationality, rational ignorance and rational irrationality.

The incompetence of voters and the absence of a price of the rights of government also results in misaligned incentives built into remuneration packages. Legislatures and ministers have different incentives from those of company executives. Whereas the latter are typically aligned with those of shareholders through sophisticated incentive packages often consisting of salaries, bonuses and/or stock options, such incentives are absent in legislatures and administra-

39 For an explanation of the economic calculation problem see Part Three: Economic Calculation, in von Mises (2007 [1949]). Or see, for the first version of the argument, von Mises (1935 [1920]).

tions. Performance-based remuneration is virtually absent in politics. And even if voters would be competent and committed enough to ensure that ministers and top civil servants are paid based on their performance, the absence of a price of the rights of government makes the best incentives impossible. Because the directors and executives of corporations are typically given stock options, maximising share prices is their primary goal. Giving stock options aligns the interests of managers with those of shareholder better than any other incentive system. But this does not exist in a representative democracy because its equivalent of shares, voting rights, are inalienable and thereby have no price.

Democratic systems suffer from many perverse incentives. Elected officials and their appointed administrations can be found manipulating the information supply of an ill-informed voter base, catering to the whims and prejudices of irrational voters, making false promises and delivering favours to specific groups, a practice known as clientelism. Instead of governing as efficiently as they can, representatives and their appointed administrations often go to great lengths to alter the distribution of government proceeds and to exploit informational asymmetries. Their goal is to be re-elected, which does not require optimising the governance they provide.

Because of these problems, the legislature and administration do not aim to maximise the government's financial profits, despite the potential benefits for voters. Voters are mostly unaware of the benefits of profit maximisation, lack the inventive to ensure that the legislature's interests are aligned with theirs, and do not have the expertise to appoint and effectively motivate those who would most successfully maximise profits even if they were committed. And even if government representatives would govern with the aim to maximise profits, were the right people for their positions and were given the right incentives, the economic calculation problem would still hinder them.

## A GOVERNMENT WITH VARIABLE BENEFITS

If voting rights in a democratic system can be seen as inalienable shares in the government, then what are their dividends? A 'voter's dividend' may sound strange to those familiar with democratic systems. One would think that a democratic government is not a for-profit corporation but a not-for-profit or non-profit organisation. Whether or not this is true, it is not what sets apart democracy from other types of government. Any government can redistribute its subjects' incomes. Many governments of various kinds engage in price discrimination by taxing their subjects at different rates and distribute the proceeds unevenly.

Another interesting characteristic of modern democratic systems, beside the inalienability of the rights of government, is the variability of who is to receive how much of the government's income. Whereas shareholders' rights to the income of their enterprise are fixed upon incorporation, the beneficiaries of a democratic government's income and their rights are typically variable and determined through a political process. These beneficiaries do not only include voters, they also include citizens who have not come of age yet and subjects who are not citizens. It does not matter whether democracies should be seen as for-profit cooperative enterprises with variable dividend policies or as non-profit organisations. Either of the two can be transformed into the other by changing the designation of who are to be the government's beneficiaries and how they are to benefit.

As the distribution of benefits is variable and determined by the political process, voters and their representatives seek to alter this distribution. Voters may not care much to inform themselves of corruption and efficiencies, but the distributions promised by electable representatives may be less costly to learn and can thereby greatly skew voting behaviour. All voters have an interest in voting for policies that result in a distribution of as much income to themselves as possible. As Frédéric Bastiat once wrote[40], *'the state is the great fiction by which everyone seeks to live at the expense of everyone* else'. As explained above, a voting right in a democratic system can be seen as an inalienable share that entitles the holder to a part of government income that is variable through a political process. Companies can have various classes of beneficiaries – They can issue common stock, preferred stock, debt and other rights to their proceeds. But the entitlements each of these rights confers on its holder are fixed

[40] *'L'État, c'est la grande fiction à travers laquelle tout le monde s'efforce de vivre aux dépens de tout le monde.'* Bastiat, F. (1848).

in some way. One feature of most electoral democratic systems, although not necessarily intrinsic to it, is that these rights are variable and set by the elected legislature. Whereas some 'shareholders' may have the right to large benefits under one elected government, their rights may be more limited under another. This does not imply that government officials have no interest whatsoever in maximising government profits. It implies that voters, elected representatives and administrations have no interest in maximising profits when this conflicts with their redistributive objectives, and that they will not always focus on maximising profits even when profit maximisation is compatible with their redistributive objectives.

## A GOVERNMENT WITH ALIENABLE RIGHTS OF GOVERNMENT

As explained above, the alienability of the rights of government allows their owners to transfer them in mutually beneficial ways. The ownership and use of the rights of government then converge respectively to who value them most and their most valued use. Those who are more competent and tenacious at using them profitably will end up possessing them to govern more efficiently.

If voting rights are fully alienable at the sole discretion of individual voters, they can transfer their voting rights to others. The efficient allocation of the rights of government is then no longer impeded. Many would then sell their voting rights to an accumulating entrepreneur. Using a single voting right can barely affect an election outcome, but an accumulating individual or firm would be willing to pay a good price for it because he can reap great benefits by using an amount of voting rights great enough to change the course of government. Such an entrepreneur is typically financially oriented – Alienable shares tend to end up in the hands of profit-maximising investors, at least because the people who have the capital to accumulate large numbers of shares mostly had to be financially oriented to amass this capital, and because institutional investors are almost purely financially oriented. Because of the large profits that he can make by efficiently using his rights of government, such a voter-shareholder has no reason for rational ignorance or rational irrationality. And he has much reason to sell them to an entrepreneur who can use the rights of government more profitably or is more committed. An important and perhaps the most important effect of alienability of the rights of government therefore stems from the possibility of accumulating shares in the government, which will result in large shareholders aiming to maximise the state's profitability. When shares are freely alienable, activist investors can step in to solve the issues stemming from dispersed ownership. After their work is done and a company's operations are improved, they sell their shares again such that small holdings increase again. Over time, the increase in small holdings may reintroduce problems of dispersed ownership, presenting a new opportunity to activist investors. Through this process, the degree of ownership dispersion converges to that which maximises the net benefits of share dispersion or concentration. This also applies to governments when the rights of government are alienable. Alienability solves the problems of rational ignorance and rational irrationality.

Alienability also affects the rules for distributing government proceeds. If the rights of government are alienable, shareholders will want predetermined rules for the distribution of profits. Otherwise, large shareholders can band together and appropriate all the benefits at the expense of small shareholders. To attract capital by issuing shares, a government must end the variability of benefits that is common in democratic systems. Alienability thereby also eliminates the problems stemming from the variability of benefits.

However, when those who hold the rights of government are more competent at using them and are more likely to pursue financial profits, they do not necessarily govern in ways their subjects most prefer. Depending on the conditions facing them, the pursuit of profit can also impel them to abuse their power at the expense of their subjects. Instead of treating their subjects like customers, they could treat them more like cattle. How to ensure that the rights of government are used to best satisfy the preferences of subjects will be explained in Part III.

## 5.2 PUBLIC AND PRIVATE PROPERTY

One of the roles typically fulfilled by governments is the provision of 'public goods', or 'public property', such as roads, public spaces, other infrastructure, schools, basic health care and much more. These goods are correctly seen as the property of a government – They are owned by the people who own the rights of government over the jurisdiction, but this is not what sets these goods apart. If it were, all property of voters would be public property, from their houses and vehicles to their phones and their pets. It is only those properties of which the alienability is severely limited that are considered public. Public property is property of which transfers at the discretion of owners themselves are effectively ruled out.

But this implies that much more property should be considered public than is typically done. Public property usually refers to government property, but much more qualifies as such if it refers to property which owners cannot transfer to others.

Public property therefore does not actually refer to government property. Non-governmental individuals can also provide what are commonly called public goods. For example, goods provided by a homeowner's association are public because the ownership rights over them, which are divided among homeowners, cannot be sold and accumulated freely. Decisions regarding these goods are likewise made democratically. The difference between public goods provided by a homeowner's association and those provided by a representative government is that the group of owners is much smaller in the former – It only includes the homeowners in the association. The difference is in their public, not in their publicness.

Something is a public good when the ownership rights over it are not alienable at the sole discretion of their holders. When something is easily alienable at the sole discretion of its owner, it is private property. If shareholders are limited in the sale of their shares because the approval of other shareholders is required, the privacy of their shares is limited. As explained, there exists a multitude of different possible limitations to the alienability of rights. One could perhaps consider these possibilities to be on a spectrum, with on one end purely private property, distinguished by its unimpaired alienability at the sole discretion of individual owners. On the other end, there is purely public property, distinguished by being completely inalienable. As restrictions increase, the 'publicness' of property increases.

One common way in which the alienability of property can be limited is by requiring the approval of other co-owners for its transfer and forbidding co-owners from owning more than one share or voting right. When such groups of co-owners are small, the difference from private property is negligible in practice. How they use public property then barely differs from how they use private property. First, transfers of shares or voting rights are then still possible because a small number of owners can contract with each other for approval. Shares or voting rights are then still effectively alienable. Second, how a participant votes then still significantly affects how their property is used. There is therefore little reason for rational ignorance or rational irrationality. In the extreme, we can imagine a one-person group requiring the approval of other participants for every decision, which in his case is nobody. In one-person groups, there is no difference between private ownership rights and ownership rights that require the approval of other participants to be transferred and cannot be accumulated. But as the number of participants increases, such shares and voting rights become effectively inalienable. Transferring the rights then becomes effectively impossible because the contracting cost of obtaining other owners' approval becomes prohibitively high. People who are more committed and competent at their use then cannot obtain them. Furthermore, rational ignorance and rational irrationality then starts to affect how participants use their voting rights, because each participant cannot have more than one voting right and a single vote does not affect them much if there are a multitude of other voters. The result is then effectively the same as with formally inalienable property.

Thus, if shares in a joint stock company are not freely alienable at the discretion of their individual owners but require the approval of other owners to be transferred, alienability is limited by the cost of contracting with other owners to receive their permission. This may make shares inalienable, unless the group of shareholders is sufficiently small such that contracting is possible at low cost.

Whereas restrictions on the alienability of shares in joint-stock corporations are not meant to prevent all transfers or accumulations of shares, in certain types of organisations they are instituted precisely to prevent accumulation and thereby the commercial use of shares. This applies, for example, to cooperatives. Section 11.7 explains what distinguishes cooperatives from investor-owned (i.e. private) corporations and why the representative system is the government equivalent of the consumer cooperative.

All cooperatives, whether worker-owned or customer-owned, require inalienable ownership in order to endure. Otherwise, profit-seeking entrepreneurs can accumulate these rights, which undermines the benefits of the cooperative. A socialist economy requires a prohibition of private property under the definition used in this book. It can consist of one non-profit or cooperative government that owns all the means of production or of a collection of worker-owned cooperatives that do so. The definition of private property defended here thus accords with the idea of socialism as an economic system without private property.

## NOTIONS OF PUBLIC GOODS

These definitions of public and private property differ substantially from how these terms are commonly used. However, the common definitions of private and public property are fraught with confusion, which must be avoided.

In economics, the term 'public good' is often used to refer to goods that are non-excludable and non-rivalrous, meaning respectively that people cannot be excluded from their use and that their use by one does not limit their use by another. However, these conditions are rarely if ever satisfied. Governments can exclude people from the use of most public goods through expulsion, and many goods such as public healthcare can easily be denied to some parts of the population. Many public goods are therefore not non-excludable at all. And virtually all public goods are rivalrous. Those that do not seem to be can still suffer from congestion, such as roads and other infrastructure. If the term 'public goods' is to refer to goods that are both non-rivalrous and non-excludable, then public goods barely exist if they do at all. According to the most common definition in economics, the term 'public goods' cannot refer to most government-provided goods.

The term 'public property' commonly refers to property owned by the government and managed by its agents for use by citizens. But not all subjects necessarily have access to it. Some public property may be for the exclusive use by children or the elderly, limiting access to a part of the government's subjects. That is, the 'public' can vary from small groups of neighbours to entire nations. And what goods provided by representatives, the cabinet and civil servants would qualify as public goods? Obviously, public goods only refers to goods offered as part of what is considered governance, not everything they offer in their own private affairs. But if that is its proper use, it is the inalienability of these goods that makes them 'public'. As explained in Section 4.7, governments are not unique in most of their undertakings. At many scales and in many different contexts, entrepreneurs can be found regulating human interaction, developing land and undertaking other projects that governments usually do. It is not the types of goods and services that makes them 'public' or 'private'. Otherwise, private roads and healthcare as well as many other private goods must also be called 'public'. It is the inalienability of rights over goods that makes them public. But since inalienability can exist in many non-governmental instances, public property cannot refer to government property exclusively. It must also include common goods provided by homeowner associations, for example.

Deviations from common usage are not uncommon in economic literature. For example, in the context of rent-seeking, economists use the term 'rent' to refer to something different from rent paid to a landlord. Similarly, in the literature on entrepreneurship, the definitions of 'entrepreneur' and 'entrepreneurship' do not entirely overlap with their everyday use. This will become evident in Chapter 7. These everyday definitions are vague and inadequate for academic purposes.

To avoid confusion, it is important to note here that 'property' in this book does not refer to goods, but rights. In the literature on public and private goods, it is common to distinguish the two types of property according to their attributes or their number of users. James Buchanan, for example, claimed that public goods are in fact 'club goods' because they are used by many people, and that the 'publicness' of these goods depend on the size of their 'clubs'. However, I will not make such distinctions here because they can be confusing. I argue that the mere provision of something to a large group of people does not make it public property. For example, a rental car is privately owned but can be driven by many people successively, and a restaurant is privately owned but can be patronised by many people simultaneously. These examples show that the 'publicness' of a good cannot solely depend on how many people have rights to use it. Both are usually considered private property, as are the temporary use rights over it that are sold by renting it out. If many people simultaneously have rights to use a good, that does not make it public property. Otherwise, goods used by families, restaurant visitors and hotel guests should be considered public, leaving very few private goods in the private sector. Even though the legal owner of what is in such cases considered a private good is a private individual, he may grant use rights to a group of individuals, thereby making it a club good.

Regardless of the arrangement of rights over the good, which determines to what degree it is public or private, the nature of the good itself does not change. A good is therefore not public or private because of its physical nature – The ownership rights over it make it public or private. It is therefore better to speak of public and private ownership, not of public and private goods. Goods are not in themselves public or private, but only the rights over them.

We must look at rights, why they are established in what way and what incentives certain rights bring about, since rights only serve to drive people to undertake certain actions. The confusion thereby disappears, but since there are myriad possible arrangements of rights it is still useful in the praxeology of rights to distinguish between public and private ownership.

## 5.3 DEFINING THE PROPRIETARY GOVERNMENT

Now that the possibility has been explained of a government based on private property in the rights of government, as opposed to the public property in the rights of government that characterises democracies, a term must be established to refer to such a government.

It is important to choose a terminology that does not require the claims made in the previous section to be true. If the claim that private ownership is distinguished by its alienability will not be accepted and common usage can as a result not be expected to adapt to the definition argued for in Section 5.2, the terms 'private government', 'private jurisdiction' and their conjugations could be seen as oxymoronic. As of now, 'private property' still commonly refers to non-governmental property. Using the term 'private government' in this context would therefore conflict with common usage and could thereby cause confusion. While the definition of private property as distinguished by its alienability is strictly speaking correct, this book is not intended to defend potentially controversial semantic claims.

To avoid confusion, I choose to avoid the term 'private' in defining the proprietary government. Instead, I define it directly according to the alienability of its rights of government. As explained, public rights are characterised by a specific kind of limitation to them. Their transfer has been intentionally made impossible or almost prohibitively costly, thereby inhibiting their efficient allocation and use.

Public property is property that has been limited in a specific way. Only rights that are alienable at the sole discretion of their individual owners, private rights, are therefore to be seen as complete.

A government with freely alienable rights of government can therefore be referred to as 'proprietary', yielding the term *proprietary government.* Accordingly, a government based on effective and intentionally inalienable property in the rights of government, whether this property is unified in the hands of one owner or dispersed among many voter-shareholders, would be called *non-proprietary.* The actions they take based on their rights of government are respectively called *proprietary governance* and *non-proprietary governance.* Section 11.7 explains why a representative government can also be referred to as a *governance cooperative,* which is distinguished by its inalienable ownership rights in the form of voting rights, like any other cooperative. The representative system is the government equivalent of the cooperative and the proprietary government is the government equivalent of the investor-owned corporation.

Then, while proprietary government and proprietary governance respectively refer to the owners of alienable rights of government and their use of these rights, it is also necessary to choose a term for referring to such a government's jurisdiction – the territory it rules over. In accordance with these terms, *proprietary jurisdiction* seems to be most suitable.[41] The transition from a non-proprietary to a

41 The term 'jurisdiction' can refer to some rights to govern as well as to the territory over which these rights are held. To avoid confusion, 'jurisdiction' is in this book only used to refer to a government's territory, while the rights to govern it are referred to as the rights of government. For the multiple definitions of the term. see for example the Cambridge Dictionary, which defines jurisdiction both as 'a country, state, or other area where a particular set of laws or rules must be obeyed' and 'the authority that a particular court of law or official organization has to make laws, rules, or legal decisions.' Retrieved on 28 March 2023 from https://dictionary.cambridge.org/dictionary/english/jurisdiction.

In Section 15.1, I argue for using the term proprietary jurisdiction instead of the terms 'free private city', 'entrepreneurial community' and 'charter city'.

proprietary government could be referred to as the *privatisation* of the jurisdiction.

A proprietary jurisdiction is thus a territory governed by a proprietary government. The privatisation of a jurisdiction is the transformation of the rights of government over that territory from inalienable into alienable rights, i.e. from public into private rights.

Lastly, To describe an advocate of proprietary governance and of the privatisation of jurisdictions, we can use the term *proprietarian.*

This terminology is appropriate not only for clarity and semantic reasons but also because it is etymologically correct. As will be shown later in this book, proprietary governments are not a new phenomenon. They have existed in various places and played a role in the colonisation of America and the Caribbean. This definitions in this book of 'proprietary government' and its conjugations accord with how these terms were used in history and historical literature. Proprietary governments have been referred to as such at least since the second half of the eighteenth century.[42] This also applies to the term

[42] The earliest use of the term 'proprietary government' that I could find was in the American assembly's address to the governor on 8 December 1759, in Pemberton, I. & Pemberton J, (1775), pp. 91-92.

Among others, Benjamin Franklin used the term to refer to the governments of the proprietary colonies when he pleaded for replacing the proprietary government with royal government. See his preface to Joseph Galloway's speech (Franklin, 1779 [originally published as a pamphlet on 11 August 1764]).

A definition according with mine can be found in (Salmon, 1767), p. 557: 'The third kind of government is the proprietary government, properly so called, because the proprietor is vested with sovereign authority : He appoints the governor, council, and magistrates, and the representatives of the people are summoned in his name ; and by their advice he enacts laws, without the concurrence of the crown ; but by a late statute, the proprietor must have the King's consent in the appointing a governor, when he does not so reside in the plantation in person ; and of a deputy-governor when he does ; and all the governors of the plantations are liable to be called to an account for male-administration by the court of king's-bench in England, by another statute. The only proprietary governments now in being are those of Maryland and Pensylvania.'

'proprietarian', which has been defined as 'an advocate of proprietary government'.[43] Correspondingly, and correct in the context of the most notable proprietary governments in history, *proprietarianism* has been defined as 'advocacy of proprietary colonies and proprietary government in colonial America'.[44] I am not the one who has coined these terms, only the one to revive them.

In light of discourse from the time of the proprietary governments and relating historical literature, it is correct to use these terms as they are defined here. Moreover, this terminology also conforms to textbook definitions of the terms 'proprietary' and 'government'. Something proprietary has been defined as something 'privately owned and managed and run as a profit-making organization' or 'of, relating to, or characteristic of an owner or title holder'.[45] Meanwhile, 'government' is defined as 'the organization, machinery, or agency through which a political unit exercises authority and performs functions and which is usually classified according to the distribution of power within it'.[46]

---

Use of the term continued throughout the rest of the eighteenth and nineteenth centuries, including in historical discourse. See, for example, Frost (1800). For terminology in recent historical literature, see for example the terminology used throughout Roper & Van Ruymbeke (2007).

French terminology for the proprietary government accorded with English terminology. The French term 'gouvernement propriétaire' was used as early as 1767. See Burke, Eidous, & Burke (1767), pp. 341-342: 'La seconde forme usitée dans nos plantations est appellée un gouvernement propriétaire' (p. 341). See also Petit (1771), pp. 69 and 403.

For a French dictionary from 1778 that describes the term in accordance with the definition I use, see Robinet, J. B. (1778), p. 136: 'La seconde espèce de gouvernement qui regne dans les colonies, est connue sous le nom de Gouvernement propriétaire. ...'

43 'Proprietarian.' Merriam-Webster.com Dictionary.

44 'Proprietarianism.' Wiktionary.org.

45 'Proprietary.' Merriam-Webster.com Dictionary

46 'Government.' Merriam-Webster.com Dictionary

Under these definitions, the definition of a proprietary government as a 'government based on alienable rights of government' stands firmly, since alienable ownership is what distinguishes profit-seeking investor-owned corporations from nonprofits and cooperatives, as will be explained in Section 11.7.

## 5.4 HEATHIAN PROPRIETARY ADMINISTRATION

Readers familiar with the ideas of Spencer Heath and his grandson Spencer Heath MacCallum may notice that proprietary governance as defined in this book differs from their idea of 'proprietary administration', although the two terms are semantically synonymous.[47] 'Heathian proprietary administration', which Heath and Heath MacCallum just called 'proprietary administration', here refers to the administrative entrepreneurship that is often undertaken by property owners. For example, a hotel owner can improve the experience of his guests by stopping any misbehaviour and investing in common spaces such as the lobby, and the owner of a shopping mall can maximise its value by requiring his tenants to maintain the appearances of their storefronts. Observing such cases of administration over properties in various instances, Heath claimed that most if not all tasks of government, including the provision of common goods and all regulatory matters, should be left to property owners.[48] Corporations owning large assemblies of land, and possibly properties built on it, would then govern their properties optimally to maximise the total value of their holdings. As summarised by Heath MacCallum:

[47] Heathian proprietary administration has also been argued for by Calvin Duke (2020).

[48] 'There is a beautiful … protective and creative services.' Spencer Heath, Thoughts written down around August, in Politics Versus Proprietorship (1933)

> The business rationale of land ownership, as explained (1936), derives from the fact that public services—the things that we enjoy in common rather than separately and apart from one another, things such as streets, public safety, and other community amenities—are supplied to sites rather than to individuals, and individuals gain access to them through their occupancy of those sites. Thus owners of land, when they lease or sell sites, are the market purveyors of those public services. Only thus can such services be distributed as other goods and services are, through the conventions of the market place. Only through property in land can they be freely and equitably administered by contract, which is egalitarian in the free tradition of tribalism, instead of through favor and privilege, forced levies, the corrosive status relationship of ruler and ruled by whatever name.
>
> This purely distributive function is the land owner's minimal role in society, for which he is recompensed minimally in either land price or rent. Traditionally landowners have done little more. In the entrepreneurial community, however, they are going beyond that minimal distributive function; here they produce the services they purvey, and their rewards are correspondingly greater.[49]

Heathian proprietary administration differs from proprietary governance. The former refers to a type of administrative entrepreneurship that is undertaken to maximise total net property rents, while the latter refers to the undertakings of a government with alienable, i.e. 'private' rights of government. Importantly, the term 'proprietary' in Heath's idea of proprietary administration refers to the unified ownership of properties that it requires, while in 'proprietary governance' it refers to the alienable and thereby private nature of the rights of government.

[49] MacCallum (1997)

The most common forms of Heathian proprietary administration exist at small scales. The owners or tenants of hotels, shopping malls, apartment complexes, nightclubs and restaurants all engage in it to some extent over their properties. Their administration is in some ways similar to the administrative entrepreneurship of states – Hotel and shopping mall owner-operators provide common spaces, some form of personal protection and public transport systems (lifts and escalators) to their visitors. Nightclub staff 'expel' customers from their premises when these are a nuisance to others.

Contrary to what proponents of the theory of Heath and his grandson believe, it does not deserve much appraisal in the context of political governance. Heathian proprietary administration is only viable in some small-scale cases. As the scale of such an enterprise grows, large diseconomies emerge that can only be eliminated by transferring ownership of properties to third parties, ending the 'proprietary' nature of its administration in the sense meant by Heath. The Heathian proprietary administrator therefore cannot efficiently fulfil the role of government.

## THE DISECONOMIES OF SCALE IN HEATHIAN PROPRIETARY ADMINISTRATION

Imagine a property owner who rents out his small portfolio of neighbouring properties that share a common area. To maximise the net rent he can earn, he makes sure that new tenants fit well into the community, maintains the common area and sets some rules to maintain harmony between his tenants. For example, he forbids parties after 11pm because his type of tenant prefers the ability to sleep well over the freedom to host parties. When disputes arise between tenants, he offers arbitration. He also hires a guard for security and to enforce rights if necessary. Instead of outsourcing property management to a third party, he decides to save expenses by providing all governance by himself. Initially, he thus practices Heathian proprietary administration at a small scale

Over time, he accumulates more properties. But as the scale of his enterprise grows, he can no longer manage his properties himself. He therefore decides to hire property managers to do this on his behalf. At some point, after acquiring more properties to add value to through Heathian proprietary administration, he owns a town consisting of thousands of properties, which is still smaller than some of the smallest jurisdictions in the world. His property managers are tasked with almost every aspect of maximising the net value of his properties, including regulating tenant interaction, providing and maintaining public spaces and amenities, providing arbitration and enforcement, and, possibly, developing and redeveloping properties.

In order to maximise his earnings, the owner needs to induce his property managers to maximise the total net present value of his assets. To do this, he decides to design a package of financial incentives. A fixed salary would not be efficient because it is independent of the rental value, costs and future value of the managed properties. Why would a property manager with a fixed salary do his best to make tenancy as pleasant as possible, to ensure a high standard of maintenance while minimising maintenance costs or to maximise the net value of any redevelopments he is tasked with?

To improve the incentives, the property owner considers other means. Perhaps a profit-based bonus would be adequate, based on the performance of the properties under the manager's control. However, this gives the property manager an incentive to maximise his present earnings from the properties he manages, but not to preserve their value. This incentive is therefore also poorly aligned with the interests of the owner, although better than a fixed salary. Neither a fixed salary nor a bonus based on short-term profits is therefore efficient.

Then the owner realises that there is no better way to align the interests than to give the managers full control of his properties, including the right to transfer control to others, together with a share in the value of the properties themselves. In other words, he transfers ownership of all his properties to his property managers and keeps the right to a share of the income generated by the properties. The new property owners, formerly the property managers, then maximise their own financial gain by maximising that of the original owner. Less oversight from the original owner is needed with this arrangement because the interests are almost perfectly aligned. This applies to all kinds of real estate, including land.

But as ownership of the properties is now divided among multiple property owners, the interests of one property owner may conflict with those of others. For instance, one property owner may benefit from building a loud, polluting factory near another's residential properties, decreasing the value of the latter. But since the original owner has an interest in all the properties, his interest is to maximise their total net value. While the interest of individual property owners is to disregard the negative externalities they create, that of the original owner is to regulate the actions of property owners to maximise the total net value of all properties together. For this reason, when selling the properties to his former managers, he retains some rights to regulate them in order to minimise net negative externalities. He also decides to subsidise some uses of properties to maximise net positive externalities. Additionally, he has an interest in providing infrastructure that increases total net property values. For this, he retains conditional purchasing options on all properties, i.e. the right to expropriate. He also keeps the right to provide arbitration between tenants and property owners. Finally, he installs a force of guards for security and enforcement.

The above serves to show that Heathian proprietary administration suffers from diseconomies of scale, which can only be solved by selling the properties while keeping the rights to regulate and tax them. The government, formerly the Heathian proprietary administrator, then keeps a right to most of the income generated by the properties he sells, charges the owners for the negative externalities they create, forbids some uses of which the negative externalities are too great and subsidises some uses for the positive externalities they create. For infrastructure projects, he keeps conditional purchasing options to expropriate properties when necessary. He also retains the right to adjudicate disputes between tenants and property owners, as well as a right to superior force in order to provide enforcement. In short, he holds the rights of government that governments usually have.

His interest is now to maximise the net value of the properties he governs because this is his source of income, while the interest of the property owners is to do so as well. All of them stand to benefit more from this arrangement than from any other. This arrangement is not based on unified property ownership in the hands of one firm or individual – It is the common arrangement of rights that can be found in most jurisdictions.

The larger the property owner's portfolio, the more property managers he has to hire and managers to direct those managers, and so on. In each of these principal-agent relationships, there are contracting costs and contractual imperfections. The incentives are never perfectly aligned, and aligning the incentives is costly. The more properties the owner has, the more layers in the hierarchy below him, the more principal-agent relationships there thereby are and the greater these costs. These diseconomies continue to mount as the enterprise grows.

There are costs to contracting and costs resulting from misaligned incentives. As a result, the relationship between a property owner and manager has inefficiencies – Some incentives of the property managers conflict with the owner's interests. To solve this, the property owner can draw up an explicit contract instead of transferring ownership, but this is very costly and probably imperfect. There will in practice be situations for which the contract does not contain provisions. Residual control rights, i.e. ownership, exist to minimise costs of contracting and misaligned incentives. In this case, instead of Heathian proprietary administration, transferring ownership while keeping the rights of government minimises these costs.

Heathian proprietary administration, which requires property ownership to be unified in the hands of one person or group, cannot efficiently replace the functions of the state. Insofar it is viable, it is already present in small-scale cases in which it is called 'property management'. To provide the functions of government at scale, the Heathian proprietary administrator must become a proprietary government as defined in Section 5.3.

## ADMINISTRATIVE ENTREPRENEURSHIP OVER UNIFIED VERSUS DIVIDED PROPERTY

Heath and Heath MacCallum have shown some unique strengths of proprietary administration as compared with administration over divided property. However, the above shows that proprietary administration is not always more efficient.

A property owner, whether of developments, land or both, has a financial interest in making his properties as attractive and useful as possible, insofar the value thereby created exceeds its cost. This gives him an interest in regulating externalities, provide common goods and services, regulate tenant interaction and so on, and to do so as efficiently as he can.

When property is divided among many owners, Heathian proprietary administration is absent or significantly reduced. However, individual owners can then come together and contract with each other to establish a set of rules or a body of representatives to govern them. They can also contract separately for each issue, such as when one property owner's use of his premises creates negative externalities. Those who suffer the externalities may then contract with him to buy him out of his activities. It was Ronald Coase who argued in his seminal paper that in a world without transaction costs, contracting could solve all problems of externalities.[50] From this theorem, the Coase theorem, it follows that no administration by a government, administrative entrepreneur or property owner would under such conditions be necessary. But we live in a world of positive transaction costs, which limits the viability of direct contracting and necessitates other forms of administrative entrepreneurship.

Heathian proprietary administration can also suffer, if shares in the total of unified properties are very dispersed, from shareholder passivity. For small shareholders, whose earnings do not significantly depend on the total value of the proprietarily administered assets, the benefits of actively overseeing the firm's management may not outweigh the costs. This can make the misalignment of interests between the owners and the managers greater.

Furthermore, if people own developments but not the land they are built on or some other complementary good such as common

50 In this paper, Coase (1960), p. 15, defined the term 'transaction costs' as follows: 'In order to carry out a market transaction it is necessary to discover who it is that one wishes to deal with, to inform people that one wishes to deal and on what terms, to conduct negotiations leading up to a bargain, to draw up the contract, to undertake the inspection needed to make sure that the terms of the contract are being observed, and so on. These operations are often extremely costly.'

In Section 7.7, under 'The Elimination Theorem', it will be explained why the Coase theorem is strictly incorrect because more conditions must be satisfied for all problems of externalities to be solved without government regulation.

The definition of transaction costs used in this book also accords with the more exact definition given by Douglas Allen: 'Transaction costs are the resources used to establish and maintain property rights.' See Allen (1991).

spaces, this can lead to the 'hold-up problem'.[51] That is, after development rights over land are sold and development has been completed, the landowner can raise the rent on his land, which the owner of the development cannot escape because of his property's immobility. Bargained price ceilings and leaseholds can provide a solution to this problem. However, price ceilings remove a landowner's financial incentive to maximise land values beyond the price ceiling. And leaseholds remove a landowner's incentive to maximise land values because selling the leasehold will make his income independent of the land's value for a certain time. Apart from the costs resulting from misaligned incentives between property owners and managers, proprietary administration over unified property in land without its developments can thus involve other costs, i.e. the costs of post-contractual opportunism and of contracting to limit it.

The only solution to the hold-up problem is for the Heathian proprietary administrator to own both the land and the developments on it, but this makes the misalignment of incentives between owners and property managers more costly.

Contracting between property owners, which may lead to arrangements like title deeds, is subject to myriad transaction costs increasing in the number of participants, such as the costs of bargaining and of adapting the deeds to changing circumstances. It can also result in enforcement problems, because people must be given incentives to enforce them. Creating and amending a deed is costly, and so is its termination and enforcement.

One type of solution that property owners can contract for, besides title deeds, is a representative system that can be tasked with administering their properties. Such systems are often instituted by property developers and owners when dividing their properties into separately owned units. However, this solution may suffer from principal-agent problems, rent-seeking, and other issues that also arise in representative political systems. Crucially, a representative system between landowners may deviate from the 'one man, one vote' rule. It can thereby escape the lock-in problem of representative political

51 For a description and examples of the problem, see Klein, Crawford, & Alchian (1978).

systems, i.e. the transition out of it is not as difficult as in representative political systems because the defining feature of representative democracies is the effective inalienability of its voting rights. But like title deeds, representative systems are difficult to deconstruct by large numbers of participating property owners. In both cases, because their voting rights are weighted by property owned and not distributed according to the one man, one vote rule, an entrepreneur can terminate it by accumulating the participating properties. However, dismantling the system requires large concentrations of land holdings that may be inefficient to administer.

Central to Heath's comparison of proprietary administration with contracting over divided property is the question of which is more efficient. Proprietary administration can suffer from misaligned incentives between the owners and the managers, but in many cases performs better in maximising net positive externalities, procuring common goods most efficiently and regulating the interaction of tenants to maximise total property values. It depends on circumstances whether proprietary administration over unified property or some kind of administrative entrepreneurship over divided property is more efficient. Both Heathian proprietary administration and contracting by property owners are subject to costs of contracting and costs of misaligned incentives. Property developers and owners maximise their profits by minimising the total of these costs.

## CROWDING OUT

As explained by Spencer Heath, intrusive governance can discourage economic behaviour by taxing it and can crowd out proprietary administration. It limits how much value property owners can add to land by already providing services and goods that they could offer instead, and limits the amount of money people can spend on proprietarily administered properties by limiting economic prosperity.

Which form of administrative entrepreneurship performs best depends on what minimises net transaction costs, which varies across time and place. What is most efficient can therefore only be observed imperfectly and is a matter of entrepreneurial decision making. We cannot draw any such conclusions from the world as it is.

Heath and Heath MacCallum overlooked the relative transaction costs of proprietary administration as compared to other forms of administrative entrepreneurship and governance. As a result, Heath even viewed the proprietary administrator as a substitute for the state. Although Heathian proprietary administration should be more prevalent – partly because of overly intrusive governance, stemming from the political economy of representative systems – they are not entirely correct in their appraisal of their idea of proprietary administration.

## OTHER FALLACIES IN HEATH'S THEORY

In his works, Heath at times contradicted himself. At some points he acknowledged the necessity of the state for enforcing rights while supporting the minarchist ideal of it, i.e. the minimal night-watchman state.[52] At others he argued that it must be completely replaced, including in its enforcement function, by proprietary administration and that proprietary administrators must in fact physically protect their residents from the grip of the government's apparatus of force. Whichever of these two stances was Heath's actual view, both are false. Because a state based on private ownership in the rights of government can be as efficient as any other private enterprise, and because of the natural synergy between large-scale administrative entrepreneurship and enforcement, a minimal state is unlikely to be economically efficient. Furthermore, if a proprietary administrator replaces the state in all its functions, he thereby himself becomes a state if he rules with the right to do so. Heath therefore failed to see that his supposed replacement of the state would itself be a state in all its rights and functions.[53] A proprietary administrator can never entirely replace a state without becoming one. Besides, a Heathian proprietary administrator would have significant diseconomies of scale at the size of a state, even if only a relatively small one such as a city-state.

52 'Thus government is … their antisocial perpetrations.', Heath (2021 [1957]). Chapter 12: Citadel, Market and Altar

53 'This discovery will … other attempted limitations.', ibid., Chapter 13: The Socialization of Government

Besides this, Heath committed the same three fallacies as anarchists commonly do. First, while recognising that the enforcement of rights is crucial for prosperity[54], he failed to see that enforcement inevitably involves coercion and that some coercion is therefore necessary for prosperity.[55] Second, Heath overlooked the fact that effective enforcement requires the superior power to coerce.[56] Third, he failed to see that coercive power is inevitable even though he acknowledged the need for protection and that it can therefore always be abused. What makes governments abuse their coercive power in transgression of their rights of government can therefore also make his envisioned replacement do so. Subordination to a proprietary administrator tasked with enforcement can involve coercion as much as subordination to any other kind of government.

When supporting the existence of a state, he envisioned a night-watchman state as ideal, but this would also inevitably have the power to coerce. Moreover, this minarchist ideal is incompatible with the political economy of representative democracy with universal suffrage – Under the present political system it would not even be viable in the first place. Minarchism reqruires a different type of government.

Heath also falsely believed that the value of a territory's administration can only be reaped through property ownership.[57] However, administrative entrepreneurs can also capture the value they create by levying property taxes such as the land value tax. Discretion over the use and transfer of property is not necessary for this purpose and would create unnecessary diseconomies of scale. Moreover, in those

[54] 'The first … from within.', ibid., Chapter 16: The Basic Social Pattern

[55] 'Apart from the … and social decline.', ibid., Chapter 11: Property the Instrument of Freedom

[56] 'The public services … profitless and vain.', ibid., Chapter 18: Public Services by the Community Owners

[57] 'It being accepted … vital public service.', ibid., Chapter 22: Private Property in Land Explained

cases in which Heath and Heath MacCallum observed proprietary administration in the real world, ownership of property is neither common nor necessary. For example, restaurant owners and hotel operators seldom own the buildings they administer proprietarily, but rent them.

The theory of Heath and Heath MacCallum is flawed in some crucial ways. However, they deserve credit for having shown that proprietary administration can create value and that governments must therefore be careful not to crowd it out.

CHAPTER 6.

# SUMMARY

The following is a summary of the most important insights contained in Part II.

Chapter 4 started with a theoretical examination of contract in Section 4.1, which has led to the following conclusions:

- The consequences of one's actions can be affected by the actions of others. Because of this, many human decisions are conditional on expectations about the actions of others. One category of action is cooperative action, or simply 'cooperation'. People cooperate when they take actions conditional on the actions they expect from others, which they need for achieving their own ends. Successful cooperation requires certain constraints on the actions of all individuals, often leaving only one course of action. As a result, it requires the participants to expect the other participants to fulfil their parts to it. If they do not, there is no reason for them to fulfil their own parts to it. If these expectations cannot be derived from something else, like customs, social norms and knowledge of human nature, they require contract to be created.
- Contract is the communication of intentions to take certain actions. It is intended to elicit certain actions from others, and these communicated intentions may be true or false. Contracting occurs because the outcomes of someone's actions can be affected by the actions of others, which makes him partly depend his actions on those he expects from the others and thereby the intentions they communicate.
- Contract results in rights, which are specifications of the intention to take or not to take certain actions. These rights are given to induce others to take certain actions.
- Laws, policies and treaties are collections of rights granted to and by the government. What applies to contract therefore also applies to those categories.

Subsequently, Chapter 4 moved on to explain the following:

- Actions must be congruous with the rights that have been granted. When congruity is imposed or inevitable, people cooperate in ways that all contracting participants prefer, i.e. that are Pareto improvements for them. The violation of rights, violative action, is detrimental to prosperity by undermining cooperation with mutually preferred outcomes. Congruity requires consent and requires that contracting does not involve threats to act violatively.
- Since it is inevitable that people can act violatively, some people must be tasked with enforcing rights. Enforcement is crucial for prosperity, as it ensures that actions are congruous. When rights are enforced, contracting therefore results in actions that all contracting participants prefer to occur. An advanced society, which is characterised by advanced specialisation, contracting and a division of labour, cannot exist without it.
- Subordination to such an enforcement provider can be based on consent. Subordination is consensual when people are free to end their subordination by leaving the jurisdiction, unless they have conditionally given up the right to do so.
- The people who are considered a government are distinguished by their rights of government. This bundle of rights is variable and often includes the right to superior force, the right to the superior capacity to direct the use of force in its jurisdiction. This right is needed to provide enforcement with the consent of the subordinated.
- Rights of government can also include, for example, the right to regulate product characteristics and the right to expropriate people for infrastructure projects. A government holds these rights to create value for its subjects by enabling courses of action they prefer.

Chapter 5 then addressed the following:

- A crucial feature of a right is its alienability – the ability to transfer the right to others. Without alienability, many mutually preferred cooperations are precluded and the allocation of resources to their most preferred ends is impossible.
- The conduct of a democratic government and its agents is greatly affected by the inalienability of its rights of government, com-

bined with the dispersion of voting rights across a multitude of individual holders and variability in the distribution of its proceeds.

- The fundamental difference between private and public rights, and thereby private and public property, lies in the limits on their alienability. The proper definitions of these terms conflict with how they are commonly used.
- By making a government's rights of government private, i.e. alienable at the sole discretion of its individual owners such that they can be transferred to those most capable and willing at using them most profitably, a government is made proprietary. Its jurisdiction is then privatised.
- A proprietary government behaves differently from a non-proprietary government. It typically pursues financial profit, confers different incentives to its representatives and administration, and it is much more efficient in its conduct.
- The theory of proprietary administration of Spencer Heath and Spencer Heath MacCallum is flawed. Heathian proprietary administration involves severe diseconomies of scale and therefore cannot efficiently replace governance by states. To eliminate these diseconomies of scale and fulfil the functions of the state efficiently, the Heathian proprietary administrator must become a proprietary government.

# PART III

# PROPRIETARY DEMOCRACY

CHAPTER 7.

# ENTREPRENEURSHIP AND CONSUMER SOVEREIGNTY

## 7.1 INTRODUCTION

This chapter contains a praxeological theory of entrepreneurship that differs from both common doctrine and other theories that have come from the Austrian School. While thoroughly 'Austrian' by its method, the theory in this chapter differs in several ways from both Austrian and non-Austrian theories of entrepreneurship:

- It concerns all cooperation, not only the exchange of goods, and views entrepreneurship as the preparation of opportunities for cooperation. Until now, virtually all economic literature has viewed entrepreneurship in the context of the provision of goods in exchange for an amount of some medium of exchange. It does not only apply to such cases, but to the entire category of cooperative action, including for example mating, friendship and collaboration in warfare and crime.[58]
- It does not concern 'markets', since these do not exist in reality. As will be argued, 'markets' are a fiction, convenient for simplifying and conveying ideas in business and economics but strictly incorrect and a common cause of error. It instead refers to opportunities for cooperation, which are prepared and offered

[58] The category of cooperation includes many more actions than may seem. See Section 4.1.

by entrepreneurs and are all unique and fleeting.[59] This makes the theory more realistic than both neoclassical and other Austrian theories.

- It does not take financial profit as a measure of entrepreneurial success, but preference satisfaction. An entrepreneur does not necessarily seek to maximise his profit, but always pursues preferable terms of cooperation. The terms to a cooperation are simply the actions to be undertaken as part of it, so obtaining preferable terms is simply synonymous with obtaining a preferable cooperation.[60] The ability to successfully demand better terms results in the ability to reap higher profits, but only insofar the entrepreneur values financial profit does profit contribute to the satisfaction of his preferences and will he pursue it. To satisfy their preferences, many entrepreneurs choose to forego profits. In fact, entrepreneurial action can result in financial losses but satisfied preferences, as well as financial profit but unsatisfied preferences. Concentrating on terms to cooperation makes the theory more realistic, because it does not require the assumption of the profit motive, i.e. that en-

59 Entrepreneurs drive the preparations that many cooperations require and present the resulting 'opportunities for cooperation' to their 'opportunity recipients'. Note that the term 'opportunities for cooperation' used in this book refers to those to be taken by their intended recipients. These are different from those often commonly described by economists in the context of entrepreneurship, which are those available to the entrepreneur. Such entrepreneurial opportunities are, as understood in the theory in this book, opportunities to create opportunities for cooperation. The latter kind, those the recipient is presented, is what is addressed here.

60 With different terms, it is a different cooperative course of action that takes place. Even though the actions of others as part of cooperation may be unchanged, different terms implies a different course of action of at least one participant. Better terms to a trade for a seller may be, for example, a higher price. Or it may be that the buyer comes to collect the good instead of the seller delivering it.

trepreneurs seek to maximise their financial profits. Instead, entrepreneurs seek to satisfy their preferences, which people always do when they act.
- It differs from common Austrian theories by including anti-competitive action, deception and commitment strategies as types of action available to entrepreneurs and explains how these categories differ from competitive action. Competitive action is the creation of better opportunities for cooperation than others do, while anticompetitive action makes the recipients of cooperative opportunities unable to achieve other ends they prefer, such as by limiting the creation of better opportunities by competitors or making them more costly to obtain. Deception changes the preferences of the recipients of cooperative opportunities and a commitment strategy convinces them that only certain terms would be accepted. These categories of action make the recipients of cooperative opportunities accept terms they find worse. They differ importantly in their consequences for them and for competitors. In this book, anticompetitive action, commitment strategies and deception are considered to be possible, profitable and common. Thereby, the theory contradicts the dismissive attitudes that most 'Austrians' have held to these categories of action.[61]

The main purpose of this chapter is to prove some claims about the notion of consumer sovereignty. This is crucial for the purpose of this book, most importantly because it is related to the idea of *proprietary democracy*, i.e. consumer sovereignty over governments. The notion of proprietary democracy will be explained in Section

61 It contradicts in particular Murray Rothbard's monopoly theory, according to which monopoly is only created by government interference in the actions of its subjects. I contend that monopoly is naturally ubiquitous because every entrepreneurial endeavour monopolises something, namely all the unique opportunities for cooperation it creates. Instead of studying monopoly, economists should shift their attention to anticompetitive action.

7.8. Chapter 8 explains how to maximise proprietary democracy and Chapter 9 outlines some of its benefits.

Before we proceed to the theory itself, it is important to explain some key ideas.

## THE VALUATION OF ENDS AND MEANS

When people act, they choose to bring about one outcome instead of another. Action is the use of means to achieve preferred ends. If someone perceives no means to be necessary to attain the end he seeks, he has already attained it – The outcome is expected without any necessary action.

When someone pursues some outcome, using the means and achieving the ends are part of the same outcome because having used some means is part of the state of affairs one chooses to bring about. Because people act to bring about one state of affairs instead of another, and means and ends are part of the same states of affairs, people value the means and ends together. Complementary means to the same end are therefore valued together.

If someone is willing to use certain means to attain a certain end, and a required action becomes unnecessary, that person will still be willing to perform the exact same action to obtain the other means necessary for attaining the end. This is because the outcome is the same whether one performs some action to obtain one means or another. One must therefore be indifferent between the two.

If one part of a set of complementary means becomes less costly, the costs saved thus accrue to what one is willing to sacrifice for the other means. For example, when one is willing to pay some amount of money for some factors of production, the amount by which one part of those factors becomes cheaper accrues to what one is willing to pay for the other necessary factors.

## CONSUMER SOVEREIGNTY

The notion of consumer sovereignty plays a crucial role in this chapter. According to this idea, entrepreneurs are impelled to satisfy the preferences of consumers as best as they can. The 'market process' impels them to cater to the most urgent wants of the consumers, because consumers determine the profitability of entrepreneurial endeavours by choosing to take the opportunities for exchange that they value most. Under consumer sovereignty, entrepreneurs can only get more preferable outcomes by catering better to the preferences of the people they cooperate with. That is, they can only influence cooperations to their advantage by bringing about Pareto improvements for the other cooperating parties. The theory of consumer sovereignty will be explained in Section 7.7.

Not all economists agree with the theory. As will be shown in this chapter, the account of the 'market process' on which it is based is incomplete in important ways and the theory of consumer sovereignty is thereby incorrect. In reality, consumer sovereignty has its limits. Although the consumer is largely sovereign, there are ways in which entrepreneurs do not obtain the cooperations most preferable to them by preparing the cooperative opportunities most preferable to their consumers. There are things they can do to get outcomes they prefer in ways that conflict with the preferences of those who receive their cooperative opportunities. These limits to consumer sovereignty will be explained in Sections 7.4 to 7.7.

The idea at the core of Part III of this book is the idea of 'proprietary democracy', i.e. the consumer sovereignty of people over governments. Chapter 8 will address conditions under which proprietary democracy is maximised. That is, conditions that must be satisfied such that a government can only get better terms of cooperation, and thus maximise its financial profits, by offering terms preferred by subjects. Answering this question is crucial, because the relative merit of the proprietary government depends on its results for those affected by it, which include its subjects in particular. The conditions for proprietary democracy are not as easily satisfied as the conditions for consumer sovereignty over entrepreneurs in non-governmental endeavours. As a result, special institutional arrangements must be made to maximise proprietary democracy. This will be explained in Chapter 10.

In Chapter 5 it was shown how limited alienability in the rights of government undermines the efficient use of these rights and thereby profit maximisation by governments, for better or worse. But if the rights of government are alienable and governments and their agents pursue financial profits more successfully and intentionally, how will they behave? In particular, how will they use their abilities to direct the use of force? The answer to these questions depends on the conditions under which a proprietary government exists, particularly its institutional arrangements.

Chapter 8 will explain circumstances under which proprietary democracy is maximised. But first, the notion of consumer sovereignty and its limits must be explained. To this end, this chapter casts a new look on the themes of entrepreneurship and competition.

## 7.2 COOPERATION WITH PARTLY CONFLICTING PREFERENCES

People act because they prefer the outcomes they thereby expect to bring about over all alternatives they perceive to be within their reach. By cooperating, people try to eliminate outcomes together that they view as inferior to the those they thereby expect to bring about instead. But while the participants all prefer to cooperate and thus share some preferences, their preferences do not necessarily accord completely. They all share the preference to eliminate the inferior outcomes by cooperating, but they can have conflicting preferences over the outcomes to realise together instead. While they all prefer to cooperate, their preferences can conflict over the terms of cooperation, i.e. over what specific cooperative course of action to undertake.

For instance, if two people decide to cook something together, they both prefer this over all courses of action where one or neither of the two were to cook. However, they may still disagree on the dish they are going to cook. And when someone sells something to another person, the seller may prefer to receive a higher price, while the buyer may prefer to pay a lower price. There are prices to which both would agree, so they prefer to trade with each other over not doing so at all. But they each prefer a different price.

The participants all prefer the different cooperative courses of action that can eliminate the inferior outcomes over those they expect to bring about the inferior outcomes. Thereby, these courses of action are all Pareto efficient with respect to the preferences of the participants. The courses of action eliminated through cooperation are Pareto inefficient. But some participants may prefer one Pareto efficient course of action while others prefer another.

People can influence a cooperative course of action and the resulting outcome to their advantage, away from one Pareto efficient cooperation to another they prefer. That is, it is possible to affect the terms of cooperation to one's own advantage and at the expense of the other cooperating participants. Because this results in a deviation from a Pareto efficient course of action, this always comes at the expense of other participants.[62]

## ANTICOMPETITIVE ACTION, DECEPTION, COMMITMENT STRATEGIES AND VIOLATIVE ACTION

People can affect the terms of cooperation to their perceived advantage and at the expense of others. One way to do so is by making other outcomes impossible that others would prefer. This forces them to accept outcomes they find less attractive. In other words, by removing some alternatives that people have, someone can impel them to cooperate with himself in a way he prefers. The eliminated alternative outcomes can be brought about by cooperations with others, with himself, or actions that are not cooperative at all. They can be Pareto efficient, and by eliminating them someone can ensure that another Pareto efficient outcome is brought about which he himself prefers. In this book, this is called anticompetitive action. When someone engages in anticompetitive action, he makes alternative outcomes impossible that people he wishes to cooperate with would prefer over those enabled by his own offerings. When done intentionally, someone acts anticompetitively to make others cooperate toward his own preferred outcome. If they would not prefer these alternatives, anticompetitive action would not be necessary in the first place. They would eliminate these alternatives through cooperation with him. Anticompetitive action is therefore meant to affect an eventual course of action to one's own advantage and at the expense of others.

Anticompetitive action can take various forms. For example, someone can hinder consumers from reaching competitors, or pre-

[62] As per the definition of Pareto efficiency. A Pareto efficient outcome is one from which no deviation is possible that makes someone better off without making anyone else worse off.

vent competitors from offering substitutes, or collude with competitors. Anticompetitive action includes many courses of action, some of which aimed at opportunity recipients directly and some of them aimed at competing entrepreneurs to eventually change the choices of opportunity recipients.

Besides anticompetitive action, there are more ways to move a cooperation from a Pareto efficient one to another oneself prefers. A common way is to create unrealistic expectations, in this book simply called deception. Unrealistic expectations can alter people's preferences. Unrealistic expectations can influence people's preferences and thereby lead them to choose courses of action that they would not have preferred under realistic expectations, but which the deceiver prefers. Because their expectations are unrealistic, they are unlikely to benefit from the outcome even though they preferred to take the course of action leading up to it. It often results in regret.

Deception takes various forms. One can for example obtain better terms of cooperation by making false promises if these promises are not perfectly enforced. One can also create false expectations by presenting opportunities for cooperation misleadingly without lying explicitly. For example, the advertisements of travel companies often contain pictures of crisp white beaches and smiling, friendly people, but no mention of stinking sewers or malaria infections.

It would be difficult to deny that people can be manipulated. Deception is possible and profitable.[63] There are of course mechanisms people use against deception, such as reputation mechanisms, but such mechanisms cannot eliminate deception completely.

To impel others into accepting terms more attractive to oneself, one can also try to credibly commit to these terms. Entrepreneurs often apply such commitment strategies in pricing their offerings. By asking a fixed price instead of allowing customers to bargain, they signal that bargaining with them will be fruitless and thereby

[63] Deception can form the basis of a very lucrative business. The Roman Catholic Church is perhaps the best historical example of this. The splendour of the Vatican attests to the profitability of mass manipulation.

commit to this price. Even though they would stay in business if their offering could only be sold at a lower price, they prefer to commit to these terms. Not everyone is willing to accept the terms they commit to, so they thereby exclude many cooperative opportunities that they could benefit from. However, such a commitment strategy can deliver them greater benefits. A smaller number of cooperations at better terms may deliver greater benefits than a larger number of cooperations at worse terms.

Lastly, as explained in Chapter 4, violative action and violative threats can move cooperations to courses of action other participants do not prefer. One's gain from acting violatively typically comes at the expense of someone else. Since this has been explained in Section 4.3, it needs no further elaboration here.

In all these types of action, the preferences of the cooperating parties conflict. Someone engages in them to move a course of action from one Pareto efficient cooperation to another one he prefers. This always comes at the expense of others – One obtains better terms of cooperation only by making others accept terms they find worse.

Note that the different categories of action addressed in this chapter are not mutually exclusive. The categories refer to the effects of certain actions. By having different effects at once, an action can belong to multiple categories. For instance, an action can be both competitive and anticompetitive or both deceptive and violative. Neither is it claimed that these categories are collectively exhaustive. There may still be other types of action that replace some Pareto efficient cooperations by others.

This chapter explains in what respects the interests of people are aligned with the preferences of those they provide opportunities for cooperation to and in what respects they are not. That is, it explains to what extent there is consumer sovereignty. To this end, we must first examine entrepreneurship.

## 7.3 ENTREPRENEURSHIP AND COMPETITION

### PRESENT CHOICES TO AFFECT THE FUTURE

A state of affairs is always the consequence of what has happened before, so to bring about one future state of affairs instead of another requires action before that future arrives. Meanwhile, different present actions affect the future differently. Some present actions constrain and enable future actions in some ways, other actions do so in other ways. What one does in the present can thus limit what one can do in the future.

Because people care about their future possibilities, they make their present actions partly depend on how their actions affect those possibilities. Thus, people choose courses of actions to keep open and open up future avenues for action. People make preparations to enable future actions and their resulting outcomes.

To know what preparations to make, one must know what outcomes are possible, which outcomes one prefers, what preparations they require and how to make the necessary preparations. Then, one must also practically succeed at making the right preparations. The future is uncertain, so the knowledge needed to make successful preparations is imperfect. There is therefore a risk of making preparations that are not worthwhile in hindsight. As a result, one can benefit from making preparations for a range of contingencies.

One can thus benefit from making preparations to enable a range of future actions. Different preparations are possible for different courses of actions, between which one needs to choose. To do this, one needs to know which actions and resulting outcomes can be enabled, how they can be enabled and which outcomes one prefers. When one seeks to enable future cooperations, the future preferences of people are also important.

These preparations can be costly. One must often forego some things one values to enable future actions. They are also not guaranteed to turn out to be worthwhile, as the future is uncertain. Preparation therefore involves costs and risks.

What cooperations one can engage in depend partly on the preferences of the people one is to cooperate with. The future preferences of people are therefore important information for deciding one's present actions if one wants to enable some future cooperations. Which cooperative opportunities will be worth creating also depends on their alternatives and on what one offers. If someone needs to take present actions to enable future cooperative actions he therefore needs to know the future alternatives and preferences people will have, and how he can enable these preferences to be satisfied.

## ENTREPRENEURIAL ACTION

Enabling future cooperation does not need to involve cooperation with the people it is meant for. Actions from others are not necessarily required to prepare attractive cooperative opportunities for them. The cooperative actions for which an entrepreneur seeks to create opportunities are therefore separate from the entrepreneurial actions that enable them. The preparatory actions and the cooperations they are meant to enable are two separate categories of action. The preparatory actions are driven by what is commonly called *entrepreneurship*.

Imagine a society in which the cooperations people can engage in are completely independent of what they did before. That is, what one does in the present does not affect what cooperative actions one can undertake in the future. In this society, there is no need to invest in capital goods, to educate oneself for a particular job, to produce goods in order to sell them, to advertise and so on. Even though the outcomes of one's actions would still be uncertain, this would not affect how and with whom one can cooperate. There would be no entrepreneurial risk.

Entrepreneurship is ubiquitous. Because cooperation often requires preparations, much of what people do is intended to enable it. For example, many types of work require people to have invested in their own education. To produce and sell goods, people must invest in capital goods. And to find employment opportunities, people often need to migrate. These are all examples of cooperations and the preparations they require. Entrepreneurship is the choice to enable future cooperations, and many decisions have an entrepreneurial aspect as people consider how their actions will affect what cooperations they can later engage in.

Because it cannot be fully known what cooperative opportunities can be created, what alternatives people will have in the future and what their preferences will be, the outcome of entrepreneurial action is uncertain. When an cooperative opportunity has been created by an entrepreneur, those for whom the opportunity is intended are free to choose whether to accept the offer when it is made.[64] If the entre-

[64] The entrepreneur does not need to know for whom he intends his created opportunities for cooperation. The intended recipients may have

preneur fails to provide an opportunity for cooperation that people prefer to their alternatives on terms that cover his costs, he will have to bear some or all of the costs himself. Even if people do want to cooperate with him, they may not do so in the way he had hoped. This may be because he has taken the wrong steps and failed to create the opportunity, or because he should not have decided to undertake the project in the first place because there are better alternatives. For his entrepreneurial action, intended to satisfy the wants of others, he is then not rewarded (enough) by them. He has then undertaken a project based on imperfect knowledge and failed.

If the entrepreneur's actions are wise, they will enable him to offer others opportunities for cooperation towards ends for which they are willing to do something in return that he considers worth his costs. They will then enable him to successfully demand terms of cooperation that he would find satisfactory when deciding to undertake his project. If they are not, people will not take up the entrepreneur's offer and his preparations will have been in vain.

But if those for whom the opportunities for cooperation are intended can commit themselves, before the necessary preparations are made, to doing their part in the cooperative action to be prepared, and if these commitments are binding, the consequences of uncertainty fall entirely on them. By entering into this forward contract, they now bear the risk that the preparations will fail and that the offer will not be worthwhile. In this counterfactual example, the opportunity recipients can contract in the present for all future cooperations, which gives them the risk of making commitments that conflict with their future preferences. By choosing between different forward contracts, they decide what cooperations are enabled. They now act as entrepreneurs instead of the former entrepreneur.

The more uncertainty there is, the less confident one can be about possibilities and the future preferences of others, and the less eager one is to make the necessary preparations, especially if those prepa-

known or unknown identities. Every entrepreneurial action is meant to offer opportunities for others, but the entrepreneur can intend them for definite or indefinite groups or individuals, whose existence he may not even be certain of.

rations cannot be used for other opportunities in light of new information, such as when capital goods cannot be converted for other uses. If the intended recipients of the opportunities were to make these decisions as described above and assume the associated risk, those making the preparations would be more eager, but they would not be entrepreneurs. Instead, those for whom the opportunities are intended would become the entrepreneurs. Entrepreneurship thus involves speculation and uncertainty bearing.

To be successful in his endeavours, the entrepreneur must incur costs. Not only must he make preparations for his entrepreneurial endeavours by doing things like investing in capital goods and hiring people, but he must also educate himself, keep up with technological developments, learn about the preferences of others and find out who to hire to do the work necessary to prepare the opportunities he intends to create. In all this, he is also an entrepreneur. He must decide whether to look for information, where to look for information and what to learn. These decisions do not only have uncertain outcomes. They are also costly. Investing in one's own education takes time, effort and money. Much may have to be foregone to discover profitable entrepreneurial opportunities. But he must also send information to others to offer them the cooperative opportunities he has created. This is also done with uncertain outcomes. The informational aspect of entrepreneurship is therefore also part of the preparatory entrepreneurial process. The decision to pay attention to entrepreneurial opportunities and to equip oneself with the necessary skills and knowledge to engage in profitable entrepreneurial endeavours is costly and risky. It is done to bring about a state of affairs in which one is better able to create profitable opportunities for cooperation in the future.

In short, entrepreneurship exists to enable future cooperation. Entrepreneurs decide what cooperations are enabled and what preparations are made to that end. They do so with imperfect knowledge of future possibilities, preferences and competing alternatives. Entrepreneurship thus involves speculation and uncertainty bearing. If the future were certain and entrepreneurs were perfectly aware of possibilities, preferences and the alternatives that will be available, they would not try to create offers that would not be worth at least their cost. There would be no entrepreneurial loss.

## THE SCOPE OF ENTREPRENEURSHIP

As explained above, the entrepreneurs decide what preparations are made to enable future cooperations with others. These preparations are separate from the cooperations they are meant to enable. The entrepreneurs bear the risk that the opportunities thereby created will conflict with the future preferences of the people they are intended for. The people the opportunities are intended for are then given the choice to take the opportunity. They do not have to bear the cost of creating it. This cost is borne by the entrepreneur.

The consequences of uncertainty do not affect a potential participant to cooperation if the other potential participants commit to their parts of the cooperative actions before he has to incur any costs of preparation. He is then assured of the reward for his undertakings and does not offer any opportunity at all. Instead, he is offered the opportunity by the other potential participants. His scope of entrepreneurship has thereby been eliminated by extending that scope for the others.

Let us examine this 'scope of entrepreneurship' in more detail. Typically, one party to a cooperative action assumes most of the entrepreneurial risk. This party presents the cooperative opportunities resulting from its preparations to one or more recipients, who may be consumers or other entrepreneurs. The cost of creating these opportunities is borne by the entrepreneur, who expects that those for whom they are created will value them commensurately. Consider, for example, someone who buys products from an online store. His only entrepreneurial uncertainty is to browse the Internet in search of a good that may not exist or may not be offered at an attractive price. This browsing may turn out to be fruitless, but his entrepreneurial uncertainty does not extend further. One party, the seller, assumes as much of the entrepreneurial risk as he can, while others receive the opportunities. This is the most common distribution of the scope of entrepreneurship – Only a small part of society undertakes most entrepreneurship.

But let us now change this scope. Suppose that one potential participant in a cooperation bears all the costs and uncertainties of discovering the preferences of others and knowing the possibilities for satisfying these. He does not yet make any 'physical' investments, such as investments in capital goods, but only explores preferences and possibilities and communicates proposals to others who may be interested. He therefore engages in some entrepreneurship, but he limits his scope of entrepreneurship by presenting the opportunity early to his intended recipients to obtain their commitments. Other entrepreneurs then compete by offering such forward contracts to the same intended recipients, who will then get to choose. Those who are presented the opportunities will, if they commit to them, take the risk that the project will not be as attractive as they had imagined. By making early commitments, they limit the scope of entrepreneurship of he who originally presented the opportunity and extend their own. An example of such an arrangement is an new property development. Developers usually sell many units before the projects are completed or before construction has even started. The risk that the project turns out different from how it was imagined because of false perceptions – or, conceivably, construction flaws – then falls on the buyers instead of the developer.

Let us now further reduce the scope of entrepreneurship for one participant and thereby further extend it for others. The intended recipient now also bears the costs of communicating opportunities for cooperation, e.g. the costs of advertising, contracting and so on. He pays an advertising company for its services regardless of whether he receives any attractive opportunities. If such communications turn out to be fruitless by not presenting him any opportunities he prefers to take, the recipient bears the cost without any benefit. The scope of entrepreneurship is further limited for one party by extending it for another. In this context, think for example of a catalogue that people can buy.

But the example can be extended even further. Not only are the costs of communication and production now borne by one party, but also the costs of exploring attractive opportunities before they are presented. Exploratory work to find out which opportunities can be created and which might be attractive is now also done at the behest of the opportunity recipients, regardless of its benefits. This includes, for example, market research. The opportunity recipients bear its cost of which the providers are thereby relieved. The former now get to decide who performs market research into what avenues and the results of this research may be published for entrepreneurs. The entrepreneurs are now also relieved of the risk that this exploration is not worth the cost, which the opportunity recipients now bear instead.

The above illustrates the nature of entrepreneurship. Entrepreneurship is to direct and bear the costs and uncertainty of the preparation of future cooperative opportunities. Everyone in society engages in entrepreneurship to some extent, but some more than others. Entrepreneurs fulfil a crucial role in society, a role in which some choose to specialise while others choose to be more passive. Some people take on more entrepreneurial tasks than others because it is more efficient to do so. It would be inefficient for a consumer to entirely arrange all the supply chains of everything he consumes. People specialise in entrepreneurship because there are gains from such specialisation. One entrepreneur can cater to many customers at once, instead of a multitude of entrepreneurs each bearing largely the same costs. Economies of scale therefore also stem from the cost of entrepreneurship. And if everyone took on the role of entrepreneur for every product they consumed, everyone would have to acquire the same costly information. It is therefore more efficient if some people specialise in entrepreneurship while the others are more passive in that respect. Nevertheless, everyone is to some extent an entrepreneur by deciding which advertisements to pay attention to, which shops to visit, and so on.

Hence, entrepreneurship is to create opportunities for cooperation, based on an understanding of the future preferences of others, what their alternatives will be and what possible opportunities can be created at what cost. Everyone engages in entrepreneurship to some extent, but some do more than others because this is more efficient.

## THE PURE ENTREPRENEUR

As explained above, everyone is involved in entrepreneurship to some extent, but some more than others. By taking the exercise above to the extreme, leading to the idea of the 'pure entrepreneur', one can study the role of the entrepreneur by isolating entrepreneurship from other activities. One can imagine a world where there is one group of entrepreneurs who undertake all entrepreneurial activities and another group of people who do not engage in entrepreneurship at all.

In the previous thought exercise that explains the scope of entrepreneurship, the role of entrepreneurship is largely shifted from one group of people to another by having those for whom the cooperative opportunities are intended commit to their part in the cooperation in advance of all necessary preparations. They thereby bear the risk of not preferring to partake in the cooperation when it has been enabled. The alternative they will have may be superior, or the necessary actions may prove to be inadequate. They run the risk of regretting later that they engaged in this forward contract.

We can assume that, *ceteris paribus*, they would prefer not to take that risk, nor the task of deciding which preparations are to be made for which future opportunities. Instead, they would prefer to keep the option to participate in other opportunities. Moreover, others are likely to be much more capable of minimising this risk and of minimising the cost of discovering what possible opportunities can be created, which one they will prefer and what steps are best taken to make the necessary preparations. As explained before, the resulting division between specialist entrepreneurs and others is efficient.

This brings us to the pure entrepreneur. This person decides to enter into the forward contract with the former entrepreneur, instead of the opportunity recipient doing so himself. The pure entrepreneur orders all the preparations to be made in minute detail. He does not make the necessary preparations – which include advertising and other information costs necessary to present an opportunity to others – but orders in detail what people must do to make these preparations. The pure entrepreneur hires people for market research, the development of new technologies, product development, advertising and marketing, customer service and so on. They are paid to follow his orders, regardless of whether what they do turns out to be worth the cost. The pure entrepreneur does this to provide opportunities for cooperation to others, not to himself. The former entrepreneur's pay is now independent of future preferences, possibilities and the adequacy of the preparations made. He simply follows orders. The pure entrepreneur also does not require any prior commitment from those the opportunity is intended for. Instead, they are free to decline the opportunity when it is presented to them and are thereby also relieved of all entrepreneurial risk and uncertainty. They do not in any way decide which preparations are made, only which are profitable.

The success of the pure entrepreneur depends entirely on how well he understands what cooperative opportunities can be created and what steps are necessary to create them, how well he predicts the future preferences of his target customers and what other options they have, and how well he executes his plans. In his entrepreneurial endeavours, the pure entrepreneur may hire skilled workers to do much of the necessary work, as when he hires engineers to make his capital goods. But he alone decides what opportunities for cooperation are to be created, and he alone bears the consequences of his failure to anticipate relevant facts about the future.

The example of the imaginary pure entrepreneur shows that the entrepreneur only directs the preparations that are made for cooperation and assumes the associated costs and risks. Entrepreneurship does not involve taking the actual actions that prepare opportunities for cooperation, but deciding which opportunities for cooperation are prepared, how they are prepared, and taking the risk that the wrong opportunities are prepared. For example, an entrepreneur does not make machines, build a factory and put everything in place for production. He hires people and compensates them such that they are satisfied with the terms they get. Providing labour and capital for the preparation of cooperative opportunities is not entrepreneurial, but directing their use is. To do so, he compensates those who perform the physical tasks. He bears all the costs and risks involved in the preparation, since he alone decides which cooperative opportunities are prepared.

## COMPETING OPPORTUNITIES FOR COOPERATION

An entrepreneur creates future opportunities for cooperation, and his success partly depends on what alternatives to those opportunities will exist. The cooperations others will be willing to partake in will depend on the alternatives within their reach. If he creates a cooperative opportunity, but someone else in the meantime creates a better one that will remove the need for his, his project will be in vain. The people for whom he had intended his opportunity will then choose another instead. This puts him in competition with other entrepreneurs. The cooperative opportunities he intends to create, even if they are superior to any other currently available, may be worthless by the time he has finished his preparations and presented them to their intended recipients. Another entrepreneur may, for example, prepare an offering by using a superior technology or by adapting the same technology better to consumer preferences.

The entrepreneur faces competition not only from other entrepreneurs, but also from future alternatives that are not cooperative at all. For example, a product may be rendered worthless by a costless and free technological innovation, or by others unintentionally removing the need for his offering. Entrepreneurs face competition from countless other possible actions that their opportunity recipients can take, not just the opportunities for cooperation offered by others.

Because the offerings of others can affect the entrepreneur's success, competition is often intentional. To be successful, the entrepreneur must pay attention to the cooperative opportunities offered by others. He must compete whether he wants to or not, either by enabling people to achieve more valued ends or by offering them less costly means to the same ends. The lower the value people attribute to the opportunities offered by others, the more offerings of the entrepreneur they are willing to accept. That is, the worse the offerings of others are, the better the terms of cooperation he can successfully demand. Conversely, the better his competition is, the worse the terms the entrepreneur can successfully demand. Thus, the more attractive his opportunity recipients find the terms he can offer and the less attractive the alternatives offered by others, the better the terms he can obtain. If he offers cooperative opportunities that opportunity recipients prefer over those offered by his competitors, cooperating with him will be a Pareto improvement for him and his opportunity recipients over the course of action in which his opportunity recipients cooperate with his competitors. Insofar he competes by offering better cooperative opportunities, i.e., Pareto improvements for the cooperating parties, his interests are thus aligned with the preferences of the recipients of the cooperative opportunities he creates.

Cooperation is a form of action, so it is always a means to an end. Instead of the opportunity offered by some entrepreneur, other courses of action may be preferred to achieve the same end, such as acquiring a good that has proven to be a better substitute to that offered by the entrepreneur, or by solving a defect at home without the help of a professional. The more suitable another available course of action as a substitute for the entrepreneur's offering, the larger the impact of the availability of this alternative and the conditions on which it is available on the conditions someone is willing to cooperate with the entrepreneur. For example, if an entrepreneur offers a good that is an adequate substitute for another good to achieve the same ends, a fall in the price of one will make people choose that instead quicker than if they were less substitutable. That is, the better one good can substitute for another, the more a change in the price of that good will affect what people are willing to pay for the other.

The magnitude of this effect is called the price elasticity of demand, but price is only one respect in which competing substitutes affect each other's profitability. In general terms, the better one's cooperative opportunity can substitute for another's, the more the terms which one can successfully demand depend on the terms of the competing offering.

There are two ways for a cooperation to be a Pareto improvement over another course of action. Either all terms are preferred by all participants, or some terms are preferred by some participants while others are preferred by other participants, and the cooperation overall is preferred by all participants. In the latter case, participants accept terms that they find less preferable to get other terms that they prefer. The preferable terms are then worth accepting the less preferable terms. Someone can thus obtain better terms of cooperation in some respects by offering terms in other respects that are preferred by those he cooperates with. Such a cooperation is then a Pareto improvement. For example, he can obtain a higher price for something he sells by making the opportunities he offers more attractive in other respects, such that it is a Pareto improvement for him and his opportunity recipients. Meanwhile, he can also obtain better terms as part of his preparations, such as the prices he must pay to suppliers, by offerings terms more attractive to them in other respects. Thus, what applies to the income from entrepreneurial preparations also applies to the costs incurred for them. The better someone's opportunity recipients find the terms he offers in one respect, the better the terms he can obtain in other respects, and the greater the financial profit he can thus make. In this sense, his interests are aligned with those of everyone he cooperates with, which can for example include both suppliers and customers.

One could thus conclude that whether some entrepreneurial preparations are worthwhile depends on whether the cooperations to make the preparations as well as the cooperations thereby enabled are Pareto improvements. However, there are many ways for an entrepreneur to get better terms without offering better terms in other respects. One way to do so is by making alternative outcomes impossible that the people one seeks to cooperate with would choose instead of one's own offering. This can make them willing to accept terms they find less favourable. Such actions, called anticompetitive actions, will be addressed in the following section.

## 7.4 ANTICOMPETITIVE ACTION

Besides competitive action, people can engage in anticompetitive action. Someone acts anticompetitively by making people with whom he aims to cooperate unable to obtain other outcomes that they would choose instead of his own offering.[65] He thereby makes them accept terms they find less attractive than the outcome he prevents. In other words, by removing some alternatives that people have, someone can make them cooperate with himself in a way he prefers. Such alternatives are obtained through cooperation with others, with himself, or through actions that are not cooperative at all. The outcomes that someone prevents by acting anticompetitively may be Pareto efficient, but by preventing them he can ensure that other Pareto efficient courses of action and outcomes are brought about which he prefers. When done intentionally, someone acts anticompetitively to make others cooperate toward his own preferred outcome. If they would not prefer the alternatives thereby eliminated, anticompetitive action would not be necessary in the first place. They would eliminate these alternatives by cooperating with him. Thus, when he acts anticompetitively he seeks to move an eventual outcome to his own advantage and at the expense of others. Such anticompetitive action includes action that reduces the ability or willingness of others to compete or makes competitors' cooperative opportunities more costly to get.

Hence, someone only intentionally acts anticompetitively to make outcomes impossible that he perceives others would choose over the outcomes he himself prefers, such that others will be will-

[65] Any course of action results in that course of action having been performed, so the outcomes of a course of action include the course of action itself. Preventing some outcome can thus be done by preventing some actions necessary for it, or by making a course of action lead to another outcome. Someone can thus act anticompetitively by making people unable to engage in courses of action that he expects them to prefer to undertake over his own offerings, but also by making them unable to achieve their preferred ends through those courses of action. Both count as making people unable to obtain their preferred ends.

ing to cooperate into bringing about his own preferred outcome. He then does so to replace a Pareto efficient outcome with another one, rather than to replace a Pareto inferior outcome with a Pareto improvement. Someone therefore only intends to act anticompetitively when he perceives it to be such that it is not a Pareto improvement.

If someone acts anticompetitively, he drives opportunity recipients to other Pareto efficient courses of action that involve cooperation with himself, whereas if he acts competitively, his actions lead to a Pareto improvement. An opportunity recipient would thus consent to a competitive action but not to an anticompetitive action.

Consider a situation in which a person named Andy initially plans to offer a cooperation, which would form part of an outcome A1 thereby enabled for the opportunity recipient, while his competitor named Bob plans to offer a cooperation that would lead to an alternative outcome B1. Andy correctly anticipates that the opportunity recipient will prefer B1 over A1, so Andy makes an investment resulting in an option A2 that the opportunity recipient will prefer over B1. The opportunity recipient prefers A2 over B1, so he would approve the investment if it were at his discretion.

But Andy can also perform an action that replaces B1 by an inferior outcome B2, for example by making it more difficult for the opportunity recipient to cooperate with Bob or by making it impossible or too costly for Bob to enable B1. The opportunity recipient then has to choose between A1 and B2, and he prefers A1. In this case he also chooses Andy's offering, but since he would prefer B1 over A1 and A1 over B2, he would prefer B1 not to be replaced by B2. The anticompetitive action thus harms him – The replacement of B1 by B2 and the resulting shift from B1 to A1 is not a Pareto improvement. He would therefore not approve Andy's anticompetitive action if his approval were required for it to occur.

## THE UBIQUITY OF ANTICOMPETITIVE ACTION

Every entrepreneurial endeavour has anticompetitive effects, but some more so than others. Since most goods are provided at physical places (as opposed to, for example, online services) and every place is unique and rivalrous, every choice to provide an offering at a physical place also limits the ability of others to compete.[66] For example, by opening a coffee shop, an entrepreneur precludes others from offering substitutes on the same premises. Strictly speaking, he thereby obtains a 'local monopoly'. Fierce competition will still be possible from places nearby, so the anticompetitive effect of his venture on the terms he can obtain is likely to be small. But if a coffeeshop is the only one allowed or able to sell coffee in a large park, the effect of this preclusion of competition is likely to be larger. Depending on the context, locational anticompetitive action can thus significantly affect the terms of cooperation, including prices. For example, if an entrepreneur succeeds at acquiring all coal mines in a region, only he will be able to sell coal locally without incurring high transport costs. In this case, especially if transport is generally costly, the effect on profitability is likely to be much larger than that of the coffee shop's limited local monopoly.

Some actions are competitive but not anticompetitive and some actions are anticompetitive but not competitive. For the former, think of introducing a new technique that other entrepreneurs can copy at no cost. One's actions affect what customers are willing to pay for the products of competitors, but do not keep competitors from competing in any way. For the latter, think of the possibility of patenting an existing technology. This would be purely anticompetitive because it would only prevent others from competing by using the patented technology.

Everything is rivalrous, so every entrepreneurial venture is to some extent anticompetitive. All competitive ventures therefore have anticompetitive effects, not only by the fact that every location is unique and rivalrous. To make the necessary preparations to offer oppor-

66 Strictly speaking, this example also applies to online services. Entrepreneurs, by having their website hosted on a domain name, thereby exclude others from using the same domain name. But on the internet, the effect of this anticompetitive aspect on profitability is likely to be negligible. Significant locational monopolies are more difficult to obtain on the internet than in physical space. But some anticompetitive actions on the internet can be more consequential, such as search engine optimisation.

tunities for cooperation, entrepreneurs usually use physical resources and cooperate with others. For example, a shoe manufacturer buys leather and labour to make shoes for consumers. Every such resource is strictly speaking unique, including in its place and time of provision. By acquiring those resources, the manufacturer precludes all other cooperations that require them.

For entrepreneurial projects, the time and place of provision are relevant, because opportunities for cooperation are always fleeting and unique. In order to provide a set of opportunities for cooperation, entrepreneurs must acquire certain resources and cooperate with certain people all within a certain time frame and within certain geographical boundaries. By acquiring a resource, an entrepreneur makes others unable to acquire the exact same resource and by cooperating with certain people he makes others unable to cooperate with them in certain ways at that time. And by occupying some place, someone prevents others from doing so. Therefore, every entrepreneurial venture that uses resources, a particular place or cooperation with others to create an opportunity, is to some extent anticompetitive.[67] By creating an opportunity for cooperation, one makes others unable to create the same opportunity for cooperation and probably also many similar ones. One does not only make others unable to offer the same opportunities, but also many other opportunities. If an entrepreneur acquires all of a particular resource that can be provided in a certain area in a certain timeframe, he thereby monopolises all unique opportunities that require any of those resources in that timeframe and in that area. Infinite different delineations of timeframes and areas exist, and so do therefore the possibilities for anticompetitive action.

67 This may seem to contradict the claim in the previous paragraph that some actions are competitive without being anticompetitive. But it only meant to say that an entrepreneurial endeavour, which is a set of preparatory actions, always contains some action with anticompetitive effects if it involves some use of physical resources or cooperation. This does not mean that all actions that make up an entrepreneurial endeavour are anticompetitive. Some entrepreneurial actions may not require any physical resources or cooperation and thus do not preclude any course of action by someone else.

The wider the range of opportunities are monopolised and the more substitutable those opportunities are as means to the same end for their recipients, the greater the impact of such monopolisation on the terms he can obtain. By limiting the ability of other entrepreneurs to compete with his offering, the entrepreneur thus improves the profitability of his own endeavours.

In a counterfactual world in which an infinite number of entrepreneurs could offer the same or different cooperations to exactly the same person at exactly the same place and time and using exactly the same resources, an entrepreneurial endeavour would not have to be anticompetitive. One entrepreneur would be able to offer something to someone at one place at one time, but another would be able to offer something identical to the same person at exactly the same place and time. Any number of entrepreneurs could have identical offerings at the exact same place and time, and have their rights enforced without this restricting the ability of other entrepreneurs to offer identical opportunities. But since this is physically impossible, the use of space and other resources, and even the enforcement of one's rights, is strictly speaking anticompetitive. For example, if an entrepreneur buys all the water wells in a region, he thereby gains the exclusive ability to sell water locally until new wells can be dug. If every place and resource were not unique or rivalrous, others could buy their own identical wells at exactly the same places and compete with him, so he would not be able to get more favourable terms from buying the wells. Their ability to compete with him by offering the identical water from identical wells at identical places would make his monopolisation unprofitable.

Enforcing rights is crucial for the functioning of society, so it is not argued here that this anticompetitive effect should be eliminated. But the enforcement of rights can definitely have anticompetitive effects.

## COMMON CASES OF ANTICOMPETITIVE ACTION

Anticompetitive action includes many courses of action, some of which are aimed at the opportunity recipient directly and some of which are aimed at competing entrepreneurs to eventually change the choices of opportunity recipients. For example, anticompetitive action can take the form of hindering consumers in reaching competitors, or of hindering competitors in offering substitutes, thereby leading consumers to oneself instead.

An example of anticompetitive action that harms competitors is sabotage or outright violence. A well-known example from history is the actions of the Luddites, who destroyed the machinery of industrial entrepreneurs to prevent them from competing successfully. As another example, competing gangs in the illegal drug trade often act anticompetitively by harming other gangs, resulting in local illegal drug monopolies.

Anticompetitive action can harm competitors, but it can also benefit them. When competitors' opportunities for cooperation are highly substitutable for his own, the terms an entrepreneur can successfully demand through a commitment strategy are more limited. But by colluding, competitors can get better terms. The opportunity recipients are then deprived of cooperative opportunities that they would find more attractive.

Collusion can be done by resource suppliers, for example. A notable example of this is OPEC. OPEC is a cartel of oil-producing countries that collectively keep oil prices much higher than they would otherwise be.[68] The cartel is not always stable, but it is most of the time.

## THE NOTION OF ANTICOMPETITIVE ACTION VERSUS THE NOTION OF MONOPOLY

It is common in this context to speak of 'monopoly' over some 'market'. When an entrepreneur gains a monopoly, this enables him in some circumstances to charge 'monopoly prices', which are prices above those that would exist in a 'competitive' market. Such prices

[68] As can be expected, OPEC does not call itself a cartel. Citing Investopedia.com: 'The term Organization of the Petroleum Exporting Countries (OPEC) refers to a group of 13 of the world's major oil-exporting nations. OPEC was founded in 1960 to coordinate the petroleum policies of its members and to provide member states with technical and economic aid. OPEC is a cartel that aims to manage the supply of oil in an effort to set the price of oil on the world market, in order to avoid fluctuations that might affect the economies of both producing and purchasing countries.' (Hayes, n.d.)

then result in 'monopoly profits', which are profits made by restricting the supply of a good, or in the terminology of this book, by offering fewer opportunities for cooperation.

The problem with the notion of monopoly as understood by most economists is that markets as such do not exist.[69] There are no discrete markets with homogeneous offerings because every offering is unique. There are also no discrete markets of heterogeneous offerings since offerings can vary in infinite ways. In reality, every opportunity for cooperation is unique and exists only once. No two entrepreneurs ever offer perfectly substitutable opportunities for cooperation to the same person in exactly the same way at exactly the same place and time. Therefore, every opportunity for cooperation is strictly speaking monopolised and every entrepreneur a monopolist. Every price is then a monopoly price, even though one monopoly price may be only slightly higher than its counterfactual competitive price while another is much higher. The conditions for perfectly competitive prices are never satisfied because every opportunity is unique and therefore never a perfect substitute for another.

It is better to examine the anticompetitive actions that result in what is commonly called 'monopoly' and the effects of such actions. That is the approach taken here. This section contains a theory of anticompetitive action instead of a monopoly theory. Everyone is strictly speaking a monopolist, which makes the notion of monopoly a trivial one. Nonetheless, some people intentionally engage in anticompetitive action in the form of 'monopolisation', which can have significant effects. By acquiring the exclusive ability to offer a range of substitutable opportunities for cooperation, entrepreneurs can get better terms from their preparations at the expense of their opportunity recipients. Moreover, because every opportunity for cooperation is unique, competitive entrepreneurship is itself also a form of monopolisation and thereby anticompetitive. By competing, one also acts anticompetitively even if not done intentionally. Monopoly theory overlooks this.

Monopolisation is anticompetitive, but it is by no means the only form of anticompetitive action. There are many other types of an-

69 However, I am not alone in recognising that there are actually no separate markets. See for example Kirzner (2011 [1963]), p. 23.

ticompetitive action, such as collusion. Another type, not uncommon in many underdeveloped parts of the world, is violence and intimidation.

## THE NOTION OF SOCIETY VERSUS THE NOTION OF THE MARKET

The false notion of the monopoly stems from the fallacy that there are markets for more or less homogeneous goods, which as explained above is false. There is no such thing as a 'market', 'sector' or 'industry'. But the notion of any market distinct from the rest of society, the 'market economy', is false. There is no market economy as such, nor is every potential cooperative opportunity a market in and of itself. There are only societies, which are simply groups of people. Or one could consider humanity to be one great society consisting of all people. There is also no such thing as 'trade' or 'market exchange' – There is only cooperation.

Market exchange or trade does not necessarily involve some transfer of money – Goods can also be bartered for goods. When actions are also included, either as services or as goods, 'exchange' becomes a category that encompasses all actions undertaken conditional on some actions one prefers others to take. It then encompasses all cooperation. The distinction between a 'market economy' and the rest of society or human cooperation thus rests on an arbitrary and unrealistic distinction between trade and cooperation. In reality, all trade is cooperation and vice versa. The market as a place or process distinct from society and cooperation is a fiction, albeit sometimes useful for conveying ideas.

Even though Ludwig von Mises conformed to common terminology by using the terms 'market' and 'trade' instead of the correct terms 'society' and 'cooperation', he understood early on that there is no difference between the market and society. In his words:

> It is no longer possible to define neatly the boundaries between the kind of action which is the proper field of economic science in the narrower sense, and other action.
>
> Acting man is always concerned with both 'material' and 'ideal' things. He chooses between alternatives. No matter whether they are to be classified as material or ideal.

> The general theory of choice is much more than merely a theory of the 'economic side' of human endeavors and of man's striving for commodities and an improvement in his material well-being. It is the science of every kind of human action. Choosing determines all human decisions.
>
> Out of the political economy of the classical school emerges the general theory of human action, praxeology. The economic or catallactic problems are imbedded in a more general science, and can no longer be severed from this connection. No treatment of economic problems proper can avoid starting from acts of choice; economics becomes a part, although the hitherto best elaborated part, of a more universal science, praxeology.[70]

One could argue that the notion of society is not superior to that of the market, that the notion of the market is benign even if incorrect since it is essentially identical to that of society and more useful for conveying ideas in economics. But this is not true, because in practice the notion of the market is used to refer to only some human cooperations, i.e. those which involve the trade of goods or services for some means of exchange. Other cooperations would supposedly be 'non-economic'.[71] Consequently, economists are led to measure economic output by the monetary value of goods exchanged. But some societies may rely more on cooperation that does not involve a means of exchange. Comparisons based on the monetary value of goods exchanged may as a result lead one to overestimate the differences in prosperity between societies and the degree to which societies were less prosperous in the past. Moreover, it also leads many economists to overestimate government involvement in so-

70 von Mises (1981).

71 The idea of 'non-economic action' is an oxymoron since all action seeks to 'economise' – Action is choosing between conflicting ends, involving scarce means to achieve them.

ciety, because contemporary governments only tax cooperation that involves the transfer of money. Cooperation in society does not only comprise the exchange of goods for money and the government does not play a role in that part of cooperation in society that does not.

There have been good and bad reasons to study economics in the context of the 'market', because 'market exchanges' are considered to be those cooperations in which a definite amount of some identical or highly similar objects or services is traded for a definite amount of currency. The neoclassical model, which revolves around magnitudes of price and quantity, becomes impossible without such a focus. The Austrian School has pointed out the shortcomings of the neoclassical model, but to the 'Austrians' this focus has also made sense as one of their main fields of inquiry has been the formation of prices and its importance for entrepreneurial planning. But this previously useful fiction that is 'the market' has its weaknesses. Exchanges of goods for currency are a form of cooperation, but cooperation is a much broader category of action. Concentrating on the market leads economists to miss out on insights about all other domains to which the praxeology of cooperation applies. What is in this book explained to apply to cooperation apply not only to what are commonly considered 'market phenomena', but also to areas such as mating, warfare, and crime.

Instead of fixating on the market, exchange and prices, the Austrian School could benefit from concentrating on respectively society, cooperation and terms of cooperation. The latter categories include the former, but are more comprehensive and do not suffer from the grey area between exchanges that supposedly take place on the market and those that would be referred to as 'non-market'.

## ANTICOMPETITIVE ACTION AND BARGAINING POWER

Anticompetitive action does not add more attractive options to the outcomes people can choose from, but removes them. This gives people no other choice than to accept less favourable terms of cooperation. In other words, an entrepreneur who acts anticompetitively makes people accept a cooperative course of action that is less attractive to them but more attractive to him. He does so to strengthen his position, enabling him to get better terms – It serves to improve the range of terms he can successfully demand for cooperation.

The ability of someone to successfully demand terms of cooperation he prefers is often called 'bargaining power'. This then becomes manifest in the process of contracting, not entrepreneurial preparations. But as was explained in Section 4.1, contracting only takes place in a world of incomplete information. In a world of complete information, an entrepreneur can benefit from anticompetitive action without this being evident in the form of bargaining power, as bargaining does not occur in such a world. The gains from anticompetitive action do not necessarily emerge in the bargaining process. Anticompetitive action and its costs and benefits exist both in a world of incomplete information and one of complete information. Only in a world of incomplete information is intentional anticompetitive action always meant to yield better terms of cooperation through commitment strategies.

## COLLUSION

Thus far, anticompetitive action has been addressed in the form of monopolisation, which comes at the expense of other entrepreneurs. But anticompetitive action can also benefit other entrepreneurs. Instead of competing, entrepreneurs can collude to obtain more favourable terms at the expense of their opportunity recipients. For instance, they can 'divide the market' among themselves according to segments. The entrepreneurs then commit to offering only cooperative opportunities that do not substitute well for those offered by the others. This leaves the recipients of cooperative opportunities with fewer options to achieve their ends and thereby enables the colluding entrepreneurs to successfully demand terms they prefer. They can also collude by demanding more favourable terms for themselves in unison, committing to not compete by offering terms their opportunity recipients would prefer. They often do this in the form of price fixing, instead of competing by unleashing price wars. In these cases, the benefits of anticompetitive action only come at the expense of the opportunity recipients.

Economies of scale can facilitate collusion by reducing the number of competitors who are well-prepared to compete. When there are fewer competitors, collusion becomes less costly. In some types of ventures, economies of scale and other anticompetitive forces are so strong that 'oligopolies' or even 'natural monopolies' emerge automatically.

## 7.5 COMMITMENT STRATEGIES AND DECEPTION

### DECEPTION

Apart from anticompetitive action, one can also move Pareto efficient courses of action to ones that are more favourable to oneself by sending certain information. People make choices based on their preferences and their preferences depend on their perceptions. An entrepreneur can change the preferences of those he seeks to cooperate with by changing their perceptions of their needs, their available courses of action and what they can expect from the opportunities he offers as well as from those of his competitors. It is difficult to deny that it is possible to influence the preferences of others. Religious, moral, and scientific authorities have influenced people's preferences throughout history. When a religious leader makes his followers avoid eating certain foods, does he not change their preferences? Similarly, a dietician can affect a patient's preferences by prescribing a diet. And since people can not only speak the truth but also omit parts of it and lie, can they not alter the preferences of others to their own advantage?

This objection to the notion of consumer sovereignty is common, but has been challenged. Entrepreneurs and others can influence the tastes of opportunity recipients, but one could for example contend that this is not possible if opportunity recipients do not allow this to happen. The opportunity recipients would thereby be 'sovereign' after all. In the words of Stanislaw Wellisz: '... we must either be forced to follow a leader, or we must accept an individual ethic. In either case a value judgment is involved'.[72]

Moreover, entrepreneurs must pay close attention to people's preferences. Even though entrepreneurs can influence the preferences of opportunity recipients, they cannot fully control them.[73] By choosing between cooperative opportunities as well as other alternatives,

[72] Bergson, Wellisz, & Baumol (1962)

[73] For a refutation of the notion that consumer tastes are formed by what is produced and not the other way around, see Hayek (1961).

people still determine to a great extent what entrepreneurs can successfully offer. Otherwise, entrepreneurs would not do any market research or adapt their offerings to consumer preferences.

But it would be difficult to argue that entrepreneurs cannot in any way influence the preferences of their opportunity recipients. By sending out information, whether true or false, they can affect what outcomes people expect from available courses of action. One notable example is the deliberate creation of false expectations about their own offerings. Without lying, entrepreneurs can portray their offerings as better than they are, such as when travel companies advertise their trips with pictures of crisp white beaches and friendly people, often smiling, but without any mention of the stinking sewers or the safety risks. Furthermore, entrepreneurs can deliberately make false promises. When contracts are not perfectly enforced, making false promises can deliver terms one prefers. Fraudsters are a common example and often get away with their crimes. The less effectively contracts are enforced, the more fraud one can expect to take place. There are non-governmental mechanisms to combat fraud, such as reputation mechanisms, but none are failproof and government solutions may well be superior if provided efficiently.

## COMMITMENT STRATEGIES

The terms of cooperation someone accepts depend to some extent on the terms he thinks he can obtain, i.e. on the terms he thinks people are willing to cooperate with him. These expectations can be affected by the preferences people claim to have. The preferences people claim to have affect the terms on which others are willing to cooperate and people's preferences are in general not fully aligned, so people can obtain better terms by communicating false preferences. Someone can get better terms by credibly communicating that he will only accept certain terms, while he would also accept less favourable terms.

A very common case is when entrepreneurs commit to fixed prices. By asking a fixed price instead of allowing customers to bargain, they commit to this price and signal that bargaining with them will be fruitless. They might still offer their goods if these could only be sold at lower prices, which tends to become clear when competition intensifies, but they commit to terms more favourable to themselves. They usually thereby forego cooperative opportunities that they could benefit from. They forego some Pareto improving cooperations because engaging in these would undermine their commitment strategy. An entrepreneur cannot maintain a fixed price if people learn that they can successfully bargain for a lower price – or, in general, better terms. His commitment must be credible. Foregoing mutually profitable cooperations is therefore a crucial element of such a commitment strategy.

Despite the resulting deadweight loss, such a commitment strategy can deliver them greater benefits. Everyone would rather engage in fewer profitable cooperations than any greater number of cooperations that one does not prefer over not cooperating at all. If an entrepreneur prefers to have more money over less, he will, *ceteris paribus*, therefore rather sell fewer products at a higher price, since at this price he can still make a financial profit.

Some customers are thereby left out, because they are willing to pay less than the price committed to but more than the entrepreneur's cost. But if he were to engage in price discrimination by selling the goods at a lower price to some customers, he would not be able to distinguish between those who intend to use the goods themselves and those who plan to resell them for a profit. So even if price discrimination would not communicate anything about his preferences, he would decide not to do it. By selling some goods at lower prices, he would make himself unable to sell goods to others at his commitment price. Price discrimination can be found in many cases where goods cannot be resold, such as enrolment at universities in the U.S. The benefit from mutually beneficial cooperations that would have occurred without the commitment strategy but are now foregone such that the entrepreneur can obtain better terms himself, is called deadweight loss. If contracting could remove the informational deficiencies resulting in deadweight losses at a lower cost than the deadweight loss eliminated, it would be in the interest of people to do so. Customers who are unwilling to pay the asking price would successfully negotiate with sellers to obtain the offered goods at lower prices. In a world of incomplete information, people contract when the expected benefit of contracting exceeds the expected cost. This puts a limit on the deadweight losses that can arise.

In a world with perfect and costless enforcement and either complete information or complete and costless contracting, and thus in a world with no transaction costs[74], no deadweight loss would have to arise. People could contract to eliminate all courses of action to which they have mutually preferred alternatives. That is, they could eliminate all Pareto inefficient courses of action. But because enforcement is costly and imperfect and because contracting is costly and incomplete and information is incomplete, deadweight losses are inevitable. Section 7.7, titled 'The Elimination Theorem,' will provide a proof of the theorem that leads to this conclusion.

The improvement of terms that is gained through commitment strategies depends on what terms opportunity recipients are willing to accept. This in turn depends on the availability and attractiveness of alternative courses of action, including opportunities for cooperation offered by competitors. Anticompetitive action can thus enable more fruitful commitment strategies and so can network effects and economies of scale.

## PARTIALLY ALIGNED PREFERENCES AND THE CONTRACTING PROCESS

As explained in Chapter 4, people contract to make the actions others deviate to alternatives they prefer. To achieve a deviation that all participants prefer, communicating false preferences is unnecessary since everyone prefers the deviation. Such deviations eliminate outcomes that are Pareto inefficient with respect to the preferences of the contracting parties. Nobody can therefore gain from communicating false preferences. But if someone prefers a deviation that others do not, he has an interest in communicating false preferences. Thus, if the preferences of contracting parties were fully aligned, i.e. if everyone would prefer the same courses of action over the same alternatives, and the contracting parties were aware of this, no contract would contain any falsehoods. People would only communicate their true intentions.

[74] As defined by Douglas Allen, "Transaction costs are the resources used to establish and maintain property rights." See Allen (1991).

## 7.6 OBTAINING BETTER TERMS

The ability of an entrepreneur to prepare opportunities for cooperation that yield him terms that are worth his costs depends on many factors. It depends on his knowledge of what opportunities he can create and what is necessary to create them; on what terms of cooperation these preparations can yield in light of the preferences of their opportunity recipients and the competing available outcomes; on the possibilities for anticompetitive action, commitment strategies and deception; on which course of action he prefers to take; and on how well he executes his entrepreneurial plans.

As entrepreneurs generally prefer to receive more money for their offerings and to pay less, the terms of cooperation are often importantly the prices at which he can cooperate. Obtaining better terms thus often results in a higher financial profit. But better terms can take the form of myriad aspects of the cooperations they enable. Preparations can, for example, also put the entrepreneur in a position wherein he can do enjoyable work. For instance, a retired investment banker who becomes a florist does not do so to maximise his financial profits. His financial income decreases because of his new choice of occupation, but he may find his new work much more enjoyable and find money much less important at his stage in life. The entrepreneur may also demand other aspects of cooperation to be more favourable, such as kindness from the people he cooperates with. The assumption that entrepreneurs maximise financial profit is therefore rather tenuous. However, the pursuit of better terms is inherent to the truism that people pursue the satisfaction of their preferences.

What may not be worthwhile for one entrepreneur may be worthwhile for another. One entrepreneur may not be satisfied with the meagre financial returns from his endeavour, whereas another might have enjoyed the endeavour so much that he would be willing to do it for those financial returns. In both cases the venture may be equally profitable financially, but it performs differently in the satisfaction of preferences. In fact, an entrepreneurial endeavour may even result in financial losses while still satisfying the entrepreneur's preferences. Conversely, an entrepreneurial endeavour can be financially profitable without satisfying the entrepreneur. Financial gains does not take into account the opportunity cost to entrepreneurship. For example, if an entrepreneur prefers to spend time with his family rather than the financial entrepreneurial profits he expects to be able to make, the opportunity cost exceeds the financial profit.

So what maximises financial profitability does not always maximise preference satisfaction. Rather than looking at financial profits and the prices that bring them about, we must look at the terms of cooperation. For the purpose of Section 7.7, which is about the notion of consumer sovereignty and in particular its limits, we must first examine how entrepreneurs can obtain the terms of cooperation they find most preferable.

## BETTER TERMS FROM COMPETITIVE ACTION

When an entrepreneur cooperates with others to prepare a future opportunity for cooperation, everyone who chooses to cooperate with him does so because they thereby expect to obtain terms they find satisfactory. They cooperate with him because they prefer this over the alternatives they perceive to have within their reach. If the people he prepared the opportunity for are not willing to accept it on terms he deemed sufficient beforehand, he finds the result unsatisfactory. Even when the opportunities are taken by their recipients, he is not rewarded for them to his satisfaction. Everyone he cooperates with benefits from the opportunities he gives them, as he does himself when the cost of the preparations made are sunk, but not without his disappointment from the vantage point of when he chose to undertake the project.

If all others obtain satisfactory terms from the cooperative opportunities he offers along the entrepreneurial process, and the people the opportunities are intended for obtain satisfactory terms as well, this does not mean his course of action has been optimal for them. It may be a Pareto improvement for all the parties involved, but another course of action might have been better. When he cooperates with others to prepare cooperative opportunities, he offers them the most attractive outcomes they perceive to have available. But when the opportunities have been prepared and are presented to the intended recipients, they may not value them as highly as he expected. Other courses of action could have resulted in offerings superior to the opportunities he has created. To cooperate with his opportunity recipients, he must then accept less favourable terms than those he could have obtained otherwise. Other cooperations would be Pareto superior to those he has enabled. Both he and his opportunity recipients could have been better off had he chosen another project.

What cooperations others are willing to engage in also depend partly on the alternatives they perceive to have. The terms obtained through entrepreneurial endeavours thus also depend on how well the entrepreneur competes with others and with the non-cooperative actions his opportunity recipients can undertake. The means or ends he offers to people can be obviated by superior means or ends within their reach.

By acting competitively, the entrepreneur makes preparations yield better terms to himself by making them more yield better terms to others. The more attractive the terms he offers in some respects, the better the terms he can successfully demand in return. Insofar the entrepreneur acts competitively, his interests are thus aligned with those of the recipients of his opportunities. The terms of cooperation he obtains, and thus his financial profits, improve as the terms he offers improve for his opportunity recipients.

## BETTER TERMS FROM ANTICOMPETITIVE ACTION

By acting anticompetitively, the entrepreneur does not create cooperative opportunities for people, but removes alternatives to those he offers. He makes them cooperate in ways he prefers by removing better alternatives from their reach. To improve the terms of cooperation that he can obtain from his preparations, he does things that worsen the terms obtained by his opportunity recipients and possibly his competitors. Unlike competitive action, an entrepreneur can thus only benefit from anticompetitive action at the expense of his opportunity recipients. They suffer such that he can gain. Anticompetitive action can also harm competitors, but if multiple entrepreneurs collaborate anticompetitively, the recipients of their opportunities suffer such that the colluding entrepreneurs can gain together.

An entrepreneur has no reason to act anticompetitively if he expects opportunity recipients to find their alternatives inferior to the cooperations he plans to offer them. They will then prefer the entrepreneur's preferred cooperation anyway, so anticompetitive action is then unnecessary. Therefore, if he deliberately acts anticompetitively, he only does so to make outcomes impossible that he expects his opportunity recipients to prefer over those he enables. That is, he does this to move the outcome from one Pareto efficient outcome to another. As per the definition of Pareto efficiency, his interest therein conflicts with those of the people he seeks to cooperate with.

## BETTER TERMS FROM DECEPTION, VIOLATIVE ACTION AND COMMITMENT STRATEGIES

As with anticompetitive action, an entrepreneur only deceives his opportunity recipients because he expects not to obtain his preferred cooperation otherwise. Insofar he sends correct information about his offerings to consumers and does not manipulate their expectations to their detriment, his interest is aligned with theirs. But since he can also lie and deceive in other ways, to manipulate expectations and change what people think they need, his interest partly conflicts with theirs. An entrepreneur can benefit from their unrealistic ideas and expectations by gaining from the resulting choices, which they will likely regret.

In this case, it may be less obvious that the improvement of the terms he obtains comes at the expense of his opportunity recipients. Because, when he affects their preferences, does he not change what they find better terms? In any case, his gain is likely to come at the cost of their regret later when their unrealistic expectations are proven wrong. Besides, one could argue that the ability to deceive consumers limits consumer sovereignty in any case. The importance of this will be explained in Section 7.7.

Apart from manipulating people's perceptions in other ways, the entrepreneur can gain from making false promises when enforcement is imperfect. Any gain he derives from this obviously comes at the expense of the people he cooperates with. False promises are not uncommon. If people would never perceive such gainful possibilities, no fraud would ever be committed. Perfect enforcement is impossible and would not be worth its cost even if it were possible. As was explained in Chapter 4, violative action in principle harms the people whose rights are violated. If it would not, they would consent to it and the action would thereby not be violative. As was also explained in Chapter 4, threats to act violatively have the same effect.

The interests of an entrepreneur can also conflict with those of his opportunity recipients in the process of contracting. Under incomplete information, one can credibly communicate false preferences. This can make others think that they cannot get better terms through bargaining, making them willing to accept the terms one demands. A common example of such a commitment strategy is when an entrepreneur sets a fixed price instead of allowing customers to bargain. As explained, they thereby usually forego cooperations that would have been mutually beneficial, but this is necessary to make their preparations more gainful.

## DISTORTIVE EFFECTS

The profitability of entrepreneurial preparations partly depends on the possibilities they yield for gainfully engaging in anticompetitive action, commitment strategies and deception. The prospects of obtaining such possibilities through entrepreneurial preparations can therefore affect what preparations entrepreneurs decide to make.

The more substitutable the offerings of entrepreneurs are as means to the same ends, the more the terms demanded by one impact those the others can successfully demand. And the fewer the entrepreneurs that compete, the lower their cost of contracting to collude. The number of entrepreneurs and the similarity of their offerings can therefore affect the prevalence of collusion by affecting how costly and attractive it is. The likelihood that a group of entrepreneurs will collude decreases in the number of its members and increases in the substitutability of their offerings. And the number of competing entrepreneurs itself decreases in the magnitude of economies of scale and network effects in their offerings. So the larger the economies of scale and the larger the network effects, the smaller the number of competitors and the more likely they are to collude. On the other hand, the greater the benefits from collusion, the more attractive it becomes for entrepreneurs to defect and for other entrepreneurs to compete. This negative feedback loop keeps collusion somewhat in check but does not eliminate it. If the threat of defection and new competition would be enough to prevent collusion completely, no collusion would ever have happened.

The prospect of competition itself may also be anticompetitive. By preparing some cooperative opportunities, an entrepreneur may inadvertently dissuade others from preparing competing cooperative opportunities. Others then choose not to compete because they do not find the terms they expect under competition attractive enough. This leaves the entrepreneur with fewer competing substitutes, which is bad for his recipients since it can force them to accept less favourable terms. As explained before, an entrepreneur can move an eventual cooperation to one he prefers by using a commitment strategy. This gives him more favourable terms of cooperation, albeit for a smaller set of cooperations. The more substitutable the cooperative opportunities offered by competitors are for his, the greater the impact of the terms of his competitors on the terms he can get. The smaller is then his capacity to successfully commit to some terms, even when he does so credibly. In this way, the number of competitors and substitutability of their offerings undermines the commitment strategies of entrepreneurs and thereby discourages them from competing.

Finally, it is important to address another specific type of interaction between entrepreneurs. If an entrepreneur incurs significant costs that cannot be recovered or repurposed, i.e. sunk costs, but still provide economies of scale, he thereby becomes willing to accept terms that he would not have found acceptable initially. That is, he would not find the terms attractive enough before the preparations were made, but when the costs are sunk, he finds them acceptable. The entrepreneur's new willingness to accept certain terms can then make other entrepreneurs unable to obtain terms they find satisfactory. As this can be expected in advance after observing an entrepreneur's preparations, such preparations may dissuade others from offering competing opportunities. By openly committing to preparations involving sunk costs, entrepreneurs can therefore dissuade others from competing.

The distortive effects of anticompetitive action on preparations can be shown by an example. Imagine an entrepreneur who buys all the water wells in one region. Until others can complete new water wells, he is thereby the only entrepreneur that can sell water locally. This yields him very favourable terms, making him great profits. His monopolisation of the water supply was an anticompetitive action, and his gains from being able to engage in a commitment strategy without being undercut by competitors comes at the expense of the people who buy his water. But since he pursues profits and cannot gain from this monopolisation without demanding terms he prefers, he decides to significantly increases water prices in the area, which prompts others to dig new wells. His anticompetitive actions thereby lead to more water wells being dug than necessary. His wells are enough to cater to all water buyers, but he had to increase prices in order to profit from his position, which impelled others to dig new wells. Anticompetitive action can thus lead to overinvestment.

The expected ability to act anticompetitively can also lead to overinvestment. Because having rights enforced has anticompetitive effects, companies may want to incur larger costs to be the first to invent a new technology. This is an effect of intellectual property. Intellectual property is an important institution without which consumer sovereignty could not exist. Intellectual properties are costly ideas that serve as crucial means of production, the use of which people cannot be excluded from without patents. Without the possibility of obtaining patents, they are therefore underinvested in. Intellectual property is a key component of the property rights system that enables human cooperation. But while consumer sovereignty requires intellectual property, it is also limited by its anticompetitive effects. The first to invent a new technology has the ability to patent it and thereby reap its value. If an infinite number of perfectly substitutable technologies could be invented at equal cost, protecting intellectual property rights would not have any anticompetitive effects. Another entrepreneur could offer the same opportunities at the same cost, even though he made his invention later. But this is not the case in the real world. As a result, the profitability of the idea for an entrepreneur depends on whether he can patent it sooner than another can. The anticompetitive effect of intellectual property rights may thereby impel entrepreneurs to incur higher research and development costs simply to be faster than others, even though people do not necessarily benefit commensurately by being able to use the invention sooner.

Anticompetitive action, deception and commitment strategies and the prospect of being able to engage in these types of action can therefore distort the allocation of the means of production away from what is most preferred by the opportunity recipients, which includes consumers. Because entrepreneurs can gain from engaging in these types of action, the preferences of opportunity recipients do not exclusively determine what entrepreneurial endeavours are most gainful.

## 7.7 CONSUMER SOVEREIGNTY AND ITS LIMITS

The terminology used thus far will from now on sometimes be abandoned to distinguish consumers as a certain type of opportunity recipients. What has been written in the previous sections applies to the content of this section as well.

All production is ultimately intended for consumption, whether people produce for themselves or buy consumption goods from others. In a society based on the division of labour, the production of goods for consumption is directed by entrepreneurs. To a large extent, they choose the specifications of their offerings based on the preferences of the consumers. In their role of consumers, people choose what to spend their money on according to their own preferences and thereby greatly affect what allocations of the means of production are profitable. According to the theory of consumer sovereignty, the consumer, choosing what to buy according to his preferences, fully determines what entrepreneurial endeavours are most profitable.[75] What best satisfies consumer preferences is then most profitable to provide.

### THE THEORY OF CONSUMER SOVEREIGNTY

According to the theory of consumer sovereignty, the consumers determine what entrepreneurial endeavours are most profitable thereby determine what is produced and how it is produced. The consumer controls all aspects of production, for instance what materials are used, how much is produced and where production takes place. He does this without explicitly dictating these aspects, but by choosing between different goods based on criteria that matter to him. As Ludwig von Mises described it in his *magnum opus,* Human Action:

[75] This definition accords with the definition given by William Hutt, who coined the term, in 1940:"...it simply refers to the controlling power exercised by free individuals, in choosing between ends, over the custodians of the community's resources, when the resources by which those ends can be served are scarce." See Hutt (1940).

> The direction of all economic affairs is in the market society a task of the entrepreneurs. Theirs is the control of production. They are at the helm and steer the ship. A superficial observer would believe that they are supreme. But they are not. They are bound to obey unconditionally the captain's orders. The captain is the consumer. Neither the entrepreneurs nor the farmers nor the capitalists determine what has to be produced. The consumers do that. If a businessman does not strictly obey the orders of the public as they are conveyed to him by the structure of market prices, he suffers losses, he goes bankrupt, and is thus removed from his eminent position at the helm. Other men who did better in satisfying the demand of the consumers replace him.
>
> The consumers patronize those shops in which they can buy what they want at the cheapest price. Their buying and their abstention from buying decides who should own and run the plants and the farms. They make poor people rich and rich people poor. They determine precisely what should be produced, in what quality, and in what quantities. They are merciless bosses, full of whims and fancies, changeable and unpredictable. For them nothing counts other than their own satisfaction. They do not care a whit for past merit and vested interests. If something is offered to them that they like better or that is cheaper, they desert their old purveyors. In their capacity as buyers and consumers they are hard-hearted and callous, without consideration for other people.[76]

The theory goes as follows. The revenue entrepreneurs get from the opportunities they offer – or, in common terms, the goods they offer – depends on how much consumers are willing to pay for them. The costs that entrepreneurs incur to provide these opportunities depend

[76] Chapter 15.4: The Sovereignty of the Consumers, in von Mises (2007 [1949])

on the value of the opportunities that consumers thereby have to forego. Entrepreneurs, based on their own perceptions of possibilities and consumer preferences, bid up the prices of the means of production such that only those entrepreneurs who believe to create the most valuable opportunities can acquire them. If their expectations are correct, they are rewarded with profits. If they are wrong, the value of their opportunities to consumers will not exceed their costs and profits will not follow. Instead, they will then incur losses. Financial entrepreneurial profit thus converges to the value the entrepreneur adds to the means of production for consumers. The more valuable his offering and the less valuable the offerings he thereby makes impossible, the higher his profits. What delivers the most value to consumers is thereby most profitable to the entrepreneur. This alignment of interests between entrepreneurs and consumers is called 'consumer sovereignty'. When the consumer is sovereign, the economic system can be correctly described as a democracy in which each penny is a vote.[77] Every consumer gets to affect how the means of production are most profitably allocated. Under consumer sovereignty, entrepreneurs thus maximise their profits by enabling the courses of events valued most by their opportunity recipients.[78] In the context of cooperation, I define consumer sovereignty as the condition that someone can only get better terms of cooperation by offering better terms to the people he cooperates with.

One could object that entrepreneurs do not always satisfy the wants of consumers as much as they can, because they also engage in leisure instead of work. But consumer sovereignty refers to the incentives that direct entrepreneurship, not to the preferences of en-

77 As Frank A. Fetter described it Fetter (1905), p. 394.

78 Under consumer sovereignty, entrepreneurs maximise profits by maximising the value conferred to consumers through cooperating with them. This involves not only the maximisation of value for the customers they already have, but also maximising their number of customers. Besides, consumer sovereignty disregards externalities. For example, under consumer sovereignty some people may be harmed by a pollutive production process more than the producer's customers gain.

trepreneurs. When choosing not to serve others, the entrepreneur effectively outbids them in his role of consumer for his own offering. This therefore does not violate consumer sovereignty.[79] The entrepreneur knows a more valued use of his time and effort, namely his own.

Consumer sovereignty is merely about incentives. It does not mean that entrepreneurs optimally allocate resources to satisfy consumer preferences, but that they have the incentive to do so. In terms of the metaphor given by Mises, the consumer is still the captain of the economy even though the entrepreneur sometimes does not always steer the ship as he should.

## THE INCORRECTNESS OF THE THEORY

However, as was explained previously, entrepreneurial endeavours do not necessarily yield the most favourable terms, and thus the highest profit, when they best satisfy the preferences of the people they are finally intended for. Entrepreneurs can move courses of action from Pareto efficient ones to Pareto efficient cooperations that they prefer, which comes at the expense of the people they cooperate with. In some cases, what is most gainful for entrepreneurs is therefore not most gainful for their customers. Proponents of the theory of consumer sovereignty overlook this and the resulting distortions, and that the consumer is thus not always on the winning side.[80]

[79] Hutt (1940)

[80] The originator of the idea of the consumer sovereignty, William Hutt, did recognise that consumer sovereignty is limited by the ability of entrepreneurs to profitably restrict supply and charge monopoly prices. So did Ludwig von Mises. See point 15 in Hutt (1940) and pp. 271-272 in von Mises (2007 [1949]).

Charging monopoly prices is a commitment strategy. As such, its profitability is limited by the availability and attractiveness of substitutes, and it cannot be done profitably under complete information. Crucially, in a world of incomplete information it can be enabled by anticompetitive action. But as explained in this chapter, not only does the possibility of profitable commitment strategies limit consumer sovereignty. So do

One could then still argue that the most profitable product specifications are those that consumers value most. But this is also false, because the characteristics of goods, not only the prices at which they are sold, are also subject to the entrepreneur's preferences. The ability to get better terms can lead to higher prices and thereby higher profits, but also to worse goods and services. Consumers may prefer to be served politely, for example, but an entrepreneur would perhaps rather not make the effort. Moreover, because the prospect of possibilities for anticompetitive action, deception and commitment strategies affect what preparations entrepreneurs make, entrepreneurs may overinvest in the development of some types of goods and underinvest in others. The consumer is therefore also not fully sovereign when it comes to the specifications of goods.

The problems that limit consumer sovereignty do not only exist between entrepreneurs and consumers, but also between entrepreneurs further up the supply chain. Opportunity recipients include entrepreneurs – Many entrepreneurially created opportunities for cooperation are intended for other entrepreneurs. What applies to the relationships between entrepreneurs and opportunity recipients therefore applies to both entrepreneurs and consumers in their role of opportunity recipients. The preferences of cooperating entrepreneurs do not fully accord either and the same possibilities for anticompetitive action, deception and commitment strategies also exist in their relationships. The consumer is not fully sovereign over the entrepreneur, nor is the entrepreneur over the other entrepreneurs he cooperates with.

A possible response to criticism of the notion of consumer sovereignty is that it only refers to the fact that means are always intended to serve ends.[81] Since we always use our means for our ends, this would then also apply to cases in which we supply each other's means. But this leap from consumer sovereignty in autistic action to

---

the possibility of profitable anticompetitive action by itself, of profitable deception and of profitable violative actions and threats. Mises and Hutt failed to see this.

81 See for example points 2 and 3 in Hutt (1940).

that in interpersonal action is incorrect. It is exactly the deficiencies and conflicts of interest in interpersonal relationships that limit consumer sovereignty. The limits of consumer sovereignty arise entirely from this.

## VIOLATIVE ACTION AND THREATS

Remember from Section 4.3 that congruous action is action in accordance with rights. People do not always act congruously. For there to be consumer sovereignty, action must be congruous, since it is congruity that ensures cooperative courses of action are preferred by all participants. If entrepreneurs can gain from breaking their commitments, this therefore undermines consumer sovereignty. Moreover, the ability to gain from threatening to violate rights also forms an exception to consumer sovereignty. Violative threats are made to make people do things they do not prefer over what they would have done otherwise. Successful violative threats undermine the purpose of congruity.

For the consumer to be fully sovereign, perfect congruity is necessary. And perfect congruity requires perfect enforcement. Every single contract, including informal oral agreements over small matters, would have to be enforced. But enforcement is costly, and the relative benefits of perfect consumer sovereignty over imperfect consumer sovereignty may not be worth the extra cost of bringing it about. Allowing some violative action may be more efficient than always enforcing everyone's rights under all circumstances. Therefore, achieving perfect consumer sovereignty would not be efficient even if it were possible.

In a world without perfect and costless enforcement, people can gain from violating rights and threatening to do so, which limits consumer sovereignty. Some violative actions and threats will occur and even if rights could be enforced perfectly, this would not be worth the cost. In the real world, perfect consumer sovereignty is therefore impossible.

## INCOMPLETE AND COSTLY CONTRACTING, CONTRACTUAL DEFICIENCIES AND INCOMPLETE INFORMATION

As explained in Chapter 4, under perfect and costless enforcement with costless contracting or complete information, cooperations would only happen when all participants prefer the contracted actions to happen. Nobody would intentionally communicate any false intentions because the communicated intentions would be enforced perfectly.

However, because flawlessly drawing up complete contracts is impossible or costly, contracts sometimes have deficiencies that lead to incentive problems. Contracts will always be incomplete and often also flawed. This can happen even if enforcement is perfect and costless and the communicated intentions are thereby all true. Flawed contracts create inefficient incentives, which may be too costly to correct later. Incomplete contracts can lead to situations in cooperation for which the actions to be taken had to be specified by the contract but are not. Inevitably, the incompleteness of contracts leads to situations in which some actions, although not in breach of any contract, would not be agreed to if they were expected at the time of contracting. One example of this is the hold-up problem described in Section 5.4. In hold-up situations, cooperative partners exploit sunk costs to move Pareto efficient courses of action to ones they prefer. Hold-up situations can arise when a cooperative partner has made sunk costs and can subsequently be forced to accept less favourable terms. To prevent such situations, contractual solutions are not always available or are simply too costly. Because of hold-up risk, people refrain from investing, hold higher stockpiles and spend more on contracting, insurance and so on.[82] This results in underinvestment and costlier production.

The contractual incentive system is always somewhat deficient. As a result, people choose not to partake in some mutually preferred cooperations because the incentive system to ensure that everyone fulfils his part to it is deficient or too costly. Consumer sovereignty is therefore limited by the incompleteness of information, the costliness and incompleteness of contracting and the inevitably of contractual flaws, because of the resulting sub-optimal incentives.

## THE ELIMINATION THEOREM

In Chapter 4 it has been explained that if contracts are perfectly en-

[82] Klein, Crawford, & Alchian (1978).

forced and people know this, they contract to undertake cooperative actions that they all prefer to the alternatives they perceive to have – They contract to eliminate Pareto inefficient courses of action.

But the cost of contracting can exceed the value obtained by eliminating the Pareto inefficient courses of action. Contracting is then inefficient to do. And when contracting is costless, i.e. when nothing of value has to be foregone for it, but enforcement is not costless or is inevitably imperfect, some people may still violate contracts. Even though contracts could be created at no cost, not everyone would necessarily abide by them because the government would find them too costly or impossible to enforce perfectly. Expecting no or lacking enforcement, some of the contracting parties then choose to violate contracts. In a world in which enforcement is costly or cannot be perfect, even under costless contracting, some contracting is then foregone because some potential participants expect the resulting contracts to be violated.

And if contracting is costless and enforcement is both costless and perfect, but complete and flawless contracting is impossible, some actions in accordance with contract are actually not efficient. When enforcement is costless and perfect and complete contracting can be done flawlessly at no cost, people can eliminate all Pareto inefficient courses of action through cooperation without any risk that contracts will be violated. Besides, as explained in Section 4.1, contracting is unnecessary and ineffectual under complete information.

Considering the above, we arrive at the following: When enforcement is perfect and costless, and there either is complete information or complete and flawless contracting is possible at no cost, people can eliminate all Pareto inefficient courses of action through cooperation. This theorem will in this book be called the elimination theorem, referring to the elimination of inefficient courses of action. The conditions under which inefficient courses of action can be eliminated will be called the elimination conditions. The elimination theorem is similar to the Coase theorem. According to the Coase theorem, all problems of externalities can be solved without government regulation if contracting and enforcement can be done at no cost, i.e. under zero transaction costs.[83] The elimination theorem differs from the Coase theorem by referring to the elimination of all inefficient courses of action, not only to the elimination of inefficient externalities, and also includes that complete information can substitute for contracting that is costless, flawless and complete.[84] When we add the condition that the people whose inefficient actions can be eliminated at no cost are aware of this, we obtain that people not only can but actually will eliminate all Pareto inefficient courses of action.[85] The elimination theorem will become important at multiple points in this book.

When the elimination conditions are satisfied, people can elim-

83 Under the conditions of the Coase theorem, enforcement could still be imperfect and contracts still flawed and incomplete, leading some contracts to fail and others to not be worth engaging in. For all problems of externalities to be solved without government regulation of externalities, the elimination conditions would have to be satisfied. If this is correct, this would refute the Coase theorem.

Coase defined transaction cost as follows in Coase (1960), pp. 15: In order to carry out a market transaction it is necessary to discover who it is that one wishes to deal with, to inform people that one wishes to deal and on what terms, to conduct negotiations leading up to a bargain, to draw up the contract, to undertake the inspection needed to make sure that the terms of the contract are being observed, and so on. These operations are often extremely costly.

84 For efficiency, both theorems also require that perfect enforcement and complete contracting are possible with no mistakes made. These conditions are here given explicitly, which Coase did not. But I assume that he made them tacitly.

85 Israel Kirzner once pointed this out. For an explanation of how transaction costs hamper the efficient allocation of resources and why the absence of transaction costs does not by itself result in efficiency, see Kirzner (1973), pp. 225-231. In that chapter, Kirzner pointed out that what I call 'awareness' and he called 'alertness' is also needed for zero transaction cost to result in the elimination of inefficient externalities.

inate all Pareto inefficient courses of action and thereby all deadweight losses. Exceptions to the elimination conditions enable entrepreneurs to gain from acting in ways that violate consumer sovereignty. People, including entrepreneurs, can then gainfully violate property rights or act congruously in ways that are actually inefficient. Consumer sovereignty therefore requires the elimination conditions to be satisfied. Enforcement must be costless and perfect, and there must either be complete information or complete and flawless contracting must be possible at no cost.

## GOVERNMENT AND THE DEGREE OF CONSUMER SOVEREIGNTY

The more ways there are to gainfully act anticompetitively, deceive others, and engage in commitment strategies and the more exceptions there are to the elimination conditions, the less sovereign the consumer is. The possibilities are not only binary – The degree of consumer sovereignty can vary. The larger the improvement in terms that can be obtained through anticompetitive action, deception, commitment strategies and violative action and the more flawed and incomplete contracts are, the more consumer sovereignty is limited.

Many governments therefore take action to increase consumer sovereignty. For example, a government can make anticompetitive action less gainful by sanctioning collusion and forbidding some mergers and acquisitions. By prohibiting misleading advertisements, it can reduce the possibilities for deception. It inevitably incurs costs by implementing these policies, but the benefits to the consumer may well outweigh these. It is, however, never possible to effectively suppress all such actions. Not only do all entrepreneurial endeavours have anticompetitive aspects, as explained in Section 7.4, but it is also not possible to observe and sanction all cases of deception and anticompetitive action effectively. Besides, commitment strategies cannot be prohibited at all, because it cannot be observed at what terms entrepreneurs become willing to prepare certain opportunities. Finally, as explained above, violative action and inefficient congruous actions can never be fully eradicated, nor are the benefits of enforcement always worth its cost.

There will therefore always be some limits to consumer sovereignty. Government regulations can reduce these limits but cannot eradicate them. A government can, however, rule society with the aim of maximising consumer sovereignty insofar the resulting benefits for consumers are worth the costs.

## CONSUMER SOVEREIGNTY AND EXTERNALITIES

Under consumer sovereignty, entrepreneurs can only get better terms of cooperation, and thus maximise profits, by offering terms more favourable to the people they cooperate with. Under consumer sovereignty, entrepreneurs can thus only gain by bringing about Pareto improvements for the cooperating parties. But consumer sovereignty itself does not ensure that those Pareto improvements are also Pareto improvements for everyone affected. People with whom an entrepreneur does not cooperate can still be affected by his actions. That is, entrepreneurial endeavours and cooperations that are Pareto improvements for the cooperating parties may create externalities. The elimination conditions that absolute consumer sovereignty requires would also enable people to solve all problems of externalities, but if the elimination conditions are not satisfied while other conditions for consumer sovereignty are, the satisfaction of consumer preferences can lead to problems of externalities.

For instance, a steel factory built and operated by an entrepreneur may cause pollution that harms the health of nearby residents. What optimises the terms obtained by consumers then comes at the expense of local inhabitants. As a result, the local inhabitants are more likely to move away, leaving property owners with depreciating properties. These *negative externalities* would still exist under consumer sovereignty and may outweigh the benefits of the endeavour. Conversely, a project may be net beneficial due to *positive externalities*, but will not be undertaken if these externalities cannot be reaped by those who create them.

The possibility to gain from creating negative externalities and impossibility to gain from some positive externalities therefore does not violate consumer sovereignty, but does limit Pareto efficiency. Consumer sovereignty is by itself therefore not a good measure of efficiency, even though it is an important part of it.

Even under consumer sovereignty, externalities can make some entrepreneurial endeavours gainful without being efficient. The offering most preferred by consumers can still create costs for others that exceed the value created for the cooperating parties. For instance, a bar may maximise its profits on a certain evening by hosting a heavy metal band, but its neighbours may prefer it to host a quintet that performs the works of Schubert because they want to sleep well. For hosting the quintet instead, they may well be willing to compensate the bar owner by more than the profits he thereby foregoes. This problem can be solved at no cost under the elimination conditions. Entrepreneurs could only maximise their gains, such as their profits, by maximising the total gains conferred to others, not only to their customers. If the external costs conferred to others exceed the profits made by the cooperating parties, the others could buy out the cooperating parties. If an otherwise unprofitable endeavour would add value overall by the positive externalities it creates, those who benefit from the externalities could compensate people to undertake the endeavour.

## 7.8 PROPRIETARY DEMOCRACY

In Part II it was explained that a government can rule its jurisdiction with the rights to do so – the rights of government. It was also explained that who governs a jurisdiction and how it is governed can be affected by restrictions on the alienability of these rights. If the rights of government are fully alienable at the sole discretion of their owners, such that they can be transferred freely, they tend to be held by those who can use them best and value them most. They are then likely to be held by those who can and will use them to get the best terms to cooperation possible. If the rights of government are alienable, they are therefore more likely to be held by those who use them for financial profit and are best at doing so.

In light of this, it is important to understand under what circumstances there is consumer sovereignty over governments, i.e. when the government's most gainful use of its rights of government delivers the best terms of subordination to its subjects. The purpose of Part III is to explain the potential benefits of the proprietary government and to explain how it can be given incentives to deliver these benefits, so this is an important question to answer. In particular, the answer to this question can point us to ways to increase consumer sovereignty over governments. As will become clear, the conduct

of a proprietary government and its agents, like that of a non-proprietary government and its agents, largely depends on institutional arrangements – The rule of law, the separation of powers and constitutional provisions currently exist to bind the world's non-proprietary governments in ways intended to benefit their subjects.
It has been explained in this chapter that the most gainful entrepreneurial endeavours do not necessarily deliver the best results for the people they are meant for, let alone others who may be affected. There are exceptions to consumer sovereignty and possibilities to create externalities, resulting in conflicts of interests between entrepreneurs and the people they serve, as well as others in society. This also applies to governments. What is most gainful and thus financially profitable for a government is not necessarily most preferable for its subjects or other people it affects.

The consumer sovereignty of subjects over governments is in this book called *proprietary democracy*. The literal meaning of democracy is 'rule by the people', but the term is commonly used to refer to political systems in which such democracy is significantly limited. In the representative democratic system, elected politicians and civil servants are tasked with administering the jurisdiction, not the electorate itself. After all, it would be inefficient if every citizen were practically involved in the government's administration. Additionally, democratic governments and their policies rely on the consent of the majority, not the unanimous consent of all citizens. Requiring the consent of every single citizen for every single political decision would be prohibitively costly. The type of democratic system that dominates politics today is therefore never fully democratic.

Proprietary democracy also has its limits, but it has merits that representative democracy by its design does not have. Under proprietary democracy, the interests of governments are better aligned with the preferences of those they rule. Whereas the preferences of the majority determine the outcomes of elections in representative systems, the preferences of every potential taxpayer affect what is most gainful for a government under proprietary democracy. Under proprietary democracy, every taxpayer is in power, not only the majority. Whereas people vote with the ballot under representative democracy, under proprietary democracy people vote with their feet by choosing what government to be subordinated to. Their preferences determine how governments get the best terms in the government-subject relationship, but they do not need to be involved in politics. Thereby, proprietary democracy is not less democratic, but more democratic than representative democracy, and does not suffer from the problems of public choice.

## MAXIMISING PROPRIETARY DEMOCRACY

If there is no absolute consumer sovereignty, entrepreneurs can gainfully act at the expense of the people they serve. Because proprietary democracy is the state of consumer sovereignty over governments, the types of exceptions to consumer sovereignty also exist with respect to proprietary democracy. The ways in which an entrepreneur can obtain better terms at the expense of those he provides opportunities for cooperation to are also available to governments. Governments can act anticompetitively, deceive, engage in commitment strategies and violate rights just like any type of entrepreneur. The ability to gainfully perform actions that move cooperations from one Pareto efficient course of action to another limits both consumer sovereignty and proprietary democracy.

Consumer sovereignty, and thereby proprietary democracy, can exist to different degrees. Under absolute proprietary democracy, there are no ways for a government to get better terms without giving better terms to its subjects. When proprietary democracy is completely absent, the terms it can get are completely independent of the terms it gives. Under some degree of proprietary democracy, it can get better terms by giving better terms, but also in other ways.

Importantly, there are ways to maximise proprietary democracy. The possibility to gainfully engage in certain actions limits proprietary democracy. By taking measures that make these actions impossible or fruitless, it is possible to increase the degree of proprietary democracy. Perfect democracy is impossible, whether representative or proprietary, but measures can be taken to increase it. The next chapter describes measures to increase proprietary democracy. Just like a government can maximise consumer sovereignty in the society it governs by enforcing rights, combating fraud and misleading advertising and prohibiting some types of anticompetitive action, measures can be taken to restrict proprietary governments and their agents in order to maximise proprietary democracy.

CHAPTER 8.

# CONDITIONS FOR PROPRIETARY DEMOCRACY

## 8.1 ALIENABILITY

As addressed briefly in Section 5.1, the alienability of a right is one of its crucial features. When a right is transferred to another person, this makes the right refer to that person instead of oneself. The person to whom the right is assigned can then fulfil the role that the right confers to its owner. This person may be more capable of fulfilling the role or may value it more. For example, someone may be able to use some capital goods better than their current owner can and accordingly expect more profit. He can then buy them from the owner at a commensurate price and gain from changing their use. The rights over the capital goods must be alienable for this to be possible, and the cost of transferring rights are ideally as low as possible. Cumbersome government regulations and taxes can make transferring rights more expensive or even impossible. This can prevent the efficient allocation of rights and thereby the cooperations thus meant to induce.

Not only does the inalienability of rights harm their functioning by leaving roles fulfilled by people less suitable, it also makes it more difficult to know how to allocate the means of production. When rights are inalienable, they have no prices as their exchange is precluded. Efficient prices arise from the free exchange of rights and are an important indicator of the best use of the means of production. Inalienability stifles the price system and leads to the economic calculation problem. If means of production can be traded freely, their prices converge to their values when used best otherwise. This keeps profit-maximising entrepreneurs from using them inefficiently. When means of production are not traded freely, it may seem as if any of their potential uses are costless, while this is not the case.

What is profitable when means of production are inalienable may be unprofitable if they were alienable.

Importantly, if an owner wants to sell his means of production but is kept from doing so by their inalienability, there can be no consumer sovereignty. Someone else may value the means of production more, which would be reflected in the price at which the owner could sell them if the rights over them were alienable. Both the buyer and seller prefer the transfer of rights, but they cannot effectuate it. The buyer wants to use the means of production better than the seller does by better satisfying consumer preferences, and the seller wants to give him the ability to do so. However, they are kept from making the necessary transaction.

To fulfil its role in the government-subject relationship, a government has a bundle of rights – the rights of government. It needs these rights to govern its jurisdiction. If the rights of government are inalienable, all the problems with inalienable property emerge. It is then more difficult for the government to ascertain whether its endeavours are efficient or whether a better use of its rights is possible. It cannot transfer the rights to people who are more competent, committed and who value them more highly. Consequently, they are not put to their most valued use. For proprietary democracy, the alienability of the rights of government is therefore crucial. Proprietary democracy requires governments to be proprietary.

The rights of government can also take the form of shares or voting rights. Just as rights in a firm can be divided into shares, the rights of government can be divided into shares or voting rights. A government is more proprietary the larger the part of its shares or voting rights that is alienable. To maximise proprietary democracy, the alienable part its shares or voting rights must therefore be maximised.

Proprietary democracy can only exist over proprietary governments. When governments are only partly proprietary, there can only be limited proprietary democracy. Non-proprietary systems, such as the representative system, can never be proprietarily democratic.

## 8.2 CONSENT AND CONGRUITY

As explained in Chapter 4, the congruity of actions with the rights people have granted ensures that cooperative actions are preferred by all participants. If a government can gain from violating the rights it has granted, or if the people it rules have not granted it the rights of government over them, this therefore limits proprietary democracy. The actions of a government must be based on, and be congruous with, its rights to take them. If no right has been granted to take an action, i.e. if no contracting has happened, action cannot be congruous. Nor is it necessarily violative, but it is the congruity of a cooperative course of action with rights that ensures it is preferred by all participants. The congruity of the government-subject relationship therefore requires the consent, whether implicit or explicit, of subjects to their governments' rights of government, as well as action in accordance with the rights of government and the rights of the subjects. This has several important implications.

## CONSENSUAL SUBORDINATION AND THE FREEDOM TO LEAVE

Subjects must be free to leave their jurisdictions, except where they have granted their government the right to restrict this freedom. For example, a subject may agree to his government's right to jail him if he commits a crime. If the conditions for the government and its agents to jail a subject are met, they can do so congruously.

A subject has only granted his government the rights of government over him if he chooses to be subordinated to it while being free to end his subordination, or if he has conditionally or unconditionally relinquished the right to leave. When he is free to leave, his decision to stay communicates to the government that he will abide by its rights of government – He gives tacit consent.[86] Remember

[86] Tacit consent is given when someone's preference to cooperate in a certain way can be derived from his actions, without consent being given explicitly. In law, this definition is not uncommon. See American Law Institute, Restatement (Second) of Torts, § 10A. St. Paul, Minnesota, U.S.A.: American Law Institute Publishers, 1965. "The word 'consent'… denote[s] willingness in fact that an act or invasion of an interest shall take place."; id. § 892(1) (1979) "Consent is willingness in fact for conduct to occur. It may be manifested by action or inaction and need not be communicated to the actor."

from Chapter 4 that a right is not a moral principle. It is merely a communicated intention to take, or not to take, some actions as part of a cooperation. If someone chooses to stay subordinated to a government while being free to end his subordination to it, he implicitly consents to its terms of subordination and thus communicates the intention not to break its laws. Tacit consent is also common in other contexts. For instance, when someone enters and decides to stay at a hotel, he gives tacit consent to the hotel owner's right to use force to maintain order and safety. And when someone sits down at a coffeeshop and orders an espresso, he does not explicitly communicate the intention to pay for it but does implicitly by ordering. Similarly, when someone decides to stay in a jurisdiction while being free to leave, he grants the government the rights of government it claims through its laws and policies.

Like the relationship between any customer and service provider, the subject-government relationship can also be terminated. Subjects can do so by leaving their governments' jurisdictions and gov-

---

Consent ensures that a cooperation is mutually preferred when someone only gives consent when he prefers that course of action to happen. Any action that is only undertaken when a particular course of action is preferred thus qualifies as consent to that preferred course of action. For example, when someone can be considered to only join a members' club when he has the intention to follow its rules, he consents to the rules by joining the members' club. This definition of consent thus accords with the definitions given in the Restatement (Second) of Torts cited above.

In the context of the government-subject relationship, the subject can be assumed to be at least aware of its government's existence, the law and its enforcement. As long as the subject is free to leave unless he has congruously given up the right to do so, the preference to engage in the government-subject relationship can thus be inferred from his choice to stay. He can then be assumed to prefer subordination to the government, in accordance with its laws, over leaving its jurisdiction. Besides, the subject can inform himself of the law when the government communicates it clearly – Informed consent is possible. For more on consent, see 'Consent' in Section 4.3.

ernments can do so by expelling their subjects. Governments should therefore have the right to expel their subjects, except when they have given up this right.

A government can still make leaving its jurisdiction more costly, such as by taxing travel or levying an exit tax. Subordination would still be consensual because people would legally still be free to leave, but the consequences would not differ from those of nonconsensual subordination. If leaving the jurisdiction is not prohibited by law, subordination is consensual. Making leaving more costly could have the same effect as nonconsensual subordination. Creating exit costs is, however, anticompetitive. A government has many options for anticompetitive action, with such great effects that it can virtually obtain the same terms as if consent would not be necessary. Consent is therefore not enough, especially in the government-subject relationship. Measures against anticompetitive action must also be taken. These will be addressed in Section 8.3.

## CONGRUOUS GOVERNANCE

By definition, congruity in the government-subject relationship requires that the government does not break its own laws. And by choosing to be in the government's jurisdiction, the subject agrees implicitly to abide by its laws. The law is thus partly a bundle of rights granted to the government by those choosing to be subordinated to it, but also specifies the rights of subjects. For instance, if the police suspect someone of a crime, they must follow their protocols and provide the suspect with legal aid in most countries. This is required by the law, as are other rights that governments and their agents may not violate.

The subject chooses to be subordinate to the government based on the intentions the government and its agents claim to have. They do this by making laws and policies and by engaging in agreements. If their actions are congruous, the subject can choose based on realistic expectations of their intentions and only those government-subject relationships are then engaged in that both the government and the subject prefer.

In theory, a government could circumvent the restrictions necessary for congruity by its right to change the law as it sees fit. By criminalising something trivial and subsequently incarcerating someone who engages in it, it would act congruously and within the bounds of the restrictions proposed above. This would not violate anyone's rights, as the government would have changed these rights just before. Submitting oneself to the government's rights of government would then practically give the government totalitarian rights of government including the right to arbitrarily keep one subordinated by force. However, in most cases, a proprietary government would avoid doing this as it would damage its reputation and make its jurisdiction less appealing. But under some circumstances, it could be in the interests of a proprietary government to suddenly close its borders to keep people captive in its jurisdiction. When a proprietary government changes its laws, it must thus communicate this clearly and allow its subjects to leave its jurisdiction well before the change in law is to apply. They must be able to leave its jurisdiction in time, so some reasonable amount of time must pass before the new law goes into effect.

## SUMMARY

For proprietary democracy, congruity and consent in the government-subject relationship are crucial. By entering the government's jurisdiction, subjects grant the government its rights of government. As long as they are free to leave or have conditionally given up the right to, they grant the government its rights of government by deciding to stay. Subjects thereby consensually engage in the government-subject relationship.

If the conduct of both government and subject is congruous and consensual, both parties prefer to engage in the relationship as specified in the law and other rights granted. Both government and subject must therefore abide by the law.

Finally, when the government changes the law, it must clearly communicate the change well in advance of implementation, such that its subjects can become informed of it and subsequently decide to leave.

## 8.3 ANTICOMPETITIVE ACTION

Like other types of entrepreneurs, governments can also act anticompetitively. As explained, every possibility to gainfully engage in anticompetitive action is a limitation of proprietary democracy. Several types of anticompetitive action available to governments will be addressed here.

### MONOPOLISATION

A common form of anticompetitive action is monopolisation. By acquiring the rights to use certain means, an entrepreneur makes others unable to compete by using any of those means in the same way. The larger this set of means, the more difficult it becomes for others to offer competing opportunities for cooperation.

Because of the hold-up problem and imputation problem, and possibly other reasons, rights of government cannot be held by many governments over the same territory. The larger the territory over which a government possesses rights of government, the fewer the possibilities of other governments to compete. Acquiring rights of government over a territory therefore has an anticompetitive effect. There can also only be one group of people with the supreme capacity to direct the use of force over a certain territory. This supreme capacity is therefore exclusive.[87] The larger the territory over which an entity holds this capacity, the smaller the territory over which others can. This capacity is typically held by a hegemon, which rules through its exclusive military supremacy.

Furthermore, economies of scale in governance make jurisdictions larger, which reduces possibilities for competition. There are also network effects in human settlement, called agglomeration effects. Agglomeration effects make jurisdictions more valuable for

[87] This does not mean only one government can have a right to superior force over the same territory. Only one can have the supreme power to use force, but multiple governments can have a power to use force superior to that of subjects.

subjects as their population grows. This puts governments ruling large, concentrated populations at an advantage over governments ruling smaller, dispersed populations. Additionally, in the anarchic world, the size of a government's territory and the number of its subjects contribute to its ability to protect its own military interests. This gives governments with large, populous territories an advantage, further limiting the possibilities for peaceful competition.

The factors described above have anticompetitive effects. To maximise proprietary democracy, various measures against the accumulation of territory can surely be thought of. However, there is a trade-off between allowing economies of scale and network effects to be fully captured and maximising the possibilities for competition. Jurisdictions must reach a minimum size to be made appealing. Not every single street, example, can be ruled efficiently by a different government with its own monetary system. On the other hand, a government that rules the entire world leaves no possibilities for competition whatsoever. Such a government would be able to demand terms to subordination more favourable to it, such as higher tax rates, than it could if subjects could leave to other jurisdictions. It is impossible to determine the ideal point between the two, but at least it can be concluded that there are trade-offs in this.

## COLLUSION

The author of 'Entrepreneurial Communities: An Alternative to the State', who uses the alias 'Calvin Duke', sees no threat of collusion between governments.[88] He claims that the existence of a government cartel would encourage newcomers to the market.

One problem with this argument is that a jurisdiction may not be available for a newcomer. The world is now almost entirely ruled by uncompetitive representative governments, and a competitor cannot enter the market if all territories left available for proprietary governments are ruled by a cartel. Another misconception is that such a cartel would be unstable. Calvin Duke compares government

88 Calvin Duke (2020), Part 1.1: Two Key Aspects of Real Estate

cartels with drug cartels and argues that government cartels would also be unstable. This comparison is incorrect because governments differ in important ways from drug cartels. The success of OPEC as a cartel of governments of oil-producing countries shows that government cartels can indeed be stable. Additionally, if the rule of law is firmly embedded in the incentive structures of governments, this can strengthen their cartels by binding them to treaties. Furthermore, governments have other ways to act anticompetitively besides forming cartels. Agglomerating or merging with other governments can eliminate competition as well. Such mergers and acquisitions would be in the interests of all participants.

For proprietary democracy, provisions can therefore be made against cartelisation and against agglomerations and mergers that do not increase efficiency but do have anticompetitive effects.

## GOVERNMENT INTERACTION

It stands to reason that violative action by governments against other governments is anticompetitive. In its worst form, a government seeks to appropriate or undermine another government's supreme power to use force. Alternatively, a government can make its opponent's jurisdiction unattractive for subjects by targeting property in the jurisdiction or even subjects themselves. Taking such actions is not violative if it has not recognised the other's rights of government, because it then does not violate any rights granted. However, it must be prevented as much as possible because it is anticompetitive and destructive. Apart from the pure anticompetitive effect, the anarchic interaction between governments limits proprietary democracy in other ways. These will be explained in the following section.

## CREATING EXIT COSTS

A government can increase the cost of leaving its jurisdiction, for instance by imposing travel taxes or exit levies. Subordination would still be consensual because people would legally still be free to leave, but the consequences would not be different from nonconsensual subordination. A government can act anticompetitively in many ways, with such great effects that it can get virtually the same terms as from nonconsensual subordination. Consent is therefore not enough, especially in the government-subject relationship. Measures against anticompetitive action must also be taken. Exit taxes must be prohibited and so do other actions that create exit costs without making subordination more valuable.

If a subject consents to the right of a government to create exit costs, it does not necessarily benefit from it. Because subjects cannot always know how a government can create exit costs in the future and therefore cannot always demand sufficient provisions against it, it may be beneficial to protect them. For good reason, prohibiting the creation of exit costs is not uncommon in the common law. It makes sense to make this apply to governments as well. Besides, not everyone can be subordinated voluntarily, so not everyone consents to the right to create exit costs even if consent is always informed. Children, for example, in principle do not get to choose their government.

## 8.4 ANARCHIC GOVERNMENT INTERACTION

To govern well, a government must be free to compete peacefully and congruously with other governments as its rights of government permit. However, the military capacity of governments often allows them to undermine competition by encroaching on this freedom.

The ability to gain from harming the military capacity of another government limits proprietary democracy in at least the following ways. First, as explained in the previous section, a government can harm its competitors anticompetitively by harming their subjects, damaging their properties or undermining their supreme capacity to direct the use of force over their jurisdictions. This can work in its favour even if it does not appropriate the jurisdiction of its victim.

Second, whereas congruous transfers of rights are mutually preferred, resulting in the assignment of rights to the people who use them most gainfully, appropriating a jurisdiction without the consent of its government does not require one to be better at using it or to value it more highly. This hinders the allocative function of congruous contracting and the Pareto improvements resulting from it.

Third, incurring and inflicting the costs of appropriating the right to superior force of another government, which include both the direct costs of warfare and the costs of the resulting destruction, conflicts with the preferences of subjects. The taxes they pay for military expenses and the damage to their property is generally not worth any advantage this may confer to them.

Fourth, it gives larger and more populous states an advantage over smaller, less populous states. States with more taxpayers need less taxes per subject to fend for themselves. This makes larger states, ceteris paribus, naturally more attractive to be subordinated to and puts them at an advantage in the anarchic interaction with other states. As a result, fewer states rule the world than otherwise would have, which makes collusion between governments less costly for them.

Fifth, the risk that a proprietary government will become hostile to it can encourage a hegemon or host government to limit the rights of government of a proprietary government, as well as their alienability. This has happened in some historical cases, when hereditary monarchies kept a hand in proprietary colonial governments for imperial purposes.[89]

Lastly, the threat of losing its right to superior force can move a government to encroach on the rights of its subjects. When faced with grave threats, governments have expropriated subjects and forced millions of men in conscription.[90] They often did so without the right to.

When competition has eroded profits to the point that they are absent or small, even a credible threat from a government to harm another government or its subjects could in theory force the threatened government into bankruptcy. Such credible threats could force the threatened government to increase its military expenditure while lowering its tax rates to compensate for the risk its subjects incur in

89 For a historical account of proprietary governments, see Chapter 14.

90 See North & Weingast (1989). In their words, 'When survival was at stake, the sovereign would heavily discount the future, making the one-time gain of reneging more attractive relative to the future opportunities forgone. Indeed, there is a long history of reneging under the fiscal strain accompanying major wars'. The importance of peace for congruous governance is explained well by Olson (1993) and in footnote 2, Chapter 2: Time, Takings and Individual Rights in Olson (2000), p. 50.

its jurisdiction. The threat of aggression thus creates extra costs for the threatened government while decreasing its ability to levy taxes. This puts pressures on governments that do not result from congruous and peaceful competition, which violates proprietary democracy.

In his book, Calvin Duke claims that a proprietary government would have no interest in waging war.[91] His position is based on several assumptions. One of these is that most of the government's subjects would immediately move elsewhere if the government starts a war. This is evidently false. There are countless examples to the contrary, and it becomes easier to avoid civilian casualties as military technology becomes more sophisticated, which makes fleeing less appealing. Moreover, consensually acquiring the rights of government over another government's jurisdiction may be more costly than using violence to achieve military supremacy over it. Even if the aggressing government sees some or even all of its subjects move away permanently or temporarily, the costs it saves by using violence to conquer another's jurisdiction may exceed any resulting reduction in its profits.

The interaction between states is highly anarchic. Only governments themselves can enforce their own rights. But for proprietary democracy, the interaction between governments must be peaceful insofar this is congruous with the rights that have been granted. Proprietary democracy is therefore limited by the capacity of governments to gain from using force, or threatening to do so, in violation of each other's rights of government. To maximise proprietary democracy, provisions must be made to limit this capacity insofar possible.

## GOVERNMENT SHAREHOLDERS SUBORDINATED TO OTHER GOVERNMENTS

Remember that a government is in this book defined as the people who hold rights of government over a jurisdiction. These people can take the form of shareholders in a proprietary government, for in-

[91] Calvin Duke (2020)

stance. A government can be the subject of other governments by being in their jurisdictions. Especially shareholders in a proprietary government might not reside in the jurisdiction over which they possess the rights of government. The governments they are subject to could violate their rights and can have strong reasons to do so.

If someone subordinated to government A holds shares in proprietary government B, and A or any of its allies wants to make B act differently, A could gain from appropriating the shares of the shareholder or to restrict him from using his voting rights in some way. When deciding where and how to officially incorporate a proprietary government, this risk must be taken into account. A proprietary government can also make institutional arrangements such that shareholders temporarily or permanently lose their voting rights if they are kept from using their voting rights in certain ways. It can also be arranged that the unlawful appropriation of voting rights will not be effectual by not being recognised by the agents of the proprietary government, including its executives and armed forces. Similar measures can be taken for executives and other key government agents. Their authority can be suspended if they are not free to use it in the government's interests. If shareholders in a proprietary government cannot trust in their freedom to use their shares as they wish, they can also be made anonymous. Encryption and blockchain technology could perhaps be used for this. In this way, shareholders of proprietary governments competing with the governments they are subordinated to cannot be forced to use their shares to undermine the governments they are a part of.

The nationalisation of the East India Company is an example of how other states can legally appropriate the rights of proprietary governments. After parliament had abolished its last trading monopolies in 1813 and 1833, leaving it only with governmental functions, the Crown finally nationalised it in 1858, thereby appropriating its rights of government along with its other possessions.[92]

92 See 'East India Company and Raj 1785-1858' on parliament.uk. Retrieved on 18 august 2023 from https://www.parliament.uk/about/living-heritage/evolutionofparliament/legislativescrutiny/parliament-and-empire/parliament-and-the-american-colonies-before-1765/

## 8.5 FREEDOM OF INFORMATION AND EXPRESSION

Proprietary democracy requires that people can freely inform themselves, such that they can make informed decisions about which government to be subordinated to. It is also crucial that people are free to convey the relevant information, i.e. freedom of expression, including press freedom. The free exchange of information is crucial for consumers to make choices based on information that matters to them. Essential for the cooperative process is the entrepreneurial process that precedes it. Just as specialised entrepreneurs must be free to enable cooperations, the people they cooperate with must also be, including by informing themselves. Freedom of expression and freedom of information are therefore indispensable for proprietary democracy.

Well-informed consumer decisions are necessary for consumer sovereignty to result in consumer well-being. People cannot have realistic expectation if they are not free to inform themselves and others of what to expect from their cooperative opportunities, and thus of what jurisdictions can offer them. Their decisions then cannot maximise their well-being. Restrictions on this freedom therefore have the same effect as deception. There can be no proprietary democracy without freedom of expression and freedom of information.

### STATE SECRECY

Like any other type of enterprise, governments must be able to protect their business secrets. Knowledge is a crucial and costly means of production, that an entrepreneur must be able to exclude others from in order to benefit from investing in it.[93] But how can we en-

east-india-company-and-raj-1785-1858/#:~:text=the%20company%20lost%20all%20its,taken%20over%20by%20the%20crown.
See also https://en.wikipedia.org/wiki/East_India_Company.

[93] As explained briefly in Section 7.6, intellectual properties are costly ideas that serve as crucial means of production, the use of which people cannot be excluded from without patents. Without the possibility of obtain-

sure that limiting free speech to protect government secrets does not hinder the ability of consumers to inform themselves? State secrecy allows governments to do things that subjects are uninformed of, which could make the expectations of subjects deviate from reality. For example, state secrecy may make subjects unable to inform themselves of whether there really is a rule of law in a jurisdiction. Moreover, the transparency required to assess whether the right to state secrecy is used for the right purposes is lacking because of that very state secrecy.

State secrecy can therefore limit proprietary democracy. On the other hand, it is also necessary for it. Entrepreneurs are less likely to make costly innovations if these can easily be copied by competitors. Besides, just like company secrecy does not keep customers from informing others aabout the quality of the company's offering, state secrecy does not constrain subjects from informing others about their experiences with the state. State secrets can be protected if subjects are free to inform themselves and others of what matters to them. Besides, even if a government demands confidentiality about its conduct from its subjects, it is difficult to enforce this perfectly and it is unlikely that other governments will enforce such restrictions on free speech, especially if such restrictions give their competitor unfair advantages. If subordination is consensual, people can therefore spread the truth outside of the jurisdiction. No government can pretend forever that its jurisdiction is a paradise if it is not – The truth eventually gets out.

However, there are measures that can promote proprietary democracy. To strengthen freedom of expression without compromising state secrecy, one possible measure is to restrict governments from requiring confidentiality from subjects who do not work for their governments. State secrecy should only apply to the state, its employees and its contractors. Another possible measure is to restrict governments from punishing subjects for damaging their reputations. Finally, another possible measure is to forbid governments

---

ing patents, they are therefore underinvested in. Intellectual property is a key component of the property rights system that enables human cooperation.

from owning large stakes in press companies and online platforms that are used for the exchange of ideas.

It may even be beneficial to forbid proprietary governments and their agents from holding any significant assets in media and related companies that can affect the spread and exchange of ideas. This could protect people's ability to freely inform themselves about what matters to them. Only their priorities should determine what information they are exposed to, not those of any government. Besides, the necessity of state media does not exist in a proprietary jurisdiction because its government is not a representative democratic state. Subjects do not need to inform themselves about political affairs as much as in a representative democracy because they do not elect any government officials. They only need to inform themselves of what matters to them. Moreover, platforms for the exchange of ideas have such strong network effects that it is very difficult for new players to successfully offer alternatives. As a result, much discourse concentrates on a small number of platforms, making their owners very powerful.

## RELIGION

There must also be a strict separation between the government and religious institutions. The Roman Catholic Church's success in legitimating and delegitimating governments before the peace of Westphalia of 1648 attests to the importance of this. Religious legitimation of government policy and authority can contaminate the information that people use to decide what government to be subordinated to. The practical inseparability of religion and politics in the Islamic world and the vast rents captured by the Roman Catholic Church in the past, as well as the ability of religious leaders to incite rebellion, all attest to this fact.

But secularity does not imply freedom of faith. Religious materials and institutions must be subject to the same restrictions as any other materials and institutions. It stands to reason that sedition and incitement of violence, for example, are impermissible. Besides, it can be beneficial to directly intervene in the religious beliefs of subjects, since these often form the basis for important choices. Religious beliefs and customs can significantly affect productivity and well-being.

### COMMON RESTRICTIONS

Governments should of course be allowed to censor sedition, slander, libel and information of which the spread poses a threat to anyone's safety. However, if a government can censor such expressions and protect state secrecy, as well as act effectively against (corporate) espionage, how does one know whether censorship is due when it is imposed? How does one know the government does not abuse this ability for censoring criticism against it or otherwise inconvenient information? To safeguard the ability of people to freely inform themselves, which in part requires the safeguarding of freedom of expression, certain institutional provisions must be made. These will be described in Chapter 10.

## 8.6 THE ELIMINATION CONDITIONS

For proprietary democracy, the elimination conditions must be satisfied in the government-subject relationship. That is, the contracts between a government and its subjects must be perfectly enforceable at no cost, and the government and subjects must be able to make complete contracts flawlessly at no cost or must have complete information. Then, no situations will have to arise in which contracts between governments and subjects, including laws and policies, can be profitably violated or acted in accordance with at the expense of the other party. All hold-up situations can then be prevented at no cost, for example.

The lower the cost of contracting and of enforcement and the better the contracts, the fewer the exceptions to the elimination conditions. The greater is then the degree of consumer sovereignty and thereby proprietary democracy.

The elimination conditions will never be fully satisfied, but for the sake of correctness they have to be included as they are strictly necessary for consumer sovereignty. Consumer sovereignty and thus proprietary democracy cannot be absolute if these conditions are not satisfied. However, they do not have to be for proprietary democracy to exist to a great degree. The exceptions to consumer sovereignty and thus proprietary democracy that would disappear if the elimination conditions were satisfied, are very limited. In the real world, violative action is already rate because rights are enforced and most actions are congruous as a result. Besides, incomplete and flawed contracting rarely leads to inefficient courses of action that are impossible or too costly to correct by redrawing the contract.

## 8.7 SUMMARY

In Section 8.1 it was explained that proprietary democracy requires alienability in the rights of government. This gives the following requirement for proprietary democracy:

- The rights of government must be alienable. If divided into shares, as many of those shares as possible must be alienable.

In Section 8.2 it was explained that proprietary democracy requires the actions of a government to be congruous and based on consent. This gives the following requirements:

- The actions of both government and subject must be congruous. A government that provides enforcement can impose congruity on its subjects, but not conversely. For congruous governance, some provisions must therefore be made to ensure a rule of law.
- Subjects must be free to leave unless they have consensually given up the right to do so.
- Governments must communicate changes in law and policy clearly and allow a reasonable amount of time to pass before these changes are to apply, such that subjects can inform themselves well of these changes and leave in time.

In Section 8.3 it was explained that governments can also act anticompetitively. For proprietary democracy, the capacity of a government to gainfully engage in anticompetitive action must be minimised. This gives the following requirements:

- Provisions must be made against government collusion and against government mergers and acquisitions that do not increase efficiency but do have anticompetitive effects.

- Governments must be kept from using aggression to act anticompetitively.
- Governments must be kept from levying exit taxes, as well as from taking any other actions that make leaving their jurisdictions more costly without making subordination to them more valuable.

In Section 8.4 it was explained that governments can interact aggressively and violatively and that the ability to gainfully engage in this limits proprietary democracy. This yields that:

- The possibilities of governments to gainfully aggress other government and violate their rights must be minimised.
- Provisions must be made to prevent a government from expropriating shareholders in another government and from constraining the use of their shares. To achieve this, owning shares can be made anonymous and the voting rights of appropriated or constrained shares can be suspended.

In Section 8.5 it was explained that the free exchange of information is important for making choices in one's own interests. This yields that:

- People must have freedom of information and freedom of expression, which may only be limited by state secrecy and restrictions on sedition, slander, libel and so on.
- State secrecy must only apply to the state and its employees and contractors. A government may also not punish subjects for damaging its reputation. Proprietary governments may also not require confidentiality from their subjects about conditions in their jurisdictions. Lastly, it may also be beneficial to forbid governments from owning large stakes in press companies and online platforms used for the exchange of information.
- There must be a strict separation of church and the government, but the government may intervene in religious affairs.

In Section 8.6 it was explained that proprietary democracy requires the elimination conditions to be satisfied, but also that there can still be a great degree of proprietary democracy if they are not.

CHAPTER 9.

# BENEFITS OF PROPRIETARY DEMOCRACY

The previous chapter discussed conditions that must be satisfied to maximise proprietary democracy. In the real world, proprietary democracy is inevitably limited because these conditions are never fully satisfied. Every way in which a government can get better terms to cooperation without improving the terms for its subjects is an exception to proprietary democracy. Like other entrepreneurs, governments can gain from acting anticompetitively, deceiving, engaging in commitment strategies, violating rights, exploiting hold-up situations and so on. Every possibility for a government or its agents to gain from engaging in such an action is an exception to proprietary democracy. The more these courses of action are made impossible or fruitless, the less exceptions there are. The fewer exceptions to proprietary democracy there are, the more people can receive its benefits.

The degree to which there is proprietary democracy can therefore be increased. Governments can be bound to agreements to keep them and their agents from engaging in certain courses of action, and institutional arrangements can be made such as a rule of law and a separation of powers to ensure that these agreements are upheld. This will be explained in Chapter 10. If arrangements are made to ensure that the conditions for proprietary democracy are satisfied as much as possible, the exceptions to proprietary democracy could perhaps be negligible, such that the benefits of proprietary democracy can be enjoyed to a great degree.

As explained in Section 5.3, proprietary governance brings unique benefits. Because the rights of government are alienable when a government is proprietary, they tend to be held by those who value them most and are best at using them. Additionally, alienability enables a small number of shareholders to hold large numbers of shares. When shares then become too widely dispersed, the consequences of shareholder passivity encourage activist investors to acquire large numbers of shares in the government and improve its efficiency. The administrations of proprietary governments are therefore more competent, efficient, and pursuant of financial profit.

But as explained in chapters 7 and 8, the interests of a proprietary government are not necessarily aligned with those of its subjects. Apart from the direct benefits of proprietary governance, there are therefore unique benefits of proprietary democracy. This chapter explains some of those benefits.

## 9.1 TAXATION

When comparing the proprietary system with the representative system, it is important to consider how the former would levy taxes compared to the latter. A proprietary government is more pursuant of profit, more competent at finding the best approach to taxation and less constrained by ideology and entrenched interests. This may result in significant differences.

Since a proprietary government is likely to aim to maximise the net present value of its financial profits and thereby the price of its shares, we must examine what forms of taxation would best serve to this end.

### PRICE DISCRIMINATORY TAXATION FOR EVERY ACTION

When people act, they often require certain actions from the government and its agents in order to achieve their ends. For example, contracting often requires government enforcement to be worthwhile. Without the expectation of enforcement, the contract is not necessarily abided by and less likely to be agreed to. These cooperations therefore require some government participation.

A government also provides common goods to enable certain actions by its subjects. For example, many actions involve the use of government-provided infrastructure and rely on government regulation to be fruitful. The government and its agents are therefore participants to many more cooperations than might seem. Their actions are necessary for many actions of subjects to be possible or fruitful.

A government can often tax the actions it enables. That is, it can require some other actions for allowing those actions to take place.

For enabling its subjects to attain the ends they seek, it can require other actions. This most often takes the form of demanding some financial compensation.

It is a tautology that the ends people pursue are those they are willing to forego most for. The actions people take are therefore the actions that, when taxed at the level at which they become indifferent between that action and another, yield the most in tax revenue. The actions that, in total, yield the highest tax revenue minus the costs to enable and tax, are worthwhile for the government to enable. Some actions may be most worthwhile for people to take, but not for the government to enable. These courses of action would then be inefficient. For example, people may find it worthwhile to drive on a particular road but not enough to compensate for its cost. The value of the road then does not exceed its cost.

The interests of the subject and a government are therefore in principle aligned. However, there are exceptions to the elimination conditions in government-subject cooperation. These exceptions include the costs of making and enforcing the agreements between a government and its subjects. They can be so significant that they preclude courses of actions that by themselves are Pareto efficient, thereby causing deadweight losses. If a government could tax its subjects for every action they undertake and the elimination conditions were satisfied, this would not have to be the case. As holds for all types of entrepreneurs, when a government can at no cost engage in perfect price discrimination because the elimination conditions are satisfied, it does not have to forego any cooperations to maximise its own gain.

Because the elimination conditions are not satisfied, a government cannot tax every individual subject at his willingness-to-pay for every action he takes. Instead, it usually taxes categories of actions at some general fees, or general percentages of the amount of money exchanged. Almost all cooperations in which some money is exchanged are taxed at a percentage of this amount of money. For different classes of cooperation and participants, a government typically has different rates. For example, it typically levies higher taxes for the exchange of labour for money than for the exchange of goods for money. That is, income taxes are typically higher than consumption taxes. And the more money someone makes by providing labour, the higher the tax rates he normally pays – Income tax rates are often progressive. By charging the same tax rates for various actions from which various values are derived, it taxes many actions above what people are willing to pay to take them. These actions are then prevented. Taxation without perfect price discrimination therefore causes deadweight losses. For example, the marginal tax rate for working 50 hours per week instead of 40 hours may make the provision of those 10 hours not worthwhile. General tax rates and fees result in gains lost for both the government and its subjects. But price discrimination to eliminate these deadweight losses or even some of them is either impossible or too costly. To obtain the best terms in a government-subject relationship, it is in the interest of a government to maximise the deadweight losses it eliminates, minus the costs of doing so.

By taxing actions at general rates, a government also taxes many actions below what people are willing to pay. As a result, this untaxed value accrues to the value of means complementary to these actions. As will be explained below, some of the value created by a government thereby accrues to land values.

Only under the elimination conditions explained in Section 7.7 are all deadweight losses eliminated. No Pareto efficient courses of action are then prevented.

However, if a government levies taxes for every action at the amount that people are at most willing to pay, it would lose people to other governments as these could offer better terms in the form of some limitations to their rights to levy taxes. This also applies to general tax rates for classes of people and transactions.

To keep people in and attract new residents, a government can commit to some competitive tax rates. Moving to another jurisdiction is costly, so communicating clearly what taxes will be levied at what rates can give people rights that they value, as it will decrease their uncertainty. Such limitations can therefore be valuable for people and thereby gainful for a government to commit to. If a government does not while other governments do, it gives the impression that it intends to levy taxes at rates that people would not find worth moving to the jurisdiction for.

A government is therefore likely to commit to certain tax rates in competition with other governments, also if it could engage in perfect price discrimination and tax for single every action. In that case, it would also commit to limitations to its right to levy taxes.

In levying taxes, a government is therefore not unlike any other type of company. Most entrepreneurs, from restaurants to machine suppliers, do not engage in price discrimination. They thereby forego cooperations that all participants would prefer. By using commitment strategies to price their products, almost all entrepreneurs create deadweight losses. And entrepreneurs, in competition with each other, communicate their prices to their opportunity recipients regardless of whether their prices are discriminatory. All of this also applies to governments.

## THE LAND VALUE TAX: NO SILVER BULLET

As explained in Section 7.1, what one is willing to forego for a means to an end without having to translates into what one is willing to forego for a means complementary to it, i.e. for a means that one also needs to obtain the same end. From this follows that when a subject is not charged otherwise for the actions enabled by subordination or for subordination itself, he attributes greater value to it, which accrues to the value he attributes to what he needs to attain it. To be subordinated to a government, one must be within its jurisdiction. The untaxed value of subordination to the government therefore translates into what one is willing to forego for occupying some space in its jurisdiction.

Most endeavours of a government are complementary to the properties it rules over. By not charging for subordination or taxing the actions of people separately, it lets the value the creation of which it enables, including for example by enforcing rights and providing common goods, by and large accrue to the value of the properties in its jurisdiction. However, it is crucial to understand that this refers to the subjective value people attribute to these properties, not necessarily the price it is sold for. People rarely if ever pay for something exactly what they are at most willing to pay. Not all the subjective value added by a government thus translates into the 'market value' of properties. This does not only apply to what is provided by a government. From the baker to the grocer, nobody reaps the full surplus value he creates. The law that the surplus value of a means accrues to the value of a complementary means thus does not mean that this translates into prices – Value created differs from value captured.

Because the value of something does not necessarily equal its price, the value the government adds to property does not fully translate into its price and therefore neither into how much property developers and investors value undeveloped land. Not all the value a government adds to properties in its jurisdiction can be captured – A property tends to go to the highest bidder, but the highest bidder may be willing to pay more for it than he needs to. The untaxed value of governance, which accrues to the value of the territory it governs, therefore only partly translates into the price of undeveloped land.

However, the more valuable the things a government provides in its jurisdiction, the more people are willing to pay for being subordinated to it and the more they are therefore willing to pay for property in its jurisdiction. It can therefore be expected that their willingness-to-pay for subordination at least largely accrues to property values. Much of the value of governance, if not charged or taxed for otherwise, will therefore accrue to the price of undeveloped land in its jurisdiction. And the more value a government creates, the higher the price of undeveloped land. By taxing away land values, a government can therefore capture some of the value it creates.

## THE SINGLE TAX FALLACY

Many economists have agreed that the value created by governments accrues to land prices. The 'land value tax' is also widely considered to be less distortionary than other forms of taxation. The first to believe so were notable classical economists including the French physiocrats[94], Adam Smith[95] and David Ricardo[96], and their ideas about the land value tax were later popularised by Henry George in his book Progress and Poverty.[97] Around the turn of the twentieth century, Progress and Poverty enjoyed widespread acclaim among intellectu-

94 Tideman (1994), p. 102

95 Ibid. p. 106

96 Ibid. p. 109

97 Ibid. p. 118

als and politicians, including Winston Churchill.[98] Henry George reasoned that the untaxed value created by a government accrues to land values in its jurisdiction and that a land value tax can therefore suffice as a single tax to finance all government expenditure. This idea gave rise to the 'single tax movement', which advocated such a tax to replace all others and supported that any government surplus resulting from it would be distributed to citizens as a 'citizen's dividend'.

But Henry George and the single tax movement overlooked the crucial difference between the value of something and its price. Because value differs from price, not all untaxed value created by a government accrues to land prices.[99] Those who get to occupy space in a government's jurisdiction never have to pay exactly what they are at most willing to pay for it. Therefore, not all government investment that creates more value than it costs can necessarily be paid for through a land value tax, which makes the land value tax unable to function as a single tax. George and the other proponents of the land value tax were right to see that the land value tax does not have the distortionary effects of other forms of taxation, but

98 Churchill (1909, July 17)

99 The single tax movement also overlooked that not all costs created by the government, such as those that stem from the taxation of other inputs, come at the expense of land values. Nicolaus Tideman explained this in his criticism of the physiocrats: "The Physiocrats went on to argue that, since all taxes were in the end paid out of rent, it would be sensible to replace all other taxes by a single tax on rent. However, the premise that all other taxes are in the end paid out of rent would be valid only if other inputs were supplied perfectly elastically. When other inputs have finite elasticities, taxes on them are not shifted completely to rent, and it is no longer the case that the owners of land are better off with a single tax on land. Nevertheless, one can still give the Physiocrats credit for first having the insight that taxing the rent of land is a uniquely non-destructive way for governments to obtain revenue. This idea formed part of the heritage from which all subsequent classical economists wrote about taxing land." Tideman (1994), p. 106

other forms of taxation may still be necessary to cover expenses. If a government only has the right to levy a land value tax, or if its right to levy other taxes is restricted otherwise, it may not have an interest in enabling some actions for its subjects that would be a Pareto improvement to enable.

Consider the following instance. Suppose a jurisdiction can accommodate three people while twelve people want to reside in it. The three places will go to the three of those twelve who are willing to pay most for it. Suppose the cost of governance is 100 per person, which adds up to 300 in total. The three people willing to pay most are willing to pay 150 each for subordination. Of the nine people left out, the next three willing to pay most are willing to pay 105 each for subordination. So to secure their places, the three who are willing to pay 150 each must pay at least 105. While they are willing to pay 150 each, they therefore pay some amount between 105 and 150 each.

Take, for example, the case wherein each at first pays 110. Suppose the government can invest 60 in some public infrastructure project that increases their willingness-to-pay to 200 each. By providing this common good, the government can thus create 150 in extra total value for its subjects at a cost of 60. But because the three people who are willing to pay most for being in its jurisdiction only need to pay at least what the 'next three in line' are willing to pay, the government cannot necessarily reap the value of its investment through a tax on property values. For example, of the nine people left out, the three people willing to pay most for subordination may only value the infrastructure project at 10 each. What they are at most willing to pay thus increases to 115 each. To keep their places, the three people willing to pay most must then pay at least 115 each to price the others out. Land prices therefore increase by 10 per place, so 30 in total, while the total value created through the infrastructure project is 150 and its cost is 60. The project therefore cannot be financed through a land value tax, despite that it adds more value than it costs.

If the government then decides to tax its three subjects at an extra lump sum tax of 40 each for the project and the amount of money paid for subordination thereby becomes 155 per subject, its subjects will still stay in its jurisdiction. Each of them values subordination at 200, so they prefer to stay. The project thereby becomes feasible after all. Suppose the government levies the extra tax of 40 only above an income threshold that the incomes of its current three subjects exceed but those of the nine people left out do not. This tax then does not decrease land values, because the three others left out who would otherwise take up those places are still willing to pay 115 for subordination. Because their incomes are below the threshold at which the extra tax of 40 is imposed, they would not be taxed at 40 if they were subordinated to the government. Because they are still willing to pay at most 115 for being present in the government's jurisdiction, the places still go for 115 each and land prices therefore do not change.

In short, the value created by a government does not necessarily accrue to land prices. This is because the price of a plot of land does not equal the value attributed to occupying that place by those who do, but only exceeds the value attributed to occupying it by those who are priced out of it. Their valuation of the place they are priced out of puts a lower bound on the price of that place.

The land value tax can cannot serve as a single tax. It does have unique merits, as Henry George and the classical economists explained, since a land value tax is not as distortive as other forms of taxation. However, the difference between land prices and land values creates an incentive problem. As the supply of developed properties increases, the resulting agglomeration effects[100] can be so strong that property prices increase as well. But this is only up to a certain point, beyond which a higher population density does not add significant agglomeration effects. One only needs so many nearby barbers, supermarkets, employment opportunities, restaurants and so on. Besides, people have finite budgets to spend, so what they are willing and capable to pay in rent cannot increase infinitely. Beyond that point, as the supply of properties increases, property prices must decrease. As development costs do not necessarily decrease commensurately, the decrease in property prices will from some point have to come at the expense of the residual between property prices and development costs, i.e., land prices. The increase in properties per square foot of land may at first outweigh the decrease in property prices, resulting in higher total land values. But when the decrease in property prices outweighs the increase in properties, land prices will fall. At the extreme, property prices will equal the cost of devel-

[100] For a definition of agglomeration effects, see below 'The Imputation Problem'.

opment and land prices will be zero. If the government has the right to tax land values, it therefore has an interest in limiting the supply of properties at some point, while its subjects would benefit from a further increase in supply. Limiting a government's right to impose taxes other than the land value tax can therefore encourage government policies that create deadweight losses.

## CRITICISM OF THE LAND VALUE TAX

The benefits of the land value tax are disputed, with several objections being most common. First, not all economists agree that the value of governance accrues to land rents and that the land value tax can therefore serve as a single tax. This objection was made above, but other economists have thus far pointed to empirical data that show that current land rents would not suffice to finance government expenditure. Considering the above, they have been right. Second, economists have criticised the notion that undeveloped land can be separated from developments even conceptually. This criticism holds that all land is produced and thereby belongs to the factor capital, and that capital and land are therefore not separate categories of inputs. Land would be a produced factor of production, implying that taxing it would cause deadweight losses. Third, even when the second point of criticism is abandoned, some assert that separating the value of land from that of developments is impossible in practice, making the land value tax unrealisable. Lastly, some acknowledge that land is not produced and that land values can be ascertained with sufficient accuracy, but contend that taxing land would still create distortions.

The first point of criticism finds support from economists such as Paul Krugman.[101] The notion that a single tax would be sufficient for financing all government expenditure has been tested empirically, which they point to as evidence.[102] This evidence is unnecessary because their point can be proven in the abstract, as has been done in

[101] Moore (2017)

[102] See, for a thorough treatment, Doucet (2021a).

this section. Although this objection is correct, it must be recognised that foregoing other forms of taxation increases the amount that can be spent on rent and that other forms of taxation cause greater deadweight losses.

The second contention, according to which land is a form of capital produced like any other, was made chiefly by Frank Knight.[103] A land value tax would therefore cause the same inefficiencies as a tax on capital does. The classical economists viewed land as a non-produced factor, a distinction which Knight disputed by defining production as the transformation of 'stocks' into 'flows'. This does not require any physical creation but can merely involve making something available to others, such as when land is leased. Discovering new land and making it available by establishing and selling rights over it would thereby count as production as much as developing it would. All that is paid for land would therefore be paid for the productive actions that make it available.

## THE VALUE OF KNOWLEDGE

Bryan Caplan and Zachary Gochenour later elaborated on Knight's criticism by connecting it to discovery and exploration.[104] As they explained, billions are invested every year into exploration for natural resources, which fulfils an important economic function. Without it, natural resource scarcity would inhibit current living standards. Once natural resources are discovered in a location, that location increases in value as a result. This appreciation can then be captured by the exploration company. Without this possibility, no exploration would be undertaken. A land value tax would therefore be distortive, as it would discourage exploration by taxing away the resulting appreciation.

Caplan and Gochenour were correct to compare natural resource exploration with innovation. By patenting their innovations, inno-

[103] Knight (1948 [1921]); Knight (1924); Knight (1933); Knight (1953)

[104] Gochenour & Caplan (2012)

vators acquire legal monopolies over endeavours enabled by their innovations. These monopolies yield them 'quasi-rents', without which there would be no incentive to make the innovation in the first place. Extending this to the context of discovery and exploration, they explained:

> Quasi-rents are as important to land development as they are to other applications where their effects have been long-appreciated, such as in providing incentives for technological innovation or product variety. This is fundamentally different from the case of a rent-seeking (Tullock 1967) monopolist. The pricing policies of the patent holder or landowner, for instance, will be similar to that of a monopolist: the key difference being that in order to obtain the quasi-rent the landowner engages in productive activity.[105]
>
> ...
>
> A very high tax on the unimproved value of land could drastically interfere with the dynamic nature of entrepreneurial activity: developers must earn some minimum amount from the land to cover the enormous tax, therefore they will employ the land in its obvious use. Consider as an analogy a person born with obvious athletic talent to play professional basketball. Taxing this person on their ability to play basketball is potentially inefficient since it discourages that person from ever exploring other skills that might be his comparative advantage. Worse yet would be to commit to increase his tax to the new, higher rate if he determines he has a higher-valued skill. Similarly, the landowner is discouraged from exploring new uses for the land, particularly if those new uses might mean new taxes.[106]

[105] Ibid. p. 8

[106] Ibid. p. 10

Caplan and Gochenour correctly pointed out that land value taxation can be distortive by discouraging exploration. However, they did not delve deep enough into why this is. Their paper lacks an explanation of how exploration makes land appreciate. Consequently, they conflated the value of knowledge gained through exploration with the value of the land it concerns. The value added by successful land exploration is not a part of unearned land rent, but a separate value, the value of the knowledge obtained. If this knowledge were perfectly excludable, its value would not accrue to land values. It could then be sold and charged for separately by the exploration company. But as it is not perfectly excludable and is perfectly complementary to the land it concerns as well as specific to it, at least part of its value accrues to land values. The distinction between land and capital therefore still stands. The knowledge gained through exploration is a form of capital and is difficult to separate from land, like physical developments are.

Consider the following analogy: If an invention makes a natural resource more valuable by pointing entrepreneurs to a possible use for it, does this imply that the natural resource itself is produced by the process of innovation? The natural resource would become more valuable if the invention would become widely available, but does the incremental value stem from characteristics of the natural resource itself or from the idea that is complementary and specific to it? If the idea were to become excludable, such as when a patent is granted, the increase in the resource's value would not take place to the same extent. Under perfect excludability, its value would not increase at all. The idea is therefore what has been produced, not the natural resource.

Caplan and Gochenour also argued that the problem they pointed out makes land value taxes somewhat distortive in practice. This still stands, but the distortions can be very limited. It can be specified in law that those who discover natural resources thereby obtain the exclusive right to extract them. Such a law would make the knowledge gained excludable and would thus solve the problem of distortions arising from taxing unearned land rent.

Fred Foldvary responded with an excellent refutation[107] of Caplan and Gochenour's article. In his words:

107 Foldvary (2014)

> A "site" is the extent of three-dimensional space in a location. Any improvements that are produced within a site are, by definition, capital goods. Hence the clearing, draining, and leveling of the materials in a site are capital goods, and the added value or income is a territorial capital yield. The exploration of a site is labor, and the knowledge gained is both a capital good and human capital, and not, by these definitions, land. Therefore a properly applied payment, whether to a landlord or a government, of the land rent, or equivalently of the land value, cannot take any of the gains recently due to human action. Any tax above what was the value prior to the exploration would be a tax on labor and capital yields, not on the natural resource rent.[108]
>
> ...
>
> The basic misunderstanding by Caplan and Gochenour is to use a physical rather than an economic definition of land. Caplan and Gochenour (2012, p. 3) define land as property "devoid of physical improvements such as buildings." But capital goods can be intangible. If a researcher discovers a new use for a chemical, that knowledge can have a market value even if it is not yet embedded in a tangible product. The economic meaning of spatial land excludes the knowledge produced about the site, as well as other intangible improvements such as title searches, surveying, and mapping. Caplan and Gochenour claim that there is a profit "incentive to produce more of the resource" (p. 4), but by the above definition, any item that is produced is a capital good, not land.[109]

In reality, some of the value of knowledge will accrue to the value of the resources it is complementary to, because one can never perfectly

[108] Ibid. p. 453

[109] Ibid. p. 453

exclude others from using the knowledge one produces. Some of the value of knowledge about land will therefore accrue to the land's value. This applies to inventions too. If an invention cannot be perfectly excluded from or if knowledge of the invention inspires other entrepreneurs to make a similar invention, its value partly accrues to the resources complementary to it. This does not imply that these resources must not be taxed, but it does mean that, as Caplan and Gochenour explain, a land value tax is likely to distort economic incentives at least a little. However, effective policies may be possible to limit or eliminate these distortions, such as granting the exclusive right to use knowledge about land to those who produce this knowledge. Foldvary also proposed such an approach, similar to patents:

> Hence a proper implementation of land-value taxation should let real estate entrepreneurs keep their profits that are attached to sites, but for a limited time. The issue is similar to that of patents. A patent can provide an incentive for inventors to create new products, but that incentive does not require patents with infinite durations; excessive patent protection can stifle rather than enhance inventions. Patents now provide 20 years for entrepreneurs to reap their monopoly profits. An entrepreneur who discovers or creates a new use for a site is like an inventor of a new product, and could be granted a land-use patent for a number of years. After that, the site rental gradually becomes land rent. The land patent duration should be long enough for typical entrepreneurs to be incentivized to innovate.[110]

Even though some of the land value taxed away is created by their owners, Foldvary also correctly pointed to some important government endeavours that significantly improve land values, such as safety and roads. The value of these goods, since they are complementary to land, will accrue to the value of land if not charged for otherwise. If it does not tax land commensurately, a government effectively sub-

[110] Ibid. p. 457

sidises landowners by giving out goods for free that are complementary to land. While taxing land rents inevitably causes some inefficiencies, not doing so also does.

## THE ACCURACY OF LAND VALUE ASSESSMENT

The third point of criticism that is often made against land value taxation is that the value added by developments cannot be separated from the value of land, and that this makes the land value tax unrealisable. Among others, Friedrich Hayek shared this view:

> There still exist some organized groups who contend that all these difficulties could be solved by the adoption of the "single-tax" plan, that is, by transferring the ownership of all land to the community and merely leasing it at rents determined by the market to private developers. This scheme for the socialization of land is, in its logic, probably the most seductive and plausible of all socialist schemes. If the factual assumptions on which it is based were correct, i.e. if it were possible to distinguish clearly between the value of "the permanent and indestructible powers of the soil," on the one hand, and, on the other, the value due to the two different kinds of improvements– that due to communal efforts and that due to the efforts of the individual owner– the argument for its adoption would be very strong. Almost all the difficulties we have mentioned, however, stem from the fact that no such distinction can be drawn with any degree of certainty.[111]

To the contrary, sophisticated methods exist to separate potential land prices from the value added by improvements. However, this can only be addressed empirically and requires an extensive treatment of appraisal methods, which exceeds the scope of this book. Therefore, the

[111] Hayek (1960), pp. 352-53

reader is referred to another resource.[112] At this point, it is recognised that absolute accuracy in separating potential land prices from the value of improvements is impossible. However, absolute accuracy is not necessary for land value taxation to be superior to other forms of taxation, because these are also subject to inaccuracies in addition to their distortive effects. In fact, estimates of potential land prices are less vulnerable to fraud. Proponents of the single tax do not claim that potential land prices can be separated from the value of improvements with complete accuracy. Instead, they have pointed out that such accuracy is not strictly necessary. In the words of Henry George:

> I am convinced that with public attention concentrated on one single source of public revenues, and with the public intelligence and public conscience accustomed to look on the payments required from that, not as an exaction from the individual, but as something due in justice from him by the community, we would come much closer to taking the whole of economic rent than might seem possible at present. Yet I regard it as certain that it must always be impossible to take economic rent exactly, or to take it all, without at the same time taking something more. ... Theoretical perfection pertains to nothing human. The best we can do in practice is to approach the ideal. ... Is it not better that the state should, on the whole, get something less than its exact due than that individuals should be compelled to pay more than they ought to be called upon to pay? If so, we must in any case leave a margin. This I have always seen. What that margin should be I have never attempted to formulate, and have never put it at ten per cent or at any other per cent. What I have always stated as our aim was that we should take the whole of economic rent "as near as might be."[113]

[112] See Doucet (2021b) and his company, ValueBase, which specialises in land value assessment: https://www.valuebase.co/

[113] Reprinted in Wenzer (1997), pp. 82, 83.

In the end, the accuracy of land value assessments is an empirical matter. Over time, new techniques have been developed and have become cheaper to use. Nonetheless, while the value of improvements and the value of knowledge can be separated from the value of land with sufficient accuracy, the last common objection still stands. It must be recognised that the land value tax is not as efficient as some claim it to be. Some deadweight losses are inevitable when land prices are taxed, which limits its efficiency.

## THE IMPUTATION PROBLEM

The value of land can to a great extent be attributed to the actions of governments and their agents, such as their regulations and their provision of common goods. However, the actions of others also affect land values. For example, someone can create network externalities by settling somewhere. His presence increases land values where he is, because it makes it more attractive for others to settle there as this would enable them to cooperate with him. The more people settle somewhere, the more attractive it becomes for others to follow suit. These network externalities are called *agglomeration effects*. While a government can foster them, they are largely attributable to residents themselves.

Various kinds of externalities are created by a government's subjects. For example, property developers create externalities by deciding what gets developed. The functions[114] and aesthetics[115] of their developments can significantly impact the value of surrounding properties. What a developer decides to develop on his land impacts the values of neighbouring land. When a new shopping mall is built, for example, this may make surrounding land more attractive for residents. Conversely, developing a residential neighbourhood may

[114] Such as educational functions, as shown in Wen, Zhang, & Zhang (2014). Many more papers can be found on the price effect of the presence of educational facilities; the paper cited only serves as an example.

[115] Kerpestein (2022)

make nearby land more attractive for a shopping mall developer. Therefore, a developer who develops both contributes to the 'undeveloped' value of the land he develops. It is important that governments do not tax away this increment in value, lest they discourage its creation.

Moreover, if the value added to land by the developer himself is seen as such by assessors when the developer develops both projects together, but is seen as unearned land rent when he does so separately or when different developers do so separately, this distorts incentives in favour of developing separate plots as a whole.[116] The external value of a development that confers on neighbouring properties is taxed away if it is counted as unearned land rent. If the developer develops all the neighbouring properties together, these externalities are not counted as unearned land rent. Instead, they are then considered improvements and are therefore not taxed away.

To minimise deadweight losses, the government must only tax away the value it adds to land, not the value added by others. If the government taxes away all land rents except the value that developers add through improvements, this will hamper the creation of external value.

Instead of a 100% land value tax, consider the following alternative arrangement. A government does not tax away all land rents but allows property owners to keep some of it. Suppose it ascertains that roughly 85% of the price of land results from its activities and that the rest is created by property owners, developers and its subjects. The government therefore decides to levy an 85% land value tax. This may seem efficient, but of all the value it confers to land prices it can now only capture 85%. Of all the value its subjects confer to land prices, it taxes away 85%. Both are consequently induced to underprovide external value, below the level that would be efficient. The cost of a public monument may be 90% of its value added to land prices, but since the government can only capture 85% of the value it adds, it would make a loss from building it. For a property developer, the cost of building a more beautiful building may only

[116] This problem with Georgism was pointed out by Charles Hooper in Hooper (1993) and much later again by Friedman (2023).

be 20% of what the extra beauty adds to land prices, but he can only capture 15% of this value and therefore would make a loss from building more beautifully even though it would add more value to land than it would cost. At any tax rate, the land value tax creates deadweight losses. Any land value tax at a predetermined percentage results in distortions. Only if the exact share of a property's price that is conferred to it by a government can be ascertained precisely and only this is taxed away, is a land value tax not distortionary. However, the value the government confers to property prices is impossible to observe with any accuracy.

The land value tax must, however, be compared to its alternatives. Lump sum taxes cause deadweight losses and all other taxes have distortionary effects that are likely to be more severe than those of the land value tax.

## IMPUTATION, CONTRACT AND INCENTIVES

Thus far, it has been explained that not all untaxed value of governance will accrue commensurately to land prices. To capture the full value of its governance, a government therefore has to levy other taxes besides a land value tax, such as lump-sum, income, or consumption taxes. It has also been explained that it can capture much of the value it creates through its governance by levying a land value tax and that this tax does not cause the same inefficiencies as other types of tax do, but that land value taxation still causes some deadweight losses. However, it is in the interests of both a proprietary government and property owners to contract in order to limit or eliminate these deadweight losses, such that the deadweight loss thereby eliminated, minus the transaction cost of doing so, is maximised.

Land value taxation would not cause any inefficiencies if it were possible to accurately determine how much of all land rents are created by whom. The government and the property owner could then contract such that both receive the value they themselves create. However, because accurate imputation is impossible, no contractual arrangement between a government and a property owner can give them perfect incentives. Situations will arise in which one of the two can add value but chooses not to because the contractual arrangement does not entitle him to fully capture the resulting increase in land prices.

If a better contractual arrangement can be made that will lead to more value being added, both parties have an interest in doing so. The interest of both a profit-maximising government and a property owner is to optimise their contract such that the deadweight losses eliminated, minus the cost of doing so, are maximised. Whenever a contract leads to deadweight losses, which limits the profits of both the subject and the government, and the contract can be redrawn at a cost lower than the deadweight loss thereby eliminated, both stand to benefit from doing so. That is, when both parties can thereby individually obtain more value than the costs they individually incur to do so, they benefit from improving their contractual arrangement. However, no arrangement is perfect.

In general, if contracting and the according deviation in actions is a Pareto improvement for the contracting parties, all of them prefer to undertake it. Thus, if the value the contracting parties attribute to the resulting deviation in actions exceeds the costs of contracting, all of them will prefer to undertake it.

## THE HOLD-UP PROBLEM

Property and governance are complementary to each other. Besides, the immobility of real estate makes it costly if not impossible for a property owner to move it to another jurisdiction and thereby have it governed by another government, and it is worth much less if ungoverned. As a result, there is a hold up problem between a government and property owners.[117] After a development is built on it, a government can tax a site so heavily that it takes away some or all of the gains from development. If the property owner had expected this in advance or had estimated hold-up risk to be too great, he would not have made the investment. In this hold-up situation, the property owner is left empty-handed as he cannot simply move

[117] The hold-up problem exists when someone can benefit from cooperating, but chooses not to because he fears to thereby give another party the ability to set the terms to cooperation to his own advantage. For a paper on the problem, see Klein, Crawford, & Alchian (1978).

it to another government's jurisdiction at no cost. The government and the property owner can prevent such situations by contracting, such as by specifying a maximum land tax or a minimum net rent for the owner. However, this requires perfect foresight or complete contracting if both parties are to reap the value they themselves create. With any contract, situations may arise wherein the government can add more value to a property than the maximum tax allows it to capture. Because complete contracting is impossible or costly and the contracting parties have no perfect foresight, the resulting part of total rent going to the property owner and that going to the government will deviate from the values they create. No contractual solution to the hold-up problem between the government and the property owner thus exists that does not lead to incentive problems and the resulting deadweight losses.

To align the incentives, the government and the property owner will have to renegotiate their agreement in light of new information. However, doing so may not be in their favour even when they can thereby eliminate a deadweight loss, because the cost of eliminating it may be greater than the deadweight loss itself. With respect to the hold-up problem, the same holds as does for the imputation problem – The government and the property owners benefit from optimising the contract between them to minimise deadweight loss if the values they thereby obtain exceed their costs of doing so.

## AGGLOMERATION EXTERNALITIES

The agglomeration externalities that a newcomer brings to a place confer to different extents to different local property owners. In theory, they could bargain with a potential newcomer to compensate him for the agglomeration externalities he would create. Compensating newcomers could benefit them by stimulating agglomeration effects. In reality, the transaction costs of doing so are too high. A government, however, if it is entitled to the increment in land prices that stem from the agglomeration externalities, also benefits from fostering them and can do so at much lower transaction costs. In a similar form, this is already common with shopping malls. Shopping mall developers and owners often offer cheaper tenancies to 'anchor tenants'. These are tenants whose presence makes tenancy more attractive for others. A popular department store, for example, can be an attractive anchor tenant by attracting foot traffic from which smaller shops can then benefit. If the other unit owners would have to bring in the anchor tenant, the transaction cost of doing so would be higher because of the number of parties involved. Developers can capture the agglomeration externalities at a lower cost by fulfilling this role instead.

When a proprietary government knows the profits to be made by compensating people for the agglomeration externalities their presence creates, it may do so to compete with other governments for subjects. Early movers would then be paid most as this will be necessary to lure them in. They will have to forego the agglomeration externalities of residing elsewhere and move with less certain outcomes regarding employment opportunities and so on. As the settlement grows, the agglomeration externalities created by the marginal newcomer decrease and he will therefore be paid less. By then, the risks of moving in will also have decreased and newcomers will be able to benefit from the externalities created by those who came before them, so less compensation will be necessary. As more governments compete for newcomers, their compensation to newcomers converges to the agglomeration externalities they thereby expect to reap. And, as settlements grow, the marginal net land rents that stem from the agglomeration effects brought by the marginal entrant decrease to the point at which compensating him is not worthwhile. People will not receive all the agglomeration externalities they create as not all these externalities accrue to land prices, nor will compensating them always be worth the transaction costs of doing so. However, proprietary governments, in their pursuit of the best terms they can obtain and thereby financial profits, can be expected to offer compensation in at least some cases.

In principle, the proposal of Henry George to tax away land rents and to redistribute these to the community in the form of a citizen's dividend comes down to the same. However, the community is not a homogeneous group. Some people bring more agglomeration externalities than others. A proprietary government has an interest in compensating people for the agglomeration externalities they individually create. Instead of the citizen's dividend proposed by Henry George, an informed proprietary government will compensate the community for the agglomeration externalities they bring insofar and in a way it is efficient to do so.

## THE LEAST BAD TAX?

Although it inevitably causes some deadweight losses and cannot suffice as a single tax, the land value tax has one unique property that makes it ideally suited to form the core of a government's taxation strategy. Namely, land does not decrease in supply as it is taxed more heavily. Land is virtually costless to provide and a land value tax does not tax away the actual price for which it is sold or leased, but the price that could be obtained for it. Land value taxation therefore does not discourage any leases or transfers of land. Milton Friedman once accordingly called it the 'least bad tax'.[118] By comparison, income taxes discourage the provision of labour, corporate taxes discourage investment and sales taxes discourage consumption. By making fewer cooperations take place, such taxes result in deadweight losses. Because the cooperations prevented are complementary to being present in the jurisdiction, these deadweight losses limit how much people value being there. Such taxes could thus decrease land rents by more than the taxes levied. They limit the tax base itself. Taxing away the value of undeveloped land does not affect its supply or demand. The land value tax is therefore likely to result in lower deadweight losses than other taxes do and is thus an excellent source of revenue for a government. Other taxes create higher deadweight losses, thereby decreasing the tax base by more than the land value tax does.

As explained before, the idea that a land value tax does not create deadweight losses is incorrect. However, there are ways to mitigate the resulting deadweight losses, such as by initially giving the rights to extract natural resources to those who discover them. And while any right to levy land value taxes creates deadweight losses due to the imputation problem and transaction costs, governments and landowners have an interest in limiting these deadweight losses by contracting.

Besides the direct deadweight losses, the right to levy land value taxes can give a government an interest in restricting the housing supply, thereby creating deadweight losses even if levying land value taxes itself would not do so. But a government that pursues profit also has an interest in opening its borders to immigrants. The point at which

[118] Friedman (February 6, 1978)

it then becomes in its interests to limit the housing supply is then likely to be very far away.

Besides, a proprietary government is likely to pursue profit and is therefore likely to seek to attract as many new residents as possible. To this end, it will keep its tax rates competitively low, in particular on mobile factors, such that residing and investing in its jurisdiction is more attractive than doing so in the jurisdictions of its competitors. More of the value created by the government will then accrue to land values.

Thus, compared to a representative government, a proprietary government is likely to rely more on land value taxation. Other taxes decrease the land value tax base. In the end, whether a proprietary government will primarily levy land value taxes or other kinds of taxes remains to be seen. A land value tax or other property taxes will probably play a large role, and empirical literature does confirm Friedman's claim.[119]

## THE PROPRIETARY GOVERNMENT VERSUS THE REPRESENTATIVE GOVERNMENT

In the pursuit of financial profits, a proprietary government is likely to rely in the first place on the land value tax. To minimise the resulting deadweight losses, it can pass legislation that grants the initial right to extract natural resources to those who discover them. It can also be expected to use sophisticated methods to ascertain the potential prices of land and, if possible, to what extent these prices are attributable to itself. By levying taxes accordingly, it can minimise the deadweight losses resulting from land value taxation. But through a land value tax, a government can never reap all the value it creates. It may therefore levy other taxes as well, such as lump sum taxes. However, it can be expected to keep these tax rates low, to attract new residents and investment and to avoid decreasing its land value tax base.

[119] See, for some of that empirical literature, for example the following papers. Arnold, et al. (2001); Johansson, Å., et al. (2008); Acosta-Ormaechea, S., Sola, S. and Yoo, J. (2019); Şen, H. & Kaya, A. (2023)

Some taxes may be levied exclusively on people with much to spend. The richer people are, the less their willingness-to-pay for subordination to a particular government translates into higher rents they must pay and thus higher land values. For instance, if a billionaire's tax burden decreases by $10 million per year and he pays $1 million per year in rent for his mansion, his rent is unlikely to increase to $11 million per year, even though what he is willing to pay for being in the jurisdiction has increased by $10 million per year. Rent is determined not only by demand but also by supply. If his landlord would increase his rent burden to $11 million per year, he would simply move to another mansion or build his own. By comparison, if the tax burden on lower incomes decreases significantly, the intensive competition for space by the poor will make rents increase almost commensurately. At their level of income, the poorest pay about as much in rent as they can bear. Lowering taxes on lower incomes therefore pays itself back to a greater extent through higher land value taxes while lowering taxes on the rich does to a lesser extent. The richer people are, the less of their tax savings translate into a higher land value tax base.

In some cases, a government can negotiate directly with the beneficiaries of a policy or public good. For instance, if a wealthy person has bought a plot of land and wants to have a connecting road built on government land, the government can choose to build the road first and tax the thereby appreciated land or to negotiate directly beforehand. Direct negotiation may be more profitable, because the value of the road to the rich person is likely to be much higher than its value to others. Direct negotiation is then a better option and does not have to result in any deadweight losses.

Lastly, and importantly, as a proprietary government actively pursues the best terms it can obtain and thereby maximise its tax base, it has an interest in avoiding unnecessary deadweight losses because deadweight losses commensurately decrease its tax base. To obtain the best terms, a government must maximise the deadweight losses it eliminates minus the costs it incurs to do so. A profit-maximising proprietary government can therefore be expected to take efficiency into account when determining its taxation strategy. It may impose both land value taxes and other types of tax and thereby cause deadweight losses, but will also try to eliminate deadweight losses when it can benefit from this. When a government and its subjects can individually obtain more value by improving their contractual arrangement than the costs they individually incur to do so, they all stand to benefit.

A proprietary government can thus be expected to avoid unnecessary deadweight losses. Accordingly, it can be expected to rely more on land value taxation and to tax the middle and lower classes less than a representative government does, while levying some income or luxury taxes on the rich specifically. It may also levy lump sum taxes and directly negotiate with people who are capable and willing to pay much for some government-provided goods or services. In general, it can be expected to impose lower taxes than a representative government usually does and to do so in ways that lead to much smaller deadweight losses. It will keep its tax rates competitively low to attract new residents and is not hindered by entrenched interests or political opposition in taxing its subjects. A proprietary government can thus be expected to tax more efficiently and to have lower tax rates than a representative government.[120]

## CONCLUSION

Because a government does not know the value its subjects obtain from every action they take, it cannot tax their actions directly at the level of these values. It can only impose taxes at general tax rates on

[120] A good example of a state that pursues financial profit is the Emirate of Dubai. Monarchies are not proprietary governments but do have similar incentives working on their rulers. The rulers of Dubai have been governing their jurisdiction with a profit motive, and thus with the intention of attracting subjects and investment. To this end, they have some of the lowest tax rates in the world. This has made their jurisdiction very attractive, making its population balloon from tens of thousands to millions in mere decades and both its population and GDP are still growing rapidly. Measured in GDP per capita, it is currently one of the richest jurisdictions in the Middle East. After Israel, it is the richest in the Middle East of which the economy does not primarily rely on natural resource extraction. For more information, see https://en.wikipedia.org/wiki/Economy_of_Dubai.

some classes of actions for some classes of people. In doing so, it has an interest in engaging in commitment strategies. In addition, if it only levies a land value tax, it cannot capture all the value it creates. Its interest is then to undersupply some things and to limit the supply of real estate. As a result, all government-subject relationships involve deadweight losses incurred by both the government and its subjects. As a result of taxation, undersupply and restrictions on the supply of real estate, actions are prevented that would be Pareto improvements.

Under some degree of proprietary democracy, however, a proprietary government has an interest in levying taxes more efficiently than a representative government does. It will therefore rely more on land value taxes and less on taxes that cause greater deadweight losses. Under some degree of proprietary democracy, it is also in the interests of a proprietary government and its subjects, including property owners, to eliminate much of the arising deadweight losses because these deadweight losses come at the expense of its tax base. A proprietary government, in its pursuit of the best terms it can get and thereby maximum financial profits, has an interest in optimising its contract with its subjects such that its deadweight losses thereby eliminated, minus its costs of doing so, are maximised. It is also likely to compensate people for the agglomeration externalities they create.

The fewer exceptions there are to proprietary democracy, the more proprietary governance will deliver these benefits. If there are too many exceptions to proprietary democracy, a proprietary government is likely to act differently. For example, if subordination is not consensual and if people are kept in unconditional subordination by force, it may be more profitable to govern the jurisdiction like a farmer operates his farm. People will then be treated more like cattle instead of customers. The government may force people to work and give up almost all of their income. Its tax base will then be whatever its subjects can bear. One minimises such cases by maximising proprietary democracy, i.e. by minimising the possibility to gainfully engage in actions that form exceptions to it.

## 9.2 POLYCENTRIC GOVERNANCE

Remember from Section 4.7 that the rights of government are a bundle of rights that can vary – Some governments have more extensive rights of government than others.

Multiple governments may have overlapping jurisdictions. Rights of government are then held by governments of different levels, such as the national and the municipal level. Certain rights of government are usually held together, and for good reason. For example, because a government will have no reason to govern if it cannot capture some of the value it thereby creates, rights of government typically include a right to levy taxes. Whether some rights are better held together by one government or separately by different governments depends on particular circumstances. Dividing the rights of government is a matter of trade-offs and requires context-specific knowledge to do well.

For example, on the one hand law enforcement would ideally be provided by those who make the law, because the cost of enforcement partly depends on the law itself. Some laws are more difficult and costly to enforce than others. If one government holds the right to make the law while another is responsible for its enforcement, this could create distortive incentives. For example, it could encourage the government that holds the right to make laws to make laws that are more costly to enforce even if this is not efficient. Other laws might add more value. One could think the right to make laws would therefore ideally be held together with the rights and responsibility to provide law enforcement. On the other hand, lower-level governments could be better at providing enforcement while higher-level governments could be better at law making. Law making often requires extensive research and expertise, while the provision of enforcement may require local knowledge. As is already common, it may then be better if municipal governments provide enforcement while higher-level governments engage in law making.

There are good reasons for a government to have overlapping jurisdictions with other governments.[121] Lower-level governments may

[121] For a seminal paper that argues for polycentric governance, see Ostrom, Tiebout, & Warren, (1961).

be better at adjusting their offerings to the preferences of subjects. Competition between multiple lower-level governments may make the entire jurisdiction of the higher-level government more attractive. It may result in fewer economies of scale because of the multitude of smaller jurisdictions resulting from it, but allows proprietary governments to provide a wider range of offerings within their jurisdictions. They can thereby better adjust their offering to the various preferences of different kinds of subjects.

In theory, there can be many overlapping jurisdictions, varying according to the preferences of local subjects. In some parts of its jurisdiction, a government can sell or lease rights of government to one lower-level government, while in other parts such lower-level governments can transfer some of their rights on to other governments. Important trade-offs, like the trade-off between capturing economies of scale and tailoring the offering to more types of subjects, as well as the trade-off between expert law making and using local information, are commonly made in dividing rights of government.

A government can divide its rights of government by transferring them in some policy domains while keeping them in other policy domains. Local governments can, for example, have rights of government with respect to public aesthetics, local public amenities such as roads, urban planning and moral issues such as religious laws. The higher-level government then keeps the rights of government in other domains, such as criminal law. Many other divisions are possible and the ideal division for each jurisdiction depends on the context.

Governments of different levels can be found in almost every country. Local, regional and state governments are common variants and some countries have another level by taking the form of federations, such as the United States. Their divisions of the rights of government allow governance to be better adjusted to the preferences of subjects. In representative democracies, governments at all levels typically take the form of the representative system. To maximise proprietary democracy, they must all be proprietary governments because all rights of government must be alienable.

As explained in Section 4.6, governments that provide enforcement have a right to superior force. Rights to superior force can also be held by multiple governments over the same territory. For example, a municipal government may only be allowed to have its own police force while a higher-level government, such as a regional or national government, keeps the right to military supremacy. The lower-level government then has a right to superior force vis-à-vis its subjects, while the higher-level government has a right to superior force vis-à-vis the lower-level government. This can discourage the lower-level government from acting violatively.

## IMPUTATION, CONTRACT AND INCENTIVES

Like governments and property owners, governments with overlapping jurisdictions face the hold-up problem and the imputation problem. They have hold-up problems because their offerings are complementary, their jurisdictions are fixed in place and they are subject to sunk costs and switching costs. They have an imputation problem because it is neither possible to determine the value of governance perfectly, nor separately for every government or property owner. Because of these problems, what was explained in Section 4.7 to apply to the relationship between an enforcement providers and administrative entrepreneurs and was in Section 9.1 explained to apply to the relationship between governments and property owners, also applies to the relationship between governments with overlapping jurisdictions.

Because of the hold-up problem, a division of the rights of government whereby governments have the right to levy taxes freely over the same jurisdictions inevitably creates distortive incentives and the resulting economic inefficiencies. The imputation problem prevents them from reaching a solution where each can capture the value they create. To prevent inefficiencies, governments must therefore be restricted in their freedom to levy taxes if they have overlapping jurisdictions.

Imperfect incentives are inevitable. However, as with the relationship between a government and a property owner, the arrangement that gives subjects the governance they value most will maximise the range of terms that subjects are willing to accept for governance, and thereby the taxes they are willing to pay. Governments with overlapping jurisdictions therefore have an interest in optimising their contracts such that the total net value created for subjects, and thereby the total net tax base, is maximised.

Incentive problems can only be prevented if the interests of the governments involved are strictly aligned or if the elimination conditions are satisfied. Giving governments with overlapping jurisdictions shares in each other could well be the best viable solution to aligns the interests of the respective parties to a large extent. A higher-level government then owns a substantial share in the lower-level government, or vice versa. In any case, the respective parties can remove inefficient incentives through contract, but never completely.

The contractual problems explained in this section limit proprietary democracy, but governments with overlapping jurisdictions always have an interest in rearranging their rights if it increases their total combined tax base by more than the cost of contracting. Under some degree of proprietary democracy, this total combined tax base to some extent depends on the terms to subordination that subjects receive. Governments with overlapping jurisdictions then maximise profits by optimising their contracts such that the net value thereby created is maximised. Whenever such governments can rearrange rights such that the resulting increase in value for subjects exceeds the cost of contracting and any other resulting costs, they can all profit from doing so.

In short, the relationship between governments with overlapping jurisdictions is subject to the same problems that exist between a government and a property owner and between an enforcement provider and an administrative entrepreneur. Their incentives resulting from their contracts are inevitably somewhat distorted. Proprietary democracy is consequently limited. However, if it exists to some degree, the respective parties have an interest in optimising their contract such that the resulting net value is maximised.

## PROPRIETARY DEMOCRACY VERSUS THE PRINCIPLE OF SUBSIDIARITY

It is currently common for governments to divide rights of government according to the 'principle of subsidiarity'. According to this principle, governance must be as localised as possible – All tasks that lower-level governments can perform must be performed by them and higher-level governments must only take on tasks that lower-level governments cannot. However, this principle is not necessarily efficient. There may be policy domains that can be devolved to lower-level governments but in which higher-level governments are more competent or efficient.

Under some degree of proprietary democracy, a higher-level proprietary government receives the best terms from subjects by regulating lower-level proprietary governments such that the total value conferred to subjects is maximised. Transferring some of its rights of government to multiple governments and thereby creating multiple lower-level jurisdictions may intensify competition and thereby lead to better and more affordable lower-level governance for its subjects. Furthermore, the higher-level proprietary government has an interest in suppressing collusion between lower-level governments, as well as mergers and acquisitions that have greater negative anticompetitive effects than resulting synergies. The governance that maximises its tax base is that which maximises the difference between the total value of subordination to the higher-level government and the cost of governance. The cheaper and better lower-level governments provide governance, the higher the profits of the higher-level government.

For example, lower-level proprietary governments can have synergies. A highway or train line connecting jurisdictions to each other, for instance, can make these jurisdictions more attractive to invest in and move to. If projects that span multiple higher-level jurisdictions add more value to these jurisdictions than they cost, such investments will be profitable for the respective governments to make together. If such a project spans the jurisdictions of multiple lower-level governments, it is both in their interests and in the interests of the higher-level government to undertake it, because the higher-level government can capture the value of the synergies it allows to be created. The higher-level government can undertake the project, or the lower-level governments can do so in the form of a joint venture. If a joint venture is impossible or relatively costly, the governments involved could perhaps capture these synergies through a merger. To ensure that only value-enhancing mergers take place, the higher-level government can keep the right to forbid them. The interest of the higher-level government is to allow the solution that maximises the net value of its jurisdiction, whether it would be a merger, a joint venture or undertaking the project by itself.

A project can also span multiple lower-level jurisdictions and add value in total but not to each jurisdiction individually. If the value that a project adds to one or more jurisdictions exceeds the net negative externalities and opportunity costs that it creates for other jurisdictions, those who undertake the project can compensate the governments of the negatively affected jurisdictions and still profit. If the transaction costs of doing so are prohibitively high, the higher-level government could profit from undertaking the project instead. What reduces its tax base in one part of its jurisdiction then grows its tax base in another part by more, making the project profitable.

In the debate about polycentric governance, different schools of thought support different divisions of the rights of government between higher-level and lower-level governments. The polycentrists support advanced divisions of the rights of government while the (neo)consolidationists support more centralised governance. Proprietary governance offers a third way – Letting the market decide. Under some degree of proprietary democracy, the respective governments maximise profits by pursuing the option that maximises the value of subordination to them all. Proprietary governments then maximise profits by striking the right balance between the costs and benefits of polycentric governance.

## 9.3 DEADWEIGHT LOSSES AND EXTERNALITIES

### INTERVENTION

As explained in Chapter 7, an entrepreneur can do things to move the cooperative actions others are willing to partake in from one Pareto efficient course of action to another. He does so to replace a future cooperative course of action that he expects others to prefer with one that he prefers. He thereby gains at the expense of others, in particular the people he cooperates with. One way to do this is through anticompetitive action, which prevents recipients of opportunities for cooperation from obtaining more valuable outcomes. By acting anticompetitively, an entrepreneur makes people cooperate with himself in ways he prefers by making them unable to obtain outcomes that they would prefer over those he offers. Another way is the commitment strategy, through which an entrepreneur convinces opportunity recipients that they cannot obtain certain terms and thereby makes them accept terms they find less favourable. Anticompetitive action and commitment strategies can prevent valuable cooperations from taking place and thereby create deadweight losses – The value that people would have obtained from the cooperations they otherwise would have engaged in. A government can limit deadweight losses by limiting the possibilities to gainfully engage in such types of action, such as by combating fraud and collusion. The deadweight loss it eliminates then accrues to its tax base, while any cost the government's interference creates for its subjects commensurately decreases its tax base. Under any positive degree of proprietary democracy, a profit-maximising proprietary government therefore has an interest in eliminating deadweight losses by interfering in the actions of its subjects, insofar the resulting net value for subjects is positive.

This does not apply to the endeavours in which a government itself competes, i.e. governance. By engaging in anticompetitive action, deception, commitment strategies and violative action in its own endeavours, it can obtain better terms from subjects and thus increase its profits. It therefore has no interest in limiting its own possibilities to gainfully engage in those courses of action. This would be irrelevant in the absence of any exceptions to proprietary democracy, since it would have no such possibilities.

## NATURAL MONOPOLIES

If an entrepreneurial endeavour naturally has such great anticompetitive effects that they significantly affect the terms of cooperation, it results in what is commonly called a 'natural monopoly'. A natural monopoly gives an entrepreneur the ability to gainfully commit to certain terms. Many mutually preferred cooperations are thereby often foregone, resulting in substantial deadweight losses. Common 'natural monopolies' include roads and other infrastructure. But as explained in Section 7.4, every entrepreneurial endeavour is strictly speaking a monopoly. Natural monopoly is strictly speaking ubiquitous as every entrepreneurial endeavour has some anticompetitive effect. However, some endeavours have greater anticompetitive effects than others. What are commonly called 'natural monopolies' naturally preclude most competition, or competition leads to unnecessary duplication such as in the case of sewage systems and electrical grids. As a result, these endeavours can lead to great inefficiencies. They either create deadweight losses as a result of commitment strategies such as monopoly pricing, or inefficient competition because a competitive market would require two or more infrastructure networks existing side by side, or both.

For this reason, governments commonly undertake these endeavours instead. They provide and own most infrastructure. Using commitment strategies to obtain better terms for the use of infrastructure comes at the expense of their tax bases, so they have little if any interest in doing so. Besides, a representative democratic government is in principle less likely to exploit natural monopolies to its advantage, because this would come at the expense of itself as its own subjects. However, because virtually all governments are currently either representative democracies or dictatorships, these endeavours are rarely done efficiently. Infrastructure projects, for example, are typically vulnerable to corruption.[122]

One way to circumvent the problems of government corruption and inefficiency is by issuing tenders, but this requires continued government involvement, in the form of price controls or a stake in the endeavours, to prevent the 'natural monopolists' from engaging in commitment strategies. Prices and quality are then co-determined by the government, often through government-owned stakes in tender companies. However, in representative systems the oversight of government-owned stakes is not unlikely to involve corruption and inefficiencies.

Proprietary governance can solve the problem of natural monopolies because the interest of a proprietary government under proprietary democracy, in the pursuit of the best terms it can obtain, is to maximise net value for its subjects. The fewer the exceptions to proprietary democracy, the stronger this interest is. Any deadweight loss then comes at the expense of its tax base, so its interest is to provide efficiently and cheaply in its 'naturally monopolistic' endeavours. A proprietary government that holds natural monopolies in

122 The construction sector is widely reported as one of the most corrupt globally. Public works and construction repeatedly top the charts of Transparency International's Bribe Payer's Index, being perceived as the sector most likely to engage in bribery. See Hardoon & Heinrich (2011).

its jurisdiction would not engage in commitment strategies, including 'monopoly pricing', in these endeavours.

Some endeavours characterised as natural monopolies, such as especially large infrastructure works, span multiple jurisdictions. The deadweight loss then does not only come at the expense of the higher-level government that undertakes it, but also of other governments. In such cases too, however, proprietary governance gives the most efficient solution. The respective proprietary governments have a mutual interest in eliminating any deadweight loss by undertaking the endeavour together or by compensating each other for foregoing commitment strategies.

## NON-GOVERNMENTAL ADMINISTRATIVE ENTREPRENEURSHIP

In his book *Private Governance*, Edward Stringham points to cases in which governments have been proven unnecessary for the regulation of human behaviour.[123] One example is that of stock exchanges, which emerged without being established by governments. In fact, such endeavours often thrived despite government attempts to suppress them, such as the derivates trade. Many more examples of non-governmental regulation can be found today, such as regulation by online selling platforms like eBay and payment facilitators like PayPal. PayPal has developed its own fraud prevention systems because government action was inadequate. Even though government solutions were perhaps possible, PayPal's own solution was much more efficient. Another example is private arbitration. As an alternative to inefficient government courts, private arbitration has become a common way to solve legal disputes. While it was not mentioned by Stringham, Heathian proprietary administration is another form of non-governmental administrative entrepreneurship that performs important regulatory functions.[124]

Apart from administrative entrepreneurship, many other mechanisms exist to regulate human behaviour. For example, religion, hon-

[123] Stringham (2015)

[124] As explained in Section 5.4.

or and conditional community membership are often important in small and primitive communities in particular.

However, these types of endeavours and social mechanisms, whether undertaken by governments or subjects, can never fulfil all government functions because enforcement is indispensable. In the words of Douglass North:

> Economies of scale result in the beginnings of hierarchical producing organizations, with full-time workers working either in a central place or in a sequential production process. Towns and some central cities are emerging, and occupational distribution of the population now shows, in addition, a substantial increase in the proportion of the labor force engaged in manufacturing and in services, although the traditional preponderance in agriculture continues. These evolving stages also reflect a significant shift towards urbanization of the society. Such societies need effective, impersonal contract enforcement, because personal ties, voluntaristic constraints, and ostracism are no longer effective as more complex and impersonal forms of exchange emerge. It is not that these personal and social alternatives are unimportant; they are still significant even in today's interdependent world. But in the absence of effective impersonal contracting, the gains from "defection" are great enough to forestall the development of complex exchange.[125]

While governments can never be fully replaced by non-governmental entities, it is not in the interest of a profit-maximising proprietary government to crowd out non-governmental administrative entrepreneurship if government involvement is less efficient. Because the government would be worse at fulfilling such roles, crowding out non-governmental administrative entrepreneurship would increase its costs by more than any resulting increase in its tax base. Instead, its interest is to complement non-governmental administrative entre-

[125] North, (1991)

preneurship by undertaking administrative entrepreneurship insofar it is most fit for the task. If non-governmental administrative entrepreneurs are better at fulfilling some role, a proprietary government maximises its gains by allowing them to, instead of restricting them or crowding them out. This stands in contrast with a representative government, whose politicians and civil servants have an interest in keeping their jobs and in creating new jobs for their friends. Their interests are to grow the civil service and its involvement in society. It cannot be said a priori what roles a government should fulfil, but both governments and non-governmental entities fulfil important administrative entrepreneurial roles in a society. A profit-maximising proprietary government will pursue the most efficient outcome.

For example, a government makes its jurisdiction most valuable by allowing access to multiple competing adjudication providers instead of maintaining a monopoly. A profit-maximising proprietary government can therefore be expected to offer its subjects free access to non-governmental arbitration and to have the resulting rulings enforced. Politicians and civil servants in a representative democracy do not have this interest, and a judiciary has an opposing interest. Besides, a government monopoly on adjudication allows judges to let personal preferences and biases influence their rulings more than independent arbitrators can, who are kept in check by competition. In representative democratic systems, judges can therefore be expected to make more flawed and biased rulings.

## EXTERNALITIES

Many actions can create externalities that make them Pareto inefficient, while it is often too costly to contract for efficient outcomes. Externalities are often too costly to sue or contract for, whatever the law may specify. Problems of externalities are then not solved through contract because the costs of doing so exceed the benefits. Contracting can be a solution when externalities are significant enough and transaction costs, which includes the cost of bargaining, are small enough.

But if a government can solve a problem of externalities, such as by levying emissions taxes or imposing noise restrictions, it may be less costly for it to do so than it is for the people involved to solve the problem through contract.[126] A government solution then solves the externalities problem and saves subjects transaction costs, which adds to its tax base. If the costs of contracting are so high that they prevent any solution from subjects themselves, a government could perhaps still provide a net-beneficial solution. Government regulation, taxation and subsidisation of externalities could create more value than the costs of doing so. Under some degree of proprietary democracy, a proprietary government obtains the best terms by regulating, subsidising and taxing externalities such that the total net value of externalities conferring to its own jurisdiction is thereby maximised. Negative externalities that affect its jurisdiction commensurately decrease the location value of its jurisdiction by making it less attractive to be present in it. The converse holds for positive externalities - Positive externalities accrue to the location value of its jurisdiction. Under some degree of proprietary democracy, a proprietary government therefore maximises its tax base by maximising the net positive of the externalities that confers to its subjects.[127]

However, there are also externalities that affect other jurisdictions. These externalities can be created by the government itself or by its subjects. Think, for example, of greenhouse gas emissions and the contamination of rivers used for drinking water and irrigation in other jurisdictions. Contrary to intra-jurisdictional externalities, a government does not necessarily profit from maximising the net positive of these inter-jurisdictional externalities.

For positive inter-jurisdictional externalities, it may be sufficient for governments and their subjects to know how the externalities they create affect other jurisdictions and to speculate on the basis of this knowledge. For example, if industrial facilities to be built in jurisdiction A will make it more attractive to settle in a nearby jurisdiction B, the government of jurisdiction A and the developer will be the first to know about the plan. They can then buy properties in jurisdiction B to capture the external value conferred to B. Alternatively, the govern-

126 Coase (1960), p. 17.

127 Or minimise the net negative of these externalities. The meaning is the same.

ments of both jurisdictions can contract to ensure that positive externalities are not underproduced. They can agree to transfer back to the creators of the externalities some of the external value that confers to their tax bases. If an activity can add net value by the positive externalities it creates for people in other jurisdictions, but is not profitable for the person undertaking it if he cannot capture some of these externalities, the respective governments have an interest in contracting such that the beneficiaries compensate him commensurately.

But for governments to have the right incentives to minimise net negative externalities, they must contract with each other. One might think that making proprietary governments liable for the externalities they allow to be created will lead to efficient outcomes, since this will impel them to extend this liability to the creators themselves. As Ronald Coase explained, however, it is not necessarily efficient to make the producer of negative externalities liable for them. Doing so may discourage the affected people from taking sufficient measures if they can.[128] It may not be efficient to make governments liable for external costs created in and transcending their jurisdictions, because these external costs may also depend on the actions of those who bear them. If those who bear the costs are fully compensated, they have no interest in minimising them. So making the producer of negative externalities liable for them may not always lead to efficient outcomes, but neither does not doing so. This also applies to the governments that allow the creation of externalities – Making them liable is not necessarily efficient, but neither is the opposite.

However, under some degree of proprietary democracy, proprietary governments always have an interest in contracting such that the resulting incentives maximise the total net value of subordination to them. If a contract impels a government to stop an activity that could produce net value if those who bear the external costs would make the right adjustments, redrawing that contract could be beneficial to all. What Coase explained to apply to the creators of externalities also applies to the governments that host them – It is in their interest to make the contractual arrangements that lead to the maximisation of net positive externalities minus the cost of contracting.

[128] Coase (1960)

In short, under some degree of proprietary democracy, a government maximises its tax base by maximising the value that people attribute to being present in its jurisdiction. In some ways, this requires offering better terms to subjects, which gives it an interest in maximising the net value of all externalities that confer to everything and everyone in its jurisdiction. Regarding externalities created in and transcending its jurisdiction, it then has an interest in contracting with other governments in order to create the incentives that maximise net external value.

## 9.4 CORRUPTION AND PROTECTIONISM

Corruption is the exploitation of a principal-agent problem by a government agent at the government's expense. Agents, such as elected officials or civil servants, may for example give favours to friends with government money or hire their own companies as government contractors at excessive fees. A proprietary government is more likely than a representative one to suppress those forms of corruption, because it is more capable at doing so and does not have any reason for rational ignorance or rational irrationality. If shares become too dispersed and the resulting shareholder passivity leads to an increase in corruption, activist investors gain an interest in buying up large numbers of shares in the proprietary government and combating corruption to increase profits. A proprietary government therefore does not suffer much from such cases of corruption. It is as likely to suffer from corruption as any other private corporation is.

### ANTICOMPETITIVE CORRUPTION

Chapter 7 described ways in which an entrepreneur can shift cooperations to be undertaken from actions preferred by other participants to actions preferred by himself. It is not uncommon for government agents to deliberately facilitate such actions. For example, by erecting trade barriers, imposing cumbersome regulations and granting licenses at their own discretion, they can give some people an advantage over others. Naturally, this comes at the expense of the people entrepreneurs give cooperative opportunities to and often also at the expense of their competitors. It also commonly results in deadweight losses.

Government agents involved in these schemes typically benefit by being bribed by the people they give favours to, which takes various forms. They may, for example, receive donations for their election campaigns or covertly accept private gifts. Governments do not suffer any costs from this form of corruption directly, because it does not lead to higher costs of governance. Indirectly, however, they still do.

As a result of this form of corruption, opportunity recipients are prevented from engaging in cooperations that they prefer and competitors are usually disadvantaged. Whether a government agent acts anticompetitively on behalf of people or merely facilitates anticompetitive action or commitment strategies, the consequences for opportunity recipients are the same. Opportunity recipients are prevented from obtaining outcomes that they would prefer. Thereby, deadweight losses are often created.

Importantly, an entrepreneur only engages in corrupt schemes because he expects the people he intends cooperate with not to prefer them otherwise. That is, the deviation in resulting cooperations is in principle not a Pareto improvement. If it were, the entrepreneur could simply contract with the opportunity recipients to bring about the deviation he prefers.

Thus, corruption that benefits some entrepreneurs comes at the expense of others and can create deadweight losses. Under some degree of proprietary democracy, a government can therefore never gain from it because the resulting deadweight losses come at the expense of its tax base.[129] Its interest is therefore to combat corruption insofar the marginal deadweight loss thereby eliminated exceeds the marginal costs of doing so. The costs of corruption to its subjects would equal or exceed the benefits to entrepreneurs and government agents.

[129] As was explained in Section 7.1, the surplus value of a means accrues to what one is willing to forego for other means complementary to it for the attainment of the same ends. As a result, when a mutually preferred cooperation is precluded, the resulting deadweight loss commensurately decreases the tax base of the government in whose jurisdiction the cooperation would have taken place.

The above applies to cases where the prevented cooperations would have taken place in the jurisdiction of the corrupt government. That is, the people affected are subjects of the government whose agents participate in the scheme. However, they may also be subject to other governments. Domestic entrepreneurs can for instance monopolise, with or without the help of a government, the global trade in a certain commodity. Historical examples of such monopolies exist and some were government-supported, such as those of the trading companies that were given legal monopolies to trade in certain areas. Two particularly successful examples are the United East India Company, commonly known as the Dutch East India Company, and the English East India Company. The former held a government-granted monopoly on the trade of several spices and on trade with Japan, which it maintained for over a century. By monopolising the spice trade, it could keep the prices of many spices high in Europe and thereby make enormous profits.[130] The latter was also given an unfair advantage by its government, which allowed it to monopolise trade with India, making it the chief provider of saltpetre in Europe. Both were authorised by their governments to defend their monopoly by force at their own discretion.

This could lead one to believe that proprietary democracy does not motivate against such favours to producers. That is, favours that give entrepreneurs an unfair advantage abroad, yielding them extra benefits that exceed the harm they do to domestic consumers. However, this is only seemingly so. Any profits made abroad from corruption, as well as any resulting deadweight losses, inevitably come at the expense of the tax bases of foreign governments. Foreign governments therefore have an interest in contracting with the government that gives the entrepreneur his advantage. They can compensate the advantaged enterprise and its supporting government for ceasing their anticompetitive actions. All parties stand to benefit from eliminating the deadweight losses through contract if the deadweight losses thereby eliminated exceed the cost of contracting.

130 van Boven (2006), p. 14

## PROTECTIONISM

Protectionism refers to government policies that restrict international trade to help domestic industries. They are intended to have anticompetitive effects on entrepreneurs from foreign jurisdictions. Thereby, they reduce the number of entrepreneurs with competing offerings within the jurisdiction, which facilitates collusion between them. Protectionist policies are usually advocated and justified with the argument that they support domestic jobs and enterprises. They do, but only by keeping foreign competitors from providing better offerings to domestic opportunity recipients. Domestic producers therefore only gain by making domestic opportunity recipients suffer a cost equal to or exceeding their gain.

Protectionist policies do not affect foreign opportunity recipients because these policies do not exclude them from any opportunities. Only domestic opportunity recipients and foreign producers are harmed.[131]

Protectionist policies harm both domestic opportunity recipients and foreign producers and benefit only certain domestic producers. Such policies therefore do not originate from a genuine commitment to improving welfare. Instead, these distortive policies are caused by corruption and the power of interest groups. A proprietary government has no interest in catering to special interests, but only in maximising its tax base. Under some degree of proprietary democracy, this requires it to minimise net deadweight losses. Some government policies may unintendedly give domestic producers an advantage, such as policies to protect consumers. These policies harm foreign competitors who offer products that are less safe for use. However, they benefit foreign competitors if their products are safer. They are therefore not driven by protectionist aims.

What holds for other forms of anticompetitive corruption and government actions that create deadweight losses therefore also

[131] Producers here refers to entrepreneurs, labourers, capital owners and landowners, who together provide all the factors of production. Anticompetitive action is undertaken by entrepreneurs, but everyone who takes part in their preparations can benefit from it.

holds for protectionism. No government can profit from it, because the resulting deadweight losses commensurately decrease its tax base. Under any positive degree of proprietary democracy, a profit-maximising proprietary government will therefore refrain from protectionist policy making.

## PROTECTIONISM AND ANARCHIC GOVERNMENTAL INTERACTION

In the real world, in which governments can always harm each other to some extent, proprietary democracy is inevitably limited. The world at large exists in a state of anarchy, which can encourage governments to make protectionist policies. For example, it can give governments an interest in rerouting strategic supply chains. Procuring military equipment and essential goods domestically may be more expensive, but allowing the supply chains of these goods to pass through the jurisdictions of geopolitical opponents may make the government vulnerable to sabotage. And governments can weaken geopolitical opponents by imposing embargos and economic sanctions and preventing certain exchanges of knowledge. As a result, global trade is unlikely to be completely free in an anarchic world, even if the world's states would all be proprietary.

Free trade has become more prevalent over the decades, resulting in a more globalised world and higher economic output. However, protectionism has still been present and has in some intergovernmental relationships reared its head once again. In recent years, the emergence of new geopolitical contenders has created an interest in 'nearshoring', i.e. the rerouting of key supply chains to the jurisdictions of less hostile governments.

Under proprietary democracy, such economically inefficient policies would never be implemented. There would naturally be free trade, with the only exceptions being those that governments perceive to add net value for their subjects.

In summary, a proprietary government never has an interest in having protectionist policies to privilege some producers over others. Policies to protect consumers may have protectionist side-effects, but these will not be aimed for. Such policies are intended to benefit subjects, not harm them. However, a proprietary government can have an interest in having protectionist policies to defend or aggress against other governments, even though this harms its tax base. This attests to the importance of preventing intergovernmental aggression to increase proprietary democracy, which was explained in Section 8.5.

## 9.5 RESTRICTIONS TO THE CHOICE SET

Under consumer sovereignty, entrepreneurs can only obtain better terms, and thus maximise their profits, by giving better terms to those they cooperate with. If consumer sovereignty is limited, some of their gainful actions lead to deadweight losses, which commensurately come at the expense of the tax bases of governments. It is therefore in the interest of a proprietary government to govern in a way that maximises consumer sovereignty, insofar the marginal value thereby conferred to its subjects exceeds the marginal cost of doing so.

However, this does not mean that it is not in its interest to restrict the choice set. People may find a certain jurisdiction more attractive to be in if they can thereby trust that their actions do not have bad consequences for them. For example, a government that regulates what materials goods may contain, based on a good understanding of the health risks posed by certain materials, may thereby make its jurisdiction more attractive to be in. Similarly, a government that strictly regulates addictive substances and strictly enforces its restrictions on such substances is likely to thereby make its jurisdiction more attractive for raising children. Parents who wish to raise their children without access to acquire unhealthy and addictive substances may be willing to pay more to live under a restrictive government than a liberal one. People often limit their freedom of choice intentionally. For example, someone may do so by going to a rehabilitation clinic. Government restrictions may likewise be very valuable. Limiting consumer freedom, if done well, is a valuable government service. Under any positive degree of proprietary democracy, it is in the interest of a proprietary government to restrict what entrepreneurs are allowed to offer such that the resulting value, minus the costs thereby created, is maximised.

One could contend that subjects can inform themselves of the important features of products and that non-governmental solutions exist to perform this function. For example, some people have specialised in making product reviews and organisations exist that inspect products to see whether the claims of producers stand the test of scrutiny.

What was explained in Section 9.2 about non-governmental administrative entrepreneurship also applies to such solutions. Except for the freedom to choose one's jurisdiction, proprietary governments are under some degree of proprietary democracy impelled to constrain consumer freedom only insofar their subjects prefer them to. If non-governmental solutions are better than governmental solutions, it is more profitable for a government not to crowd them out or to provide any substitutes. Besides, non-governmental solutions cannot replace government-imposed restrictions completely. Someone who would rather live or raise his children in a jurisdiction where addictive substances are out of reach, for example, cannot rely on non-governmental solutions.

One could also contend that restrictions on consumer freedom limit consumer sovereignty. But consumers must also be free to restrict themselves. For example, when a passenger boards a ship, he voluntarily submits to the captain's authority and the restrictions this puts on his freedoms. This is not seen as a violation of his freedom because he consents to it by boarding the ship, and it is necessary for making the voyage go orderly. Correspondingly, if a government-subject relationship is consensual and congruous, limitations to consumer freedom do not violate consumer sovereignty. The consumer voluntarily limits his own freedom to satisfy his own preferences.

## 9.6 MONETARY POLICY

Currencies are subject to very strong network effects – The more people use a particular means of exchange, the more useful it becomes as such. Despite this, the state can in principle still decide what currency is used in its jurisdiction, except for rare cases such as transactions between criminals or under hyperinflation. Governments have thus been able to establish natural monopolies for the currencies issued by their central banks.

The elected administrations of representative governments and their central banks, which are not always independent, have strong political incentives to channel new money to voter bases, and to artificially create credit booms to make people feel richer, suppress unemployment and stave off recessions. They have this interest despite the resulting harm to economic output and stability over the long term. Representative systems only encourage their incumbent rulers to seek rents and to try to win the next elections, not to maximise long-term prosperity.[132]

Proprietary governance can be a solution to this problem. A proprietary government has no reason to manipulate the money supply because its real profits depend on real economic output. Its directors are unlikely to discount future prosperity as much as elected officials do, because their incentives are likely to be aligned well with shareholder interests. A proprietary government and its directors maximise their incomes by maximising the present value of the tax base, which depends on the present value of the economic prosperity of its subjects.

[132] This feature of the representative system was also observed by Friedrich von Hayek. See von Hayek, F.A. 1990. Denationalisation of Money: The Argument Refined. 3rd ed. London: Institute of Economic Affairs.

In his words: 'Once governments are given the power to benefit particular groups or sections of the population, the mechanism of majority government forces them to use it to gain the support of a sufficient number of them to command a majority. The constant temptation to meet local or sectional dissatisfaction by manipulating the quantity of money so that more can be spent on services for those clamouring for assistance will often be irresistible.' (p. 103)

And, under the title 'Good national money impossible under democratic government dependent on special interests', Hayek explained: 'I do not think it is an exaggeration to say that it is wholly impossible for a central bank subject to political control, or even exposed to serious political pressure, to regulate the quantity of money in a way conducive to a smoothly functioning market order. A good money, like good law, must operate without regard to the effects that decisions of the issuer will have on known groups or individuals. A benevolent dictator might conceivably disregard these effects; no democratic government dependent on a number of special interests can possibly do so.' (pp. 117-118)

As a solution to manipulations of the money supply, some people look optimistically toward cryptocurrencies. Unlike traditional currencies, the quantity of a cryptocurrency cannot be manipulated by anyone, making it immune to government interference. But cryptocurrencies have their weaknesses, in particular that a trade-off must be made between their safety and their efficiency. And eventually, governments can suppress the use of cryptocurrencies by force. A representative government's administration would strongly oppose a cryptocurrency that seriously threatens its access to cheap credit or its power over the money supply, and has strong means to suppress its use.

People who seek to end the credit inflations created by central banks will therefore not find their solution in cryptocurrencies, but should consider supporting the privatisation of jurisdictions instead.

## 9.7 A COMPARISON WITH REPRESENTATIVE DEMOCRACY

When there are exceptions to proprietary democracy, i.e. when a government can gain from acting in ways that come at the expense of its subjects, it can also still gain from acting in ways that create value for them. It only has no shared interests with its subjects when the terms on which it can govern people are completely independent of their preferences or when it can fully dictate their preferences. When proprietary democracy is limited, a government will therefore still have an interest in acting in the ways explained in this chapter. Nonetheless, it is important to minimise exceptions to proprietary democracy, such that a government does not have an interest in acting at the expense of its subjects. Under some degree of proprietary democracy, and it is difficult to imagine a way in which there could be none at all, proprietary governance thus delivers the benefits explained in this chapter. The only exceptions being those where the governmental courses of action that deliver these benefits conflict with the actions that form exceptions to proprietary democracy.

## PROPRIETARY DEMOCRACY VERSUS REPRESENTATIVE DEMOCRACY

The benefits addressed in this chapter are all but absent under representative democracy. By its institutional nature, representative democracy inevitably leads to ideologically motivated policies, ineffective and inefficient governance, corruption and protectionism, inefficient taxation and bureaucracy, and many more problems that are intrinsic to the representative system.

If voters in representative systems were as competent and committed in selecting the right representatives as shareholders typically are in selecting their directors, these problems would not occur. But due to the institutional nature of the representative system, they are not. If voting rights were alienable, things would be different. These rights would naturally end up in the hands of the most competent, committed and appropriately educated for making the jurisdiction as profitable as possible. As a result, corrupt and inefficient politicians and civil servants would be removed from their positions, and polarising and fearmongering political campaigns would be fruitless. These are just some of the benefits.

The directors of companies are not elected for their ethnicity, religion or ideological creed, but for their competence and commitment. Through sophisticated incentive packages, their interests are aligned as well as possible with those of their shareholders. Politicians, on the other hand, are selected according to other criteria, including their race, their religion and the favours they promise to their voters and donors. When they are elected, their interest is to only look ahead to the next election and to maximise the rents they reap from their positions, not to maximise the value of the shares and stock options they would typically have as directors. As a result, representative government administrations are some of the worst performing organisations. They are notoriously inefficient and many have failed at creating even the most basic institutional preconditions for economic development. The representative state has a system of bad incentives that attracts demagogues and parasites. The corporation, on the other hand, has a system of incentives optimised for profit.

Insofar the maximisation of profit is done through courses of action that form exceptions to proprietary democracy and thereby comes at the expense of subjects, representative democracy may be a superior political system for subjects, as well as non-subjects affected by the actions of the government and its agents. But this does not make the representative system superior in general. Proprietary democracy has benefits that representative democracy does not. The next chapter explains how both systems can complement each other in a 'hybrid system' to provide the best of both worlds. Since the systems can co-exist in the hybrid system and therein deliver many of their benefits, proprietary governments would ideally play a role in every jurisdiction.

CHAPTER 10.

# INSTITUTIONAL ARRANGEMENTS

To ensure that the conditions for proprietary democracy are satisfied as much as possible, proprietary governments and their agents must be restricted in their conduct. Government shareholders and their agents must not act in ways that form exceptions to proprietary democracy. However, they do not necessarily have an interest in restricting themselves from doing so.

When establishing a proprietary jurisdiction, it is therefore important to subject the proprietary government to an incentive system. This chapter describes two such systems.

One is the self-limiting system, which grants and denies certain rights to a government and its agents to discourage them from acting in ways that form exceptions to proprietary democracy. Constitutional laws, for example, can forbid legislators from introducing laws that take away the freedom to leave or freedom of expression of subjects.

This system requires the rule of law. Other institutional provisions in the self-limiting system, such as children's rights, freedom of expression and the freedom to leave, are ineffective without the rule of law. The rule of law requires an independent judiciary and a functionally independent apparatus of enforcement. Shareholders and their direct agents, i.e. the legislative branch, must not be able to appoint judges and enforcement officials and must be punishable for undermining their independence or undermining the necessary restrictions.

The term 'self-limiting' thus refers to a combination of institutional arrangements that are in large part already common in current political systems. These arrangements include more than the rule of law and the rule of law is crucial for other arrangements to be effective. The arrangements are brought under one term here only for convenience.

Another is the hybrid system, in which a proprietary jurisdiction overlaps with one or more jurisdictions of other kinds. For example, a proprietary government may have overlapping jurisdictions with a representative democratic government that has the right to superior force over the proprietary government's agents. The proprietary government is then a lower-level government with respect to the representative government. If a proprietary government or its agents violate rights, the representative government's agents can then intervene. The representative government then has the usual problems of public choice, but these problems can be limited by transferring most of the rights of government to the proprietary government. The problems of public choice then do not affect the policy domains governed by the proprietary government. Thereby, an optimal combination of the proprietary system and the representative system can be created.

## 10.1 THE NECESSITY OF INSTITUTIONAL ARRANGEMENTS

### THE ABSENCE OF A FAIR ARBITER

As explained in Section 8.5, governments are often in a state of anarchy. Because some government must have military supremacy over a jurisdiction, the interaction between governments is often anarchic. Nobody but states themselves can enforce their rights and keep each other at peace. For this reason, politics is often compared to organised crime. Like governments, criminal organisations cannot rely on a group of people with military superiority to enforce their rights. Criminal organisations also interact in anarchy. A drug lord cannot sue another in the state's courts for damage inflicted to his property or to enforce a deal the other has reneged on. Consequently, they create local monopolies and alliances by force and punish unreliable partners with brutal violence. In many parts of the world, governments interact similarly. At the international level, it is mostly a game without rules, despite attempts to establish an international legal order.

This also applies to the government-subject relationship. In principle, a government can violate the rights of its subjects with impunity. Whereas the baker and the supermarket cannot force their customers into nonconsensual cooperation, the government can. Because enforcement is provided by those who have the superior capacity to direct the use of force, that which enables effective enforcement provision also enables them to force their subjects into subordination without consent. Stronger states are better at securing life and property, but can thereby also act more easily in ways that conflict with proprietary democracy.

In this respect, governance stands out from almost all other kinds of enterprise. If, above the level of governments, there would exist a benevolent entity with supreme power over the world's governments, none of this would be a problem. The omnipotent and fair arbiter in the 'governance market' would ensure that government-subject relationships are consensual and that governments interact peacefully and congruously. Unfortunately, no such arbiter exists. The only arbiters, insofar there are any, are states themselves. In the anarchic international system, governments can keep their subjects in captivity without significant repercussions. It is simply in the nature of the game.

However, there have been attempts to mitigate the problems of anarchy. One strategy has been to transform states into representative democracies. According to democratic peace theory, these are less likely to aggress each other, resulting in a more peaceful world.[133] As Woodrow Wilson once stated, to justify the United States' active participation in the first world war:

> … we shall fight for the things which we have always carried nearest our hearts—for democracy, for the right of those who submit to authority to have a voice in their own governments, for the rights and liberties of small nations, for a universal dominion of right by such a concert of free peoples as shall bring peace and safety to all nations. …[134]

The peaceful and congruous interaction between states that is necessary for proprietary democracy is thus naturally absent. Perhaps representative democracy would lead to more peace, but democratic peace theory is contested. Representative democracy could also make it easier for radicals to come to power, which could make representative democracy more likely to lead to war instead of less likely.

[133] Democratic Peace Theory, Wikipedia.org. Source included in the reference section.

[134] As he stated in his address to Congress on April 2, 1917, in which he argued for a declaration of war on Germany.

## PROPRIETARY DEMOCRACY

To maximise proprietary democracy is to minimise the ability of governments and their agents to gainfully engage in courses of action that come at the expense of their subjects. To this end, institutional arrangements are necessary that keep governments and their agents from undertaking these courses of action. The courses of action to be discouraged include:

- Violative actions and threats
- Any action through which a government can harm or threaten to harm another government without the right to do so.
- Limiting, without the right to do so, the freedom of subjects to end their subordination by leaving the jurisdiction.
- Implementing laws or policies before a reasonable period of time has passed after their announcement. All subjects must be able to leave in time before the implementation of a new law or policy.
- Restricting freedom of speech or freedom of information more than is necessary for effective governance. Permissible restrictions include restrictions on libel, slander and sedition and include state secrecy for state employees and contractors.
- Colluding with other governments, or merging with or acquiring other governments, in situations in which its anticompetitive effects make this on net harmful to subjects.
- Appointing the heads or staff of religious institutions. Religious institutions may, however, still be restricted in their freedom to spread religious ideas.

Another necessary measure is that shareholders temporarily or permanently lose their voting rights when another government restricts their freedom to use these rights or appropriates their shares completely.

Some of these restrictions are difficult to implement. For example, how does one know when a foreign government poses a sufficient threat to justify military action against it? How much time must pass before a new law goes into effect after it has been announced? When do the harmful anticompetitive effects of a merger or acquisition exceed its economies?

Minimising the exceptions to proprietary democracy may be difficult in practice. More research is certainly needed on this subject. This book is the first attempt to address the idea of consumer sovereignty over governments and to explore the restrictions to be put on proprietary governments and their agents. Not all necessary restrictions may be known and restrictions may be difficult to put in place. However, measures for proprietary democracy can and must be taken if proprietary jurisdictions will be instituted. This chapter serves to describe two types of 'incentive systems' that can be used to this end. Without such an incentive system, proprietary democracy is doomed to fail.

## INCENTIVE SYSTEMS

Remember from Chapter 4 that assignments of rights, when effective enforcement is expected, function as incentive systems to induce cooperative courses of action. An effective incentive system to constrain a government and its agents can be created by allocating the proper rights to the right people. Its effectiveness depends on the incentives that are thereby given to the individuals that perform functions as or for governments.

Rights are meaningless without effective incentives to act in accordance with them. A state has an interest in having the rights of its subjects enforced because this enables valued cooperations to take place in its jurisdiction and thereby makes its jurisdiction more attractive to be in. For providing enforcement, a government can obtain some terms from the people whose rights are enforced. Without enforcement, advanced economic prosperity would not be possible and its tax base would as a result be smaller.

However, the incentives that a government creates for its subjects do not necessarily exist for itself. A government does not necessarily have an interest in acting congruously and there is often nobody who can force it to do so. There is often no fair arbiter that oversees the government. It is possible, however, to submit a government and its agents to an effective incentive system that keeps them from acting at the expense of its subjects. This chapter explains two such systems, of which at least one must be instituted to ensure that the conditions required for proprietary democracy are and remain satisfied.

## 10.2 THE SELF-LIMITING SYSTEM

Effective incentive systems can be installed by governments themselves. For a time, many hereditary monarchs bound themselves to constitutions and the separation of powers. They thereby effectively instituted self-limiting systems. The term 'self-limiting system' refers to government systems wherein the rule of law has been established and authority is constrained through an adequate allocation of rights. By the resulting incentives, these constraints preserve the rule of law and the rights of government and discourage governments and their agents from using their powers in certain ways.

A proprietary government needs an effective incentive system that establishes the rule of law, in order to ensure that its shareholder rights are upheld by its directors and to give investors the confidence to lend it money and invest in its jurisdiction. A proprietary government must also be vigilant that the rule of law does not erode over time, which can occur if its directors can change its constitution. Once that has happened, the government cannot be sure that its shareholder rights will be upheld. History is replete with cases in which a ruler sent someone to rule over a territory on his behalf, after which the agent did not uphold the agreement and broke away with his fiefdom. The breakaway states could do so because of their control over the local military. As shown by Stephen R. Brown in his book *Merchant Kings*[135], this was also not uncommon for historical proprietary governments. The local agents of the trading companies' directors could at times ignore orders with impunity. Because of the agent's military authority, the relationship between a government and its agents is subject to a principal-agent problem that does not exist in other business relationships. In other shareholder-agent relationships, shareholders can resort to a government to enforce their rights. But in this context, there is often no government that can make the agent uphold the shareholders' rights, at least not without incurring a great cost. Therefore, incentive systems must be put in place that constrain the agent in his command over the state's apparatus of force. This is in the interest of the proprietary government itself.

[135] Brown (2009)

However, it is not in a government's self-interest to allow any measures that increase proprietary democracy, or to keep the rule of law in place in all respects. It is not in its interest to restrict itself and its agents from acting anticompetitively, violating subjects' rights to leave and so on. Such violations of proprietary democracy are especially attractive if competition with other governments is so intense that profits are otherwise much lower.

Some believe that the rule of law is meaningless because the state both writes its laws, interprets them and enforces its interpretation. However, it is not 'the state' that has discretion over legislation, adjudication and enforcement. Each of these matters are at the discretion of different individuals, each with their own preferences and incentives. By assigning certain rights to each individual, an incentive system can be created to discourage them from abusing their power. If this were impossible, no democratic system would ever have lasted. Besides, while these incentive systems can 'erode' over time, it may be possible to design incentive systems to counteract such erosion.

A potential weakness of the self-limiting system is the ability of proprietary governments and their agents to undermine the rule of law once they perceive it to be in their interests. For instance, once a government has gained enough military power to gainfully violate the rights of other governments, it may attempt to undermine the rule of law that was established to prevent such violations. This is not difficult if the rule of law is reversible, such as when it is only included in an amendable constitution. Under certain circumstances, such as when competition between proprietary governments is so intense that profits are significantly reduced, this could be an attractive way to increase profits. To counteract this problem, it may be possible to make the rule of law irreversible, or perhaps conditional on approval by referendum, and to allow victims of a government's violative actions to sue it in foreign courts and lay claim to its foreign assets. It is also important that a government and its agents are punished if they break the law.

The self-limiting system is not a new invention. Every functional representative system is self-limiting. Representative systems contain institutional arrangements to establish a rule of law and to preserve these systems. Such institutional arrangements can also be made to maximise proprietary democracy. For proprietary democracy, it is important to create a separation of powers – A functionally independent judiciary and a functionally independent apparatus of enforcement. The government and its agents must be prevented from appointing judges and enforcement officials, and must be punishable for undermining this functional independence. Collusion between members of the different branches of government to violate the law must also be punishable. To prevent such collusion, it may also help to elect new directors in a predetermined election cycle. Besides, as in any other well-designed political system, new laws, policies and treaties must pass an independent supreme court to determine whether they conflict with the law.

A self-limiting proprietary government is therefore in some ways similar to a representative system. In both, the government and its agents are restricted such that they do not abuse their power. The difference between the self-limiting proprietary system and the self-limiting representative system lies in the alienability of their shares or voting rights. In the self-limiting proprietary system, these rights are alienable and thereby can end up in the hands of to those who can and will use them best.

## 10.3 THE HYBRID SYSTEM

Another way to constrain a proprietary government is to install what is in this book named the *hybrid system*. A hybrid system consists of governments of different types, in this case proprietary and non-proprietary, with overlapping jurisdictions. In particular, it can take the form of a representative democratic government and one or more proprietary governments, with the former having military supremacy over the latter. The proprietary government then has a *relative* right to superior force[136] over its subjects, while its subjects as an electorate

[136] 'Relative right to superior force' refers to a right to superior force held over subjects by a 'lower-level' government, while a 'higher-level' government holds a right to superior force over the agents of the lower-level government. The lower-level government can then provide enforcement, while the higher-level can enforce rights on the lower-level government, as well as their subjects, under certain conditions. In this way, lower-level governments can be made to prevented from violating rights and from aggressing each other.

form a representative government that owns a right to superior force over the proprietary government's agents. As in any other polycentric political system, in the hybrid system the higher-level government has policy discretion in some policy domains while the lower-level governments has policy discretion in other policy domains. In its most likely form, in which the higher-level government is representative, the higher-level government can for example have policy discretion in the field of criminal law, human rights and defence, while the lower-level proprietary governments have policy discretion over the rest. Compared to a fully proprietary system, this combination offers the unique benefits of representative democracy. For example, as some claim, representative democracy discourages violent intergovernmental conflicts.[137] The hybrid system allows the representative system to deliver its unique benefits, including its reluctance to use force against another government or to violate the freedom to leave, and to impose restrictions on the lower-level proprietary governments. These restrictions can include, crucially, those that increase proprietary democracy. The representative government then provides the benefits of representative governance in its policy domains while the proprietary governments provide the benefits of proprietary democracy in their own policy domains. Public choice problems, i.e. the problems that are intrinsic to the representative system, such as corruption and bureaucracy, are also likely to arise. But these are mitigated by transferring extensive rights of government to the lower-level proprietary governments. All policy domains under the control of proprietary governments are insulated from the problems of public choice – the problems of representative democracy. Of course, the hybrid system requires sufficiently well-functioning institutions in the representative government. If these institutions are very dysfunctional, a completely independent proprietary government in a self-limiting system could be better.

A hybrid systems can involve governments at various levels. Many polycentric systems have a national government as well as regional

[137] According to democratic peace theory. See Democratic Peace Theory, Wikipedia.org. Source included in the reference section.

and local governments.[138] The number of governments of a certain level can vary, but so can the number of levels. The more governments and levels of government there are, the higher the cost of contracting between them, but there may be benefits that outweigh these costs. For more on polycentric governance, see Section 9.2.

The representative government in a hybrid system must of course have the institutional arrangements necessary to uphold the rule of law and preserve representative democracy. Otherwise, it will not deliver its benefits and may not even last. Furthermore, to prevent corruption involving or affecting the proprietary governments, the agents of the representative government, which includes ministers and parliamentarians, must be kept from owning shares in proprietary governments and from controlling voting rights in proprietary governments on behalf of their electorate. The agents of the higher-level representative government must be unable to exert control over the proprietary government beyond any lawful restrictions – They may only restrict it insofar the representative government's rights of government allow this.

While the hybrid system has benefits that a self-limiting fully proprietary system does not have, it also has weaknesses that the latter does not have.

First, checks and balances and the limiting power of a constitution tend to erode over time.[139] Thus, the usual problems that arise in representative systems, such as corruption and bureaucracy, could grow over time, as well as encroachment on the rights of the lower-level proprietary governments.

Second, the relationship between a higher-level representative government and lower-level proprietary governments is subject to the hold-up problem and the imputation problem, which were ex-

[138] As well as organisations which only engage in administrative entrepreneurship, i.e. governance but without enforcement.

[139] As can be seen in the United States, constitutions can be liberally interpreted as government-appointed judges see fit. Secondly, constitutions can be changed by incumbent politicians. The players of the game get to change the rules, which cannot be good.

plained in Section 9.2. These problems inevitably result in some distortive incentives. Whereas the agents of a proprietary government naturally have a strong interest in improving the contract with the representative government, the agents of the representative government do not as much. The latter, i.e. elected politicians, are instead interested in electoral victory and extracting rents.

Third, those countries that need proprietary governance the most do so because their states have weak institutions. Through proprietary governance, a country can reduce corruption and stop widespread violations of rights. Establishing a hybrid system could therefore mitigate these problems, but it is also important for proprietary governments to compete peacefully on a 'level playing ground' – The representative government must not favour one proprietary government over another. However, since countries with corrupt states need proprietary governance the most, those that need it the most are the least likely to maximise proprietary democracy in a hybrid system.

Finally, whereas a higher-level representative government can use force to dismantle a proprietary government's apparatus of force if the latter's agents violate rights too often, it can probably only do so at a large cost. This could give the proprietary government the ability to violate rights to an extent with impunity. In a hybrid system, it can therefore be beneficial for proprietary democracy if the proprietary government is also self-limiting..

To keep the proprietary and representative governments in a hybrid system from violating rights, one solution could be to make them hold large amounts of assets in multiple foreign countries. Victims of corruption can then sue the corrupt governments at foreign courts in countries with better institutions and claim financial compensation. If the integrity of one or some of these courts seems to be lacking, legal action can be taken at another court. For instance, if courts in the United States are found to be unreliable, claimants could seek justice at a Swiss or Singaporean court.

Another way to prevent a higher-level representative government from violating the rights of a proprietary government or its subjects is to allow the latter to become subordinated to another representative government, or to become independent, by referendum. This creates a way out of a failing representative system and may keep the representative government and its agents in check. The representative government and its agents do not want to lose territory, so they can be expected to avoid triggering a break-away referendum.

## RESCINDING RIGHTS OF GOVERNMENT

A proprietary government in a hybrid system must own its rights of government, meaning that they cannot be rescinded without its consent. Otherwise, the representative government *de facto* still holds this policy discretion and only lends it to the proprietary government. By rescinding this policy discretion, it can then extend its regulatory scope as it wishes, which undermines the purpose of privatising a jurisdiction. Policy discretion that can be rescinded by the higher-level government under any conditions is no meaningful policy discretion. Alternatively, the representative government could keep the option to acquire policy discretion at a pre-specified price under pre-specified circumstances. This limits the proprietary government's ownership of its policy discretion, but the proprietary government is still the owner. In such cases, the hybrid system can therefore still be considered as such. But the disadvantages of such an arrangement are obvious – The proprietary government can be less confident in using its rights of government and people are less likely to invest in its jurisdiction.

CHAPTER 11.

# LIMITATIONS OF PROPRIETARY DEMOCRACY

## 11.1 PREFERENCES VERSUS WELL-BEING

Even if absolute proprietary democracy were possible, there would still be strong arguments against it. For example, preference satisfaction may not always benefit well-being. Under proprietary democracy, a government can only obtain better terms by giving better terms to its subjects. To better satisfy its own preferences, it must then better satisfy the preferences of others. However, satisfying the preferences of others may not actually make them better off. For example, some people have a strong preference for using hard drugs and some others have a strong preference for self-mutilation. It would be difficult to argue that the satisfying these preferences is good for their well-being. Similarly, some people may prefer to be subordinated to a government that strictly imposes Islamic law. This may restrict them so much that it is difficult for them to be happy, but they may prefer this by expecting it to make them more likely to enter paradise when they die.

Furthermore, even if people do pursue happiness in this life above all else, they may fail to do so. A hedonist may prefer to live in a jurisdiction where addictive substances are freely available, but may eventually be less happy as a result. In the end, people may fare better if their freedoms are restricted in some ways.

Lastly, how are we to define well-being? Should we adopt a hedonistic definition? Or does well-being depend on physical well-being instead of the pleasures we experience? And if well-being comes from pleasure, are all pleasures equal? The proper definition of well-being is still contested.

Proprietary democracy does not necessarily maximise welfare. Proprietary democracy makes governments unable to get better terms without better satisfying the preferences of their (potential) subjects. These preferences can be ill-informed and irrational. They might also not result from the aim to maximise well-being. Even if they do, one's notion of well-being may differ from that of others. If we adopt a hedonistic definition of well-being, people must have hedonistic preferences and be infallible in satisfying their preferences if proprietary democracy is to maximise hedonistic well-being. However, these objections also apply to representative systems. If preference satisfaction does not necessarily lead to well-being, this equally invalidates representative democracy.

## PROPRIETARY TYRANNY

The difference between the maximisation of value and the maximisation of well-being is illustrated by the following scenario. Imagine someone rich enough to acquire the rights of government over a proprietary jurisdiction does so to realise his vision of an ideal society. In his utopia, everyone must follow his dress code and eat his favourite food every day. He changes the official language to his favourite one, Esperanto, and forbids all others. All buildings must be designed in his favourite style, brutalism, and all venues must play thrash metal on their speakers. There is no economic freedom – His 'utopia' has a planned economy. People are poor and miserable. Obviously, not many people would like to live in such a jurisdiction. Most people choose to leave, but he does not care how many people he rules over.

Using his own fortune, he acquires a jurisdiction in which many people already live. As he realises his vision, his policy changes impact their lives dramatically. Their livelihoods and investments are wound up in the jurisdiction and they are thus harmed greatly by his actions. His laws and policies make their lives more difficult and harm their investments. Nonetheless, his acquisition of the jurisdiction and his use of it are 'economically efficient'. He has acquired it legitimately and does not violate anyone's rights by using his policy discretion as he wishes. His policies destroy much value for his subjects, but he is willing to forego the profits he could otherwise obtain – He personally values his policies more than his subjects value other policies.

Value is thus not the same as well-being. Proprietary democracy may maximise value but does not always maximise well-being. A government may be unwilling to forego mistreating people regardless of what its victims offer in return. As long as it does not violate their rights, the government's treatment of its subjects is 'efficient'.

To maximise well-being, the rights of government may therefore have to be limited. Either the rights themselves must effectively be limited, e.g. when a government's rights do not allow it to impose religious rules, or ownership should be kept from some who wish to use it in ways that are bad for well-being, or both.

History is replete with dictatorships and hereditary monarchies that were violent and oppressive rather than cooperative and liberal. Their aim has not always been to make their jurisdictions as attractive as possible to live, work and invest in. This contrasts with the responsive, innovative and customer-focused governance that one would expect from a proprietary government today.

Like many historical cases of extortionate taxation, it seems reasonable to partly ascribe this to the constant violent threat of contending governments from within and outside the jurisdiction. Threats to a ruler's power and life can be expected to raise his time preference. Even though high taxation may cost him subjects and make those who are left less productive, he prefers this over losing his jurisdiction and his life. Under proprietary democracy, such conditions would be absent.

But even proprietary democracy does not guarantee against tyranny. The sometimes tyrannical behaviour of hereditary monarchs can also partly stem from them being satisfied with their wealth, leading them to focus on other, ideological objectives. For instance, a hereditary monarch could prefer to persecute a religious minority he considers heretics, rather than maximising his financial profits by making his jurisdiction as attractive as possible to them. Especially if he believes this to increase his chances of entering heaven, he may use his power in this way. Even under proprietary democracy, tyranny thus cannot be ruled out as a consequence of privatising a jurisdiction.

As Scott Alexander explained in an article critical of Mencius Moldbug's 'neocameralism':

> There's another important aspect here too. Reactionaries – ending up more culpable of a stereotype about economists than economists themselves, who are usually pretty good at avoiding it – talk as if a self-interested

> monarch would be a rational money-maximizer. But a monarch may have desires much more complicated than cash. They might, like Henry, want to marry a particular woman. They might have religious preferences. They might have moral preferences. They might be sadists. They might really like the color blue. In an ordinary citizen, those preferences are barely even interesting enough for small talk. In a monarch, they might mean everyone's forced to wear blue clothing all the time.
>
> You think that's a joke, but in 1987 the dictator of Burma made all existing bank notes illegitimate so he could print new ones that were multiples of nine. Because, you see, he *liked* that number. As Wikipedia helpfully points out, "The many Burmese whose saved money in the old large denominations lost their life savings." For every perfectly rational economic agent out there, there's another guy who's *really* into nines.[140]

A jurisdiction is privatised by making the rights of government over it alienable. They can then be transferred freely, such that they can be allocated to the people who value them most and can best use them in ways others value most. If a jurisdiction is proprietary, the rights of government over it can thus be bought if the buyer offers conditions attractive enough to the seller. Meanwhile, rights of government can be expected to be very valuable to the power-hungry, the ideologically motivated and the aspiring tyrants. In fact, they can be expected to be willing to pay more for these rights than those who merely intend to use them for financial profit. There is therefore much reason to restrict the very alienability of the rights of government that characterises the proprietary government. One potential restriction could be to limit the portion of shares one individual or family is allowed to own. The well-being of thousands is then less likely to depend on the sanity of one person or a small group of people.

[140] Scott Alexander (2013)

On the other hand, a wider dispersion of shares can make the problems of public choice re-emerge due to the rational ignorance and rational irrationality it may encourage. It may be better to carefully examine the motives of those who seek to acquire rights of government and to prevent the acquisition if these motives are likely to be detrimental to well-being. In the hybrid system, transfers of rights of government can be made to require approval by agents of the representative government, such as a special agency or parliamentary committee. This can put a healthy check on these transfers. However, this can lead to the usual problems of nonprofit and cooperative systems. Those who acquire large numbers of alienable shares tend to be intelligent, pragmatic and financially motivated. They do not typically adhere to radical ideologies such as communism or national socialism. But over time, unowned institutions and cooperatives are often captured or drift away ideologically.

Ideally, rights of government would be alienable, but only to people who would use them for financial gain within reasonable moral bounds.

## 11.2 THE NONCONSENSUALLY SUBORDINATED

As Chapter 8 explains, consent and congruity are essential for proprietary democracy. But consent is not always possible. Not everyone can choose what government to be subject to. This includes young children, for example.[141] Whether or not children are to be

[141] Ludwig von Mises did not see children as acting beings: "The newborn child is not an acting being. It has not yet gone the whole way from conception to the full development of its human qualities. But at the end of this evolution it becomes an acting being." From Chapter 1: Acting Man, The Prerequisites of Human Action, in von Mises (2007 [1949]).

Mises' point is reasonable, although it seems difficult if not impossible to ascertain at what point in its development a child becomes an acting being. The young are given increasing freedoms as they mature,

seen as capable of making choices is irrelevant, because in any case they are unable to make choices to their own benefit. It is therefore justified to make choices on behalf of children, a right and responsibility that naturally falls on their parents.

But imagine, for example, an orphaned child. One that has no further family and whose parents have not made any provisions for the possibility that their child would become orphaned. Without any restrictions, the proprietary government then has unrestricted control over the child, allowing it to do as it pleases. The amount of taxes it can expect the child to pay over his lifetime could be less than his market value. In that case, it would be most profitable for the government to sell the child to the highest bidder, which would probably lead to the child being abused. This would of course be gravely immoral and must therefore be prevented. The exploitation of children is illegal but is unfortunately also profitable, which is why this problem persists.

This problem does not only affect orphaned children. Some children have parents who are unable to raise them. For example, some parents suffer from such severe mental health problems or addictions that they neglect their children or even pose a danger to them. In such cases, the proprietary government can also decide over the child, but must not have free reign in doing so.

Besides children, provisions must be made for people who have never had the ability to voluntarily choose for their subordination, such as those who reach adulthood with a severe mental impairment. People who develop such a condition as adults could have prepared for the risk, so it is not necessary to make any special provisions for them.

The category of people for which special provisions must be made is thus the *nonconsensually subordinated*.[142] The nonconsensually

depending on their own capacities. Their freedoms are typically given to them gradually by their parents according to their level of maturity.

[142] Nonconsensual cooperation is cooperation for which consent has not been given, but against which also no unconsent has been given. Unconsent is the denial of consent and is different from non-consent.

subordinated, including children in particular, must have the right to shelter, nutrition, education, safety and health care, which a government must be obliged to provide. Proprietary democracy does not encourage governments to do so, so provisions for this must be fixed in law. When the government-subject relationship relies on consent and subjects are able to consent to their own benefit, these provisions are unnecessary.

## 11.3 THE WELFARE STATE VERSUS THE PROFIT MOTIVE

If there are diminishing marginal returns to income for well-being, income redistribution could be utilitarian. A poor person would then satisfy more urgent needs with an increment of income than a rich person would with the same increment. Therefore, redistributing money from the rich to the poor could increase total well-being. But a proprietary government has no interest in redistributing income from the rich to the poor. Redistribution does not enlarge its tax base, but harms it.

Moreover, under proprietary democracy each penny functions as one vote, while money is not equally distributed. Whereas the 'one man, one vote' rule holds in a representative democracy, it does not under proprietary democracy. The rich have more to spend and will therefore be more valued customers to proprietary governments. Proprietary democracy could thus lead to worse conditions for the poor and the weak.

Furthermore, because privatising jurisdictions intensifies competition in the domain of governance, it could make governments competitively lower their tax rates to attract subjects. People who pursue their own financial self-interest would then move to where they are taxed least. Such states already exist, such as the Principality of Monaco and the Emirate of Dubai. Privatising jurisdictions would ex-

---

Non-consent is the absence of both consent and unconsent. See '5. Non-consent' in Bell (2011), pp. 26-27.

pand the possibilities of companies and people with large incomes to move to low-tax jurisdictions. This could undermine welfare states. Competitive pressures between governments bring many advantages, but if welfare states must survive such that the weak are taken care of, the net result might not be beneficial.

From a utilitarian perspective, the privatisation of jurisdictions could therefore worsen conditions for many people. But as Section 11.5 will explain, this does not have to be.

## 11.4 OTHER POTENTIAL OBJECTIONS

### UNGOVERNED PEOPLE

In addition to those addressed thus far, other valid objections to proprietary democracy can be expected. One such concern is that a proprietary government would not provide its goods and services to everyone because not everyone can afford them. Governance comes at a cost, and not everyone is productive enough to cover it. Providing governance to them is unprofitable, so a profit-maximising government would leave them in anarchy. Or it could even attempt to get rid of them, in order to make room for others or to prevent them from committing crimes and being a nuisance to tax payers.

However, if some people derive less value from governance than it costs to provide to them, it is efficient to leave them ungoverned.[143] It is profitable to govern them if governance would increase their prosperity by more than its cost. If a proprietary government leaves people in anarchy, the anarchy they are in is therefore probably efficient. The protection of property, for example, matters less for people who do not own much.

They might be better off if they were governed, as people would be better off if they would get what they desire but cannot afford. However, the problem is to be solved by income redistribution. The

[143] For a more elaborate argument for this, applying to both ungoverned people and ungoverned territories, see Leeson (2007).

poor can then choose how to spend the income that is redistributed to them. If they prefer to spend it on governance, governance will be most profitable to provide to them. This problem can thus be solved by a hybrid system with a welfare state.

## BANKRUPTCY AND UNGOVERNED TERRITORIES

Another possible objection is that a proprietary jurisdiction could end up ungoverned if its proprietary government goes bankrupt. The jurisdiction then lacks basic government services such as enforcement. However, a representative government is more likely to go bankrupt because it is typically less efficient. Its jurisdiction is then as anarchic and rife with problems as a failing proprietary jurisdiction would be. Moreover, its representative nature prevents entrepreneurs from acquiring its rights of government if it goes bankrupt. This prevents others from governing its jurisdiction better, thereby keeping the jurisdiction in its poor state.

If a government goes bankrupt, it is either because its territory should not be governed at all or because it governs poorly. In the former case, governance is inefficient to provide in that territory and thereby unprofitable for a proprietary government. Bankruptcy is then a necessary outcome, preventing governance from being provided where it should not. For example, it would be inefficient to provide government goods and services in places that are difficult or impossible to inhabit, such as the Sahara Desert. In the latter case, the proprietary government goes bankrupt because of mismanagement. Another proprietary government can then acquire its shares or merge with it. Alternatively, the proprietary government corporation can be liquidated and its rights of government can be sold to a more competent or committed entrepreneur. The jurisdiction can then be governed better and thus profitably. Alienability in the rights of government can thus solve the problem of government bankruptcy.

Proprietary governments are less likely to fail than representative governments. They are more likely to govern well because proprietary rights of government naturally end up in the hands of those who value them most and are best at their use. Because they are more competent and committed at governance, relatively few failed proprietary states will exist. And if a proprietary government does mismanage its territory, the alienability of its rights of government allows more competent and committed people to acquire them. Because of its proprietary nature, shares in a failed proprietary government are quickly acquired and its organisation improved, or its rights of government are acquired and used better. A proprietary jurisdiction is thus unlikely to remain under a failing government for long. By contrast, if a representative government fails, the inalienability of its rights of government prevents others from acquiring them and governing the jurisdiction better. Its territory is then not officially anarchic because its rights of government are officially still owned by someone, but in reality its capacity to provide basic services like enforcement has collapsed. As a result, criminal organisations come to the fore.

After bankruptcy, but before another entrepreneur acquires the shares in a government or its rights of government, basic services must still be provided. To this end, a proprietary government can buy insurance or create a special fund such that its residents will not be left without essential services if it goes bankrupt. This is in its own financial interest, since its jurisdiction would be worth much less if left without basic services. When enforcement is no longer provided, for example, criminal organisations often take control, prompting people to leave and making it costly to re-establish order. Provisions to prevent this can greatly benefit its liquidation value.

## 11.5 THE HYBRID SYSTEM FOR THE BEST OF BOTH WORLDS

To every problem with proprietary democracy that has been addressed in this chapter, the hybrid system provides a solution. When preference satisfaction is bad for well-being, such as when people are irrational or ill-informed, the relevant policy discretion can be kept by the representative government. Thereby, proprietary governments can for example by prevented from legalising addictive substances.[144] Furthermore, the conditions for proprietary democ-

[144] In theory, a proprietary government would regulate drugs such that nobody can obtain addictive and life-destroying substances, while rela-

racy can never be fully satisfied. Possibilities for anticompetitive action and deception, for example, can never be eliminated completely. It could therefore be wise to subject proprietary governments to higher-level representative governments, such that the latter can intervene in the actions of the former if these actions conflict with proprietary democracy. And whereas a proprietary government has no interest in redistributing income, a representative government and its agents do. While proprietary governance has unique benefits, representative governance thus also has a role to play.

The hybrid system can be adapted for various purposes and conditions. Over one jurisdiction, proprietary governments may have extensive policy discretion, including for example in criminal law and moral matters, while over another jurisdiction this may fall under the authority of the representative government. To obtain the unique benefits of both the proprietary system and the representative system, a representative government could devolve most of the rights of government to proprietary governments while keeping a right to levy taxes, redistribute income, ensure that lower-level rights of government are not transferred to people with bad intentions, control addictive substances, decide over moral matters, take measures in favour of proprietary democracy, protect the rights of the nonconsensually subordinated and so on..

Proprietary democracy is not necessarily always utilitarian. The representative system may deliver utilitarian benefits that proprietary democracy does not. The hybrid system, however, offers a way to optimally use both systems for various objectives. Representative and proprietary governance each have unique costs and benefits. A well-designed hybrid system strikes the right balance between both systems and thereby delivers the benefits of both to optimise governance for its specific context. All political factions, except anarchists and communists, should therefore support of some role for proprietary governance. It is not related to any specific political ide-

---

tively harmless drugs are available and the underage can obtain neither. This would make its jurisdiction more attractive to live in, raise children in and visit, while preventing a loss of taxpayers to addiction and death.

ology. It is not a libertarian or 'right-wing' idea, nor one of any other political ideology. Profit maximisation by a proprietary government and income redistribution by a representative government can, for example, co-exist in a hybrid system. And, in countries where rulers want to ensure that religious norms will be imposed, a hybrid system can be created in which a theocratic body keeps certain rights of government. In any context and for every purpose, a hybrid system can provide the best of both worlds. Proprietary governance therefore has something to offer to every country.

Furthermore, the problems that are not solved by either a hybrid or fully proprietary system are equally inevitable in a fully representative system. For example, representative governance can descend into tyranny as much as proprietary governance can. What makes alienable rights of government attractive for people who should not own them also makes positions of power in representative systems attractive to them. Moreover, a proprietary government is less likely to elect a tyrant than a representative government because it is typically less irrational and better informed. And while people can choose the wrong jurisdiction to move to, this problem is equally present with representative systems, in which people are also fallible as voters.

A hybrid system could also include a hereditary government. A hereditary monarch has little interest in maximising his financial income at the expense of everything else. While typically pursuing financial income to a great extent, he also has a strong interest in seeing his country flourish even in ways that do not maximise his income, and in redistributing money to his people or to charitable causes. He could also ensure that lower-level proprietary governments compete fairly and do not fall into the wrong hands.

In cases where democracy is unsuitable, such as where the electorate would be highly radicalised, a hybrid system could instead consist of only hereditary and proprietary entities. As Chapter 13 explains, such a system would be the logical successor to the feudal system, in which rights of government were typically inalienable. Now that the reasons for their inalienability no longer exist, lower-level rights of government can become alienable while rights of government at the sovereign level remain inalienable to prevent them from falling into the wrong hands.

Lastly, a hybrid system could also consist of all three systems: the proprietary, the democratic and the (hereditary) monarchical. Each government is then given the policy domains it is best suited for.

## 11.6 THE PROPRIETARY SYSTEM VERSUS THE REPRESENTATIVE SYSTEM

As explained in this chapter, proprietary democracy is not perfect. For example, while proprietary democracy leads to more efficient governance in terms of preference satisfaction, this may not actually maximise well-being. In addition, proprietary democracy will not lead to income redistribution, even though it may be utilitarian. However, a hybrid system can optimally deal with any shortcomings of proprietary democracy and the problems then remaining are equally present in representative democracy. For every representative system, there is thus a superior alternative in the form of a hybrid system.

### THE SUPERIORITY OF PROPRIETARY DEMOCRACY

In his book *Free Private Cities: Making Governments Compete For You*, Titus Gebel compares representative democracy to his idea of the 'free private city', his variant of the proprietary jurisdiction. By imagining a representative system that provides automobiles, which is typically done by private corporations, he illustrates how the two types of institutions differ:

> Imagine you live in an automobile democracy. In an automobile democracy, everyone has the right, but also the duty, to buy a car. What this car looks like, how it is motorized, what interior and what color it has, has been decided by the democratically chosen car-government. This also determines the price you have to pay. Both are often unpleasant. Then another government is elected with other preferences that it imposes on car buyers. There is constant hitting and poking about what this single car is like; countless manufacturers and suppliers maintain lobbyists in the capital so that their products are built into the car model of the respective government. Shifting interest groups, which prefer different types of engines, are also trying to influence parliament and government. Countless autopolitical groups claim that they are unable to pay the full price and therefore try to get discounts.

> A few years ago a second type of car was introduced, which is more simply equipped and cheaper. Many intellectuals criticize that this has created a two-tier society. But everyone agrees on one thing: the system may have shortcomings, but there is no better one. Because what would be the alternative? Only an auto-dictator or king of cars, however, who is not democratically elected and determines what type of car there must be for everyone at what price. They had that before, and nobody wants to go back to that system. The idea that people can choose the car they like best from countless different offers and manufacturers, with the equipment they like best, is completely unthinkable for the citizens of automobile democracy. This idea is so bizarre that it is not even discussed in public.
>
> In fact, we live in such a system! One simply replaces the word "automobile" with "state services and activities". Taxpayers must finance subsidies for uneconomical technologies, state television stations and military missions abroad, chairs for gender studies and theology, even if they reject all this. Citizens will continue to be forced to take out pension, health and nursing care insurance, whether they like it or not. You may not purchase light bulbs, powerful vacuum cleaners, plastic bags or cigarettes without warnings. And the list of prohibitions and commandments is getting longer every year. In other words, citizens are not customers but subjects. Why is that so and why don't most people object?[145]

One can create an automobile democracy by setting up a consumer cooperative that manufactures cars. A consumer cooperative is a customer-owned business, in which the owners usually have one voting right each. As Section 11.7 explains, the representative system is in fact a consumer cooperative that provides governance.

145 Gebel (2018)

Why do automobile cooperatives not exist? If representative democracy is the best political system possible, why does it rarely exist for other entrepreneurial endeavours? Why are the world's most innovative and successful firms not run by representatives elected by their respective customer bases? If the consumer cooperative truly functions better than any alternative, it would have prevailed over other types of corporations. But alternatives to the private corporation are rare and seldom efficient. In this thought exercise, Gebel points to some of the myriad problems intrinsic to the representative system. Interest group politics and inefficiencies are only two of many recurrent problems. In the proprietary system, these problems are non-existent.

Most successful companies cater to the preferences of their consumers and are run by experienced entrepreneurs or visionary innovators. Their customers do not decide what is produced or how it is produced. Nor do their customers elect any representatives to play a role. They do not vote by ballot for one phone or car to be produced instead of another. Instead, consumers 'vote with their feet'. By choosing between different offerings, they impel entrepreneurs to cater to their preferences, to produce efficiently, to eliminate corruption as much as possible and to prevent ideology to play any role in entrepreneurial decision making. This stands in stark contrast with governance cooperatives. Cooperatives are rare, which proves that capitalist institutions are generally better at maximising value for consumers than any other democratic system. Proprietary democracy merely extends the highly successful capitalist system, and the conditions for its proper functioning, to the domain of governance. Governance as a service, efficiently provided by for-profit corporations.

As Section 5.1 explains, the differences between proprietary governance and democratic governance eventually stem from inalienability of the rights of government, combined with a wide dispersion of voting rights and variability in the rights to government proceeds. Due to the inalienability and wide dispersion of voting rights, voters are characterised by incompetence, ignorance and irrationality. As a result, representative systems are particularly vulnerable to incompetence, corruption, irrational and ideologically motivated policies, bureaucracy and interest-group politics. Due to the variability in who and what tax revenues are to be spent on, electoral politics is also characterised by clientelism and constant battling over resources.

This contrasts starkly with proprietary governance, especially under proprietary democracy. The relative benefits of proprietary governance are substantial. They include the virtual elimination of corruption and bureaucracy, the drastic increase in efficiency, more professional and non-ideological policy making and the complete elimination of electoral political phenomena, such as clientelism and pork-barrel voting. Under some degree of proprietary democracy, a government can be expected to cater much better to the preferences of subjects than governments currently do. It will tax much more efficiently in order to minimise deadweight losses. It will more efficiently divide rights of government with governments at different levels. It will regulate externalities with the aim to maximise total net value. It will forego protectionist policies and eliminate corruption such that the net value thereby created is maximised. It will restrict the freedom of consumers in ways they prefer. For the satisfaction of the preferences of subjects, no form of democracy is superior to proprietary democracy.

Moreover, in contrast to representative democracy, proprietary democracy can succeed regardless of the culture of its subjects. To function well, representative democracy requires subjects to have a 'democratic culture' that fosters political participation. Voters must inform themselves of political matters, debate and vote, and tolerate opposing viewpoints. Representative democracy is therefore only suitable for certain populations, while proprietary democracy can succeed everywhere.

As explained in this chapter, proprietary democracy is neither perfect nor perfectly feasible. As was also explained, however, the inadequacies of proprietary democracy can be optimally dealt with in a hybrid system and for every representative system there is a superior alternative in the form of a hybrid system. Besides, measures can be taken to maximise proprietary democracy, such that few exceptions to it exist.

## PROPRIETARY DEMOCRACY FOR PROGRESSIVE IDEALS

Since proprietary democracy requires privatising the rights of government, it will be vehemently attacked by ideological opponents. In particular people on the left side of the political spectrum, who often oppose free and private enterprise, can be expected to be hostile to it. Moreover, many outspoken progressives, including many academics, directly owe their livelihoods to state subsidies. Without the representative system, many of them will only be able to sustain themselves by providing low-skilled labour.[146]

However, it must be understood that proprietary governance has something to offer to every jurisdiction, in every context. All the benefits of the representative system, such as the welfare state and the asserted democratic peace, can be kept intact. In fact, for some of the left-wing ideals, the proprietary government is simply superior. Proprietary governments can be expected to govern more efficiently, which leaves more wealth to give to the poor and will lead to more efficient production, higher capital accumulation and thereby a lower cost of living for everyone. Besides, the directors of a proprietary government are more likely to comply with climate treaties than the representatives and ministers of a representative government. Representative government officials can benefit from breaching treaties, as the penalties for doing so typically only follow after their term. For shareholders in a proprietary government and their directors, all future cash flows are important.

And whereas politicians in representative systems have no interest in fostering social cohesion in the long or short term, proprietary governments do. A proprietary government benefits from racial and religious tolerance and will actively foster it. To make its jurisdiction as attractive as possible to as many people as possible, it must make its subjects accept all kinds of newcomers and vice versa. This contrasts starkly with the incentives of politicians in multicultural societies with representative systems, who gain from stirring up racial and religious antagonism, portraying newcomers and minorities

146 Those whose livelihoods depend on the representative system, including chiefly bureaucrats and politicians in particular, as well as other beneficiaries of this system, will be very critical of proprietary democracy. Not only have they self-selected into their positions partly because they believed in the merits of this system, but their incomes also depend on it. I am not the first to recognise the principle that incumbents tend to be hostile to institutional change, see for example Weber (1947), pp. 318-319.

as threats and discriminating against them in favour of their own ethnic and religious voter bases. From Lebanon to Nigeria, the world is replete with examples of such tribalist politics.

Multicultural societies therefore have much to gain from proprietary governance. In proprietary jurisdictions, multicultural populations can flourish better than anywhere else. This is evident in the Arab world, for example. Ruled by hereditary monarchs, whose interests are similar to those of proprietary governments, the Arab world was more ethnically harmonious than ever since. Under hereditary monarchy, Jewish, Christian and Muslim merchants befriended and traded with each other throughout the region. After representative democracy was installed, it did not take long before Lebanon descended into civil war, Coptic Christians were driven out of Egypt and every Jewish community in the Arab world was decimated. In the Arab world, it is not coincidentally the hereditary monarchies that are now most inviting to immigrants, as evidenced by United Arab Emirates and Saudi Arabia.

Whereas hereditary monarchies are not proprietary governments, they do equally have a long-term orientation and tend to prioritise the maximisation of financial profit more than representative governments do. Under proprietary governance and profit-maximising hereditary monarchy, ethnic minorities are consequently treated better than in many representative democracies. In fact, one could even go as far as to say that an event like the shoah would never have occurred under a profit-maximising proprietary government. No profit-maximising proprietary government would massacre its most civilised, economically productive and culturally advanced ethnic group.

On the contrary, it would attempt to inspire other groups to follow the successful minority's example. It would mould the culture and beliefs of its subjects to make them more productive and create a society that others want to join. A profit-maximising proprietary government would actively combat subversive beliefs, bad manners and detrimental cultural habits. Like the hereditary monarchs and aristocrats of the past, it would civilise its subjects such that they can perform well and flourish. In this respect, whatever makes its subjects more prosperous increases its profits. Because after all, this is what maximises a proprietary government's tax base.

Not only does a proprietary government have an interest in fostering harmony between different ethnic and religious groups, in general it will not disregard the preferences of any tax-paying minority. To a proprietary government, minorities matter as much as majorities do because they pay taxes like anybody else. This difference between profit-oriented entrepreneurs and politicians in representative systems has been explained by Ludwig von Mises:

> In the political democracy, only the votes cast for the majority candidate or the majority plan are effective in shaping the course of affairs. The votes polled by the minority do not directly influence policies. But on the market no vote is cast in vain. Every penny spent has the power to work upon the production processes. The publishers cater not only to the majority by publishing detective stories, but also to the minority reading lyrical poetry and philosophical tracts. The bakeries bake bread not only for healthy people, but also for the sick on special diets. The decision of a consumer is carried into effect with the full momentum he gives it through his readiness to spend a definite amount of money.[147]

## CONCLUSION

Proprietary democracy has its inadequacies, but these can be avoided by incorporating proprietary governments into hybrid systems. The inadequacies then remaining are equally present in any representative system. Furthermore, proprietary governance and proprietary democracy bring unique benefits. For every context, a hybrid system is therefore possible that is superior to a fully representative system. Proprietary governance can thus make every society more prosperous. The poorest societies in particular, because their poverty is especially due to bad governance.

Besides, privatising jurisdictions can serve progressive ends. A proprietary government has an interest in fostering harmony between

[147] The Sovereignty of the Consumers, in Chapter 15: The Market, in von Mises (2007 [1949]), p. 271

ethnic and religious groups and welcoming immigrants. It also has a stronger interest in complying with treaties, civilising its subjects and serving the needs of every minority. Above all, it will increase prosperity, leaving more to redistribute to the poor.

## 11.7 THE REPRESENTATIVE SYSTEM AS THE GOVERNANCE COOPERATIVE

By assigning ownership in organisations to different classes of people, different types of organisations can be created. These include investor-owned firms, cooperatives and nonprofits. Governments can also take these forms.

### THE PURPOSE OF THE COOPERATIVE

As explained in Chapter 7, there are ways for entrepreneurs to shift cooperations away from those preferred by their opportunity recipients to those they themselves prefer. In all entrepreneurial endeavours, consumer sovereignty is therefore limited. In some types of endeavours, or 'markets', it is more limited than in others. The limitations come at the expense of opportunity recipients, which can be both consumers and producers.

To address this problem, people can form cooperatives. A cooperative is an enterprise owned by its customers. It is an organisation in which its customers possess the residual control rights, which allows them to elect its managers. Cooperatives are typically not-for-profit and serve to provide them the goods and services they would otherwise procure from entrepreneurs. In a cooperative, they themselves play the role of entrepreneur and provide themselves with what they need. Because a cooperative's owners and opportunity recipients are in principle the same people, there is no reason for the owners to act at the expense of their customers – They are their own customers. Crucially, their ownership rights in the cooperative are not freely alienable because the cooperative could otherwise come under the control of other entrepreneurs and lose its cooperative character. Voting rights cannot be accumulated – Cooperatives are typically instituted with the one-member-one-vote rule. Sometimes, the weighting of a participant's voting rights depends on the magnitude of his patronage to the cooperative.[148]

Cooperatives are instituted when the relative costs for opportunity recipients are lower than the costs they would incur if investor-owners were to own the company. Investor-owners could gain from acting at their expense, such as by engaging in deception or anticompetitive action. The relative costs of a cooperative depend on various factors. For example, its participants must not be too numerous, dispersed or transitory. Only then will they make the effort to oversee the organisation's managers well. Otherwise, they will have little interest in exercising effective ownership. Rational ignorance and rational irrationality will then emerge – Participants then barely benefit from informing themselves well or abandoning bliss beliefs such that their ownership rights are used better. The organisation is then managed poorly while its managers have much freedom to exploit principal-agent problems. Moreover, the participants in a cooperative are usually not as capable in their role of owners as investors are. Incompetent investors tend to be weeded out from their role by the losses they incur, but incompetent customer-owners are not. As a result, cooperatives are rare and usually have a relatively small number of recurring participants. However, when interacting with investor-owned firms, people bear the costs of deception, anticompetitive action and so on. The costs of participating in a cooperative may well be lower. Consumer cooperatives are instituted because consumer sovereignty is limited.

Cooperatives are common in various sectors. In the agricultural sector, for example, farmers commonly participate in cooperatives to buy fertiliser. There are large informational asymmetries between the buyers and sellers of fertiliser, which sellers can exploit. Farmers thus participate in cooperatives to protect themselves from such exploitation.[149] Social clubs are also often cooperatives.[150] Most familiar to us,

148 Hansmann (1996), p. 15

149 Ibid., Chapter 7. Agricultural and Other Producer Cooperatives, pp. 28 and 149-157

150 Ibid., Chapter 10. Clubs and Other Associative Organizations, pp. 182-194

however, is the governance cooperative, known as the representative democratic state. Consumer cooperatives are instituted because consumer sovereignty is limited, and this is also the reason why governance cooperatives have been instituted – Consumer sovereignty over governments, i.e. proprietary democracy, is limited.

## THE NONPROFIT ALTERNATIVE

Besides the cooperative and the investor-owned firm, there is also the nonprofit organisation. A nonprofit organisation has no owners. Managers can appoint their own successors and are in their roles bound to statutes and legislation. No ownership rights in a nonprofit can be accumulated because there are none. The nonprofit has similar strengths to those of the cooperative. However, it is in some cases viable when a cooperative is not since it does not need a limited number of recurring customer-members to perform its functions, which a cooperative does. To still avoid the relative costs resulting from investor-owned firms when the conditions for a well-functioning cooperative are absent, a nonprofit can be instituted.

As Henry Hansmann explains:

> … these firms without owners typically arise where there is at least one class of patrons for whom both the costs of contracting and the costs of ownership are quite high, with the result that there is no class of individuals to whom ownership of the firm can be assigned without severe inefficiencies. This class of patrons is usually a significant group of the firm's customers. The high costs of contracting facing those customers are typically the result of severely asymmetric information. More particularly, nonprofit firms commonly arise where customers are in a peculiarly poor position to determine, with reasonable cost or effort, the quality or the quantity of the services they receive from a firm. As a consequence, assigning ownership to anyone other than these customers would create both the incentive and the opportunity for the customers to be severely exploited. Yet at the same time, the customers are so situated that the costs to them of exercising effective control over the firm are unacceptably

> large relative to the value of their transactions with the firm. The solution is to create a firm without owners-or, more accurately, to create a firm whose managers hold it in trust for its customers. In essence, the nonprofit form abandons any benefits of full ownership in favor of stricter fiduciary constraints on management.[151]

One could also imagine a nonprofit government – A government without voters in which the residual control rights are held by a 'council of wise men'. This council is then constrained by a statute in the form of a constitution and the members of the council are as much subject to it as anyone else is.

## THE ASSIGNMENT OF OWNERSHIP

Ownership can be assigned to different classes of people who interact with the firm. In cooperatives, it is assigned to customers. In investor-owned firms, it is assigned to investors. Ownership is in principle assigned to those who value it most, which depends on its relative cost to different people. Alternative contractual solutions are never perfect and can still lead to actions at the expense of some parties. If, for some party, the cost of contracting and of the actions at its expense are too great, that party may prefer to interact with the firm as its owner.

> Indeed, the basic function served by giving voting control over a firm to a group of the firm's patrons is not to provide a means for conveying the patrons' preferences to the firm's management, but rather to make it more difficult for the firm to exploit those patrons as a class-that is, to prevent the firm from taking actions that will strongly disadvantage a substantial majority of those patrons. This is why, in most firms, voting control is given to a class of transacting parties who, if they were solely dependent on

[151] Ibid., p. 228

> market contracting, would collectively be subject to exploitation by the firm, either because the firm has market power, because the firm has an informational advantage over them, or because the patrons must make transaction-specific investments that will compromise their exit option once they begin dealing with the firm.
>
> In short, the principal role of voting in firms is much as it is in most democratic governments: not to aggregate and communicate preferences, but simply to give the electorate some crude protection from gross opportunism on the part of those in power.[152]

Few if any firms are owned by both their customers and their investors, because the interests of these groups conflict. Regarding the gainful actions that form exceptions to consumer sovereignty, customers have interests that directly oppose those of investors. As Hansmann explains:

> There is clearly a need for good communication between patrons and the firm, just as there is between citizens and their government. Indeed, a recurrent theme in the management literature has been the need for managers to find better means of listening to their customers, suppliers, investors, and workers. But giving patrons voting control over the firm is not necessarily a good means to this end, creating possibilities for costly conflict and skewed decision making.
>
> On the contrary, where the owners of a firm are at all heterogeneous in their interests, it is common to encounter devices designed to attenuate rather than increase the refinement and force with which electoral mechanisms convey the interests of the individual owners. For example, as we have seen, worker-owned firms with a diverse

[152] Ibid., pp. 288-289

> labor force sometimes require that directors be elected at large rather than by smaller constituencies, that they serve terms of several years rather than just one year, or that they be outsiders rather than members of the work force they represent. An extreme version of this attenuation is the formation of a nonprofit firm whose directors are charged with operating the firm on behalf of a given class of patrons but who are not elected by those patrons.[153]

Such conflicts of interests cannot be solved through contracting. One could think that provisions could be contracted to prevent the exploitation of opportunities to deceive, act anticompetitively and so on. A contract could, for example, simply forbid such actions. If contracting and enforcement would be costless and could be done perfectly, contract would be a viable solution. No ownership would be necessary. But contracts are inevitably incomplete, flawed and costly. As Hansmann explains:

> The other side of the coin is that, where a firm does have a class of patrons with highly homogeneous interests, ownership is often an attractive alternative to market contracting for those patrons. Market contracting, like politics, has its costs, and ownership can reduce those costs by removing the conflict of interest between firm and patron that lies at their root.
>
> In this there is nothing special about investors of capital. Often they are the only reasonably homogeneous class of patrons, and thus the natural owners by default. But where another substantial group of patrons has the requisite commonality of interest –whether they are workers, other suppliers, or customers – it is evidently efficient to give ownership to that group even when the potential reduction in their costs of contracting is relatively modest.[154]

153 Ibid., p. 289

154 Ibid., pp. 289-290

The people who hold the residual control rights in a firm are typically the people who value them most. A class of people who interact with the firm values ownership higher than others do when the costs they expect to bear from the firm acting at their expense are high enough relative to their expected cost of ownership. For example, most firms are investor-owned because investing usually involves greater risks than being an employee or a customer.

A consumer cooperative, which is a consumer-owned firm, is more efficient when exceptions to consumer sovereignty create greater costs for consumers than the costs of participating in a cooperative.

In a non-profit organisation, no one has residual control rights. A nonprofit is therefore more vulnerable to institutional capture and more likely to be inefficient and corrupt, because there are no owners to dissolve it. As the members of a cooperative become more transitory, numerous, dispersed or otherwise have much reason to be passive, it increasingly resembles a nonprofit. As a result, many cooperatives have the same problems as nonprofits often do.

A partnership is a firm owned by its employees. It is instituted when employees find owning residual control rights to be worth any resulting increase in costs, such as the cost of capital. If the firm is not owned by its investors, its cost of capital may well be higher because the investors then have weaker means to defend their interests. In some industries, such as professional services, capital is barely necessary and employees benefit from contributing to their brand value together and sharing marketing expenses. In such cases, it is most attractive for an employee to join a partnership. Partnerships are typically organised according to the 'one person, one vote' rule. This gives one voting right to each participant, which can be better when little capital is needed. In a partnership, an employee is given voting rights and a share in the firm's profits in exchange for his labour, his contribution to the firm's reputation and any other contribution he makes to the firm's value. The value that one participant contributes does not differ much from what another contributes, so the 'one person, one vote' rule is appropriate. Proprietary firms typically follow the 'one share, one vote' rule. This gives investors voting rights in proportion to their investment, which is appropriate because large investors have more at stake. The 'one share, one vote' rule thereby allows the firm to have a lower cost of capital. A partnership is less suitable for a more capital-intensive business because the higher cost of capital would have a larger effect on total costs. In such cases, employees can get better terms, in particular higher salaries, at an investor-owned firm.

## INSTITUTIONAL LOCK-IN

As explained above, and in Section 5.1 in the context of a government, participants in a cooperative become more passive in using their rights as they become more numerous. As a result, the organisation becomes less efficient as managers can get away with worse performance and more corruption, and becomes less likely to be dissolved even when it is efficient to do so. Dissolving a cooperative can be in the interests of its owners, as the rights of the cooperative can then be transferred to others. The participants can then use the money received for these rights, including for any capital they own, in better ways. However, the passivity of participants that prevents the efficient operation of the cooperative also prevents its dissolution. All property owned by the cooperative is thereby 'locked in' – It does not get transferred to others who value it more and is not used for its most valued ends. In the words of Hansmann:

> ...when a firm's owners do not effectively control the incumbent managers, the managers may seek to preserve their autonomy or their jobs, by substantially raising the costs of changing the firm's form of ownership. The managers are particularly likely to be successful in this regard where, as in many cooperative and mutual firms, shares in ownership are not freely marketable.[155]

The same applies to nonprofit organisations. In nonprofit organisations, nobody is allowed to reap any profits. The returns to dissolving a nonprofit therefore do not go to its managers, but must typically be used for charitable purposes. Its managers would therefore never benefit from dissolving it, and it is thus only dissolved when it goes bankrupt. Even if someone else could use the nonprofit's property

[155] Ibid., p. 46

better, it is not transferred to him. Its most efficient use is prevented altogether.

As a result of this problem, there are many nonprofits in which great amounts of capital are locked in, and whose managers have little reason to use this capital most efficiently. The nonprofit sector is thus naturally home to a class of parasites – Regardless of their performance, managers do not risk losing their positions. By their nature, nonprofit organisations are prone to rent-seeking and favouritism, are relatively favourable to ideological objectives[156] and often have incompetent members and managers. They have all the public choice problems that are common in representative democratic governments. They are notoriously inefficient, ideologically driven and poorly managed.

Nonprofits must still compete with other nonprofits and organisations of other types, which limits the degree to which their managers can parasitise them. However, many still perform worse than their for-profit counterparts. What protects these organisations from the 'discipline of the market'? What keeps them afloat? First, as explained above, nonprofits are typically not dissolved unless they go bankrupt. They can therefore survive while underperforming their for-profit counterparts. Any non-negative rate of return on a nonprofit's net capital allows it to endure and any positive rate of return even allows it to expand. As Hansmann explains, illustrating the problem with data from the hospital sector:

> ... when demand declines, nonprofit firms have much less incentive and opportunity than investor-owned firms to reduce their investment in the industry. A nonprofit firm need not – indeed, cannot – pay any return on its net capital (that is, the capital that the firm has acquired over time through donations and retained earnings). Consequently, even in the absence of any direct or indirect subsidies (such as tax exemption), a nonprofit firm can remain in operation at its current scale as long as its reve-

156 As explained by John Smoke (2021), who also points out the magnitude of locked-in capital.

nues are sufficient to cover depreciation – that is, sufficient to earn just a zero net rate of return. Any positive rate of return on the nonprofit's net capital, even if it is well below the rate of return required by the capital market, will actually permit the firm to expand. And a nonprofit's management – whose employment is at stake, who has no ownership interest in the firm's assets, and who may feel a professional commitment to supplying the type of services produced by the firm – has a strong incentive to avoid liquidating the firm in whole or in part, and to keep it going at the largest scale possible regardless of the rate of return on its invested capital. The result is that forces of competition in the product market can be quite slow in weeding out inefficient nonprofit firms; even in the absence of subsidies, nonprofits can survive and even grow when they are earning a rate of return so low as to cause an investor-owned firm to scale back or exit.

In short, capital tends to get locked into nonprofit firms. This phenomenon probably goes far toward explaining why, despite the rapid and aggressive entry of well capitalized investor-owned chains into the hospital industry after 1965, the market share of nonprofit hospitals did not decline. If nonprofits could and would disinvest as rapidly as for-profit firms, then nonprofit hospitals, which account for a large share of the GNP produced by all nonprofits in the United States, would probably have a much smaller presence in the economy. Much the same may be true for other service industries in which commercial nonprofits have a large presence, such as prepaid group medical practice (health maintenance organizations), day care, most forms of education, and banking (the latter of which we shall examine in Chapter 14). As each of these industries has expanded and matured, the severe informational problems and the supply-side subsidies that initially prompted the use of the nonprofit form have been mitigated. Nevertheless, the nonprofit firms that originally populated these industries have remained and even expanded.

> This is not to deny that informational asymmetry may continue to provide a justification for a significant non-profit presence in some of these industries. Nursing care, in particular, is arguably an industry where the potential for customer exploitation is large and is not always adequately dealt with by regulatory and reputational constraints on for-profit firms. This may help explain why, even as the nursing home industry roughly doubled in size between 1971 and 1985, the market share of nonprofit nursing homes actually increased, from 18 percent to 23 percent, over the same period.[157]

Second, nonprofits usually receive large subsidies while their for-profit counterparts do not. They are thereby advantaged in a government-created unequal playing field. Such subsidies can be found in virtually every country today.[158] As Hansmann explains, presenting the problem in an American context:

> In the United States, most nonprofit firms of any financial significance are exempt from the federal corporate income tax, and often from state corporate, property, and sales tax-

[157] Hansmann (1996), pp. 240-241

[158] The non-profit nature of most universities prevent profit-maximising entrepreneurs from owning them efficiently. They are also usually protected from for-profit competition. Many non-profit universities receive government funding or subsidies, which makes for-profit universities unable to compete successfully. Trustees and staff are thus protected both from shareholder oversight by profit-maximising entrepreneurs and from competition that forces them to provide better education at lower prices. Regulations also prevent universities from competing along some lines, such as by offering more efficient online education or offering the possibility of obtaining degrees without the education itself. Such competition, while it would benefit students, especially those who prefer to self-study or work alongside their studies, would erode much of the income of these organisations and destroy many administrative and teaching jobs.

> es as well. Further, at various times most nonprofit firms have been exempt from, or received specially favorable treatment under, Social Security taxes, unemployment insurance taxes, postal rates, the minimum wage, securities regulation, bankruptcy, copyright, laws on antitrust and unfair competition, and tort liability. These exemptions and privileges have presumably resulted in a larger nonprofit sector than would otherwise have developed.[159]

However, non-profits do not need subsidies to emerge. As explained by Hansmann:

> Even in the absence of these subsidies, however, nonprofit firms would probably still have a significant presence in the economy. Indeed, nearly all of the special legal benefits accorded nonprofits were first granted in the late nineteenth or twentieth centuries, when nonprofits were already well established in important sectors such as education and health care.
>
> Moreover, the extension of special privileges to nonprofits in any given industry has generally occurred as a response to the development of a significant nonprofit presence in that industry, and not the other way around. That is, as nonprofits have developed in new industries, such as the performing arts, health insurance, and nursing care, the scope of exemptions and other benefits has subsequently been expanded to include those classes of nonprofits. Subsidies have evidently had little role in determining the distribution of nonprofits across industries.
>
> Finally, the range of subsidies granted nonprofit firms reached its peak about 1950, and has steadily eroded since then. Nearly all the privileges and exemptions mentioned above have been scaled back or have simply been with-

[159] Ibid., p. 244

> drawn entirely from some or all nonprofits. And although these changes will presumably have some impact in the long run, they have not immediately resulted in an obvious reduction in the scope of the nonprofit sector.[160]

Non-profits may also emerge without subsidies, because their non-profit status allows their customers to trust them more than if they had owners. Customers are often too non-recurring and numerous to form a functional cooperative, and investor-owned firms cannot always be trusted because their owners have an interest in exploiting advantages at the expense of their customers. In some situations, nonprofits are more trustworthy while still being functional, allowing them to outcompete their for-profit competitors.

However, when their relative advantage disappears, they endure despite this being inefficient. As Hansmann explains:

> In nonprofit firms, and also in many consumer-owned firms in which the customers do not have meaningful control (such as life insurance and banking), capital can become locked in. These firms tend to accumulate capital beyond their needs and, conversely, fail to shed capital, or to exit the industry, when they are inefficiently large or simply inefficient.
>
> In a sense, capital lock-in is an aspect of the agency costs of management. Why, then, is this a major difference between ownership forms, while agency costs of management in general do not seem to differ greatly? The answer, perhaps, is that managers are responsive in eliminating many inefficiencies – such as those associated with unnecessarily high costs of production, or with failure to conform production to demand – because, in the face of product market competition, their organization's ability to survive, much less grow, will otherwise be threatened. But the same drive for institutional survival – whether it

160 Ibid., p. 244

derives from the managers' desire to maintain their own jobs or, less selfishly, from the excessively high salience that the virtues of their organization's services have achieved in the managers' eyes – will push managers to maintain and even accumulate capital within the firm even when it is earning an inefficiently low rate of return. And a nonprofit firm, or a proprietary firm that pays no dividends, can survive and even grow as long as it is earning any positive net return on its invested capital, even if that rate of return is far below what could be earned if the capital were employed elsewhere. As a consequence, product market discipline will not suffice to drive capital out of a nonprofit firm or out of a proprietary firm whose owners have no effective control.

It follows that nonprofit firms, and also consumer cooperatives, can survive in industries well beyond the time when other ownership forms, and particularly investor-owned firms, have become more efficient.

There is a similar problem of excessive capital accumulation within investor-owned firms. Publicly held companies that are effectively controlled by their managers frequently not only survive but invest and grow even when they are earning less than a market rate of return on their invested capital. Indeed, large publicly traded business corporations are apparently much more subject to this problem than are many types of cooperatives, such as the large farmer-owned production and supply cooperatives, or the retailer-owned supply cooperatives. With investor-owned firms, however, there is ultimately both the incentive and the mechanism to withdraw capital from the firm through a takeover of its management, by means of either a hostile tender offer or a proxy fight. These latter mechanisms are crude. But even those crude mechanisms are lacking in some common types of non-investor-owned firms.[161]

[161] Ibid., pp. 292-293

## INSTITUTIONAL CAPTURE

When the managers of nonprofits appoint their own successors and cannot be motivated by financial self-interest, they appoint their successors for other reasons. Nonprofits therefore do not only disproportionately attract people who are ideologically motivated, they also disproportionately select them. Ideologues tend to favour those who share their ideology. As a result, nonprofits naturally tend to become driven by those ideologies that are most ardently adhered to and whose adherents are most intolerant of opposing viewpoints.

Additionally, because nonprofits are not controlled by shareholders, they are particularly susceptible to corruption. Statutes are never perfect, especially when they can be changed. As a result, the managers of nonprofits can often build up entrenched interests, create unnecessary jobs for people and otherwise make themselves and their friends profit financially.

Organisations can be captured by ideologues and corrupt managers, especially nonprofits. Institutional capture can also emerge in cooperatives with many members, especially if their members are transitory. As Hansmann explained, cooperatives increasingly resemble nonprofits as their members become more numerous, transitory or dispersed.

## FREEDOM OF ENTERPRISE?

It is important that an organisation can be transformed into another form if it would thereby become more efficient. For example, it should be possible to transform a cooperative into a proprietary company or conversely. Its managers must also then have an interest in doing so. Unfortunately, in the case of nonprofits and dysfunctional cooperatives, managers have no such interest. Their institutions are thus locked in and their capital is kept from its most efficient use.

To address institutional lock-in, it may be beneficial to limit the freedom of enterprise.[162] For instance, nonprofits and cooperatives

162 Hansmann's stance on this is unclear, but he does not seem to agree. In his words: 'Freedom of enterprise is a fundamental characteristic of the most advanced modern economies. Capitalism, in contrast, is contingent; it is

could be required to dissolve after a number of years. At least, they should compete on an equal playing field with investor-owned firms, instead of being subsidised or otherwise advantaged by governments.

## REPRESENTATIVE DEMOCRACY AS A GOVERNANCE COOPERATIVE

Consumer cooperatives prevail over investor-owned firms when the exceptions to consumer sovereignty are so costly for their customers that their customers are better off as members of cooperatives. If the costs resulting from exceptions to consumer sovereignty are high enough, the costs of participating in a cooperative may well be lower. Like any entrepreneur, a government can engage in deception, anticompetitive action, commitment pricing and all other courses of action of which the possibility to gainfully engage in it limits consumer sovereignty.[163] In particular, a government can subordinate its subjects without their consent. As Chapter 8 explains, there are many exceptions to proprietary democracy through which a government can benefit at the expense of its subjects. All these exceptions result in costs for subjects. Subjects can therefore benefit from forming or joining consumer cooperatives that provide governance, i.e. representative democratic systems. In a consumer cooperative, its patrons possess the residual control rights, in the form of voting rights, typically according to the 'one member, one vote' rule. This also applies to representative systems – Subjects typically have voting rights according to the 'one man, one vote' rule. As the members of a governance cooperative, i.e. its electorate, they own the rights of government.

The proprietary government is the government equivalent of the investor-owned company. This book explains its benefits in particular

simply the particular form of patron ownership that most often, but by no means always, proves efficient with the technologies presently at hand.' Ibid., p. 297.

163 Or, as I call it in the context of the government-subject relationship, proprietary democracy.

if the conditions for proprietary democracy are satisfied[164], while also explaining that these conditions are impossible to fully satisfy and that the representative system still has some relative benefits in any case.[165] However, many benefits of proprietary democracy also emerge if it only exists to some extent. Consumer sovereignty is always somewhat limited, but from the general prevalence of proprietary firms over cooperatives it follows that the former generally create more value than the latter. Cooperatives are the exception, not the rule, because they involve greater costs. Furthermore, a hybrid system consisting of both the proprietary and the representative system could deliver the benefits of both.[166] Therefore, at least lower-level jurisdictions should be privatised, and all policy domains that are better governed proprietarily should be devolved to proprietary governments.

## LOCKED-IN GOVERNANCE COOPERATIVES

The lock-in problem is even more consequential in governance cooperatives. All of the world's habitable land has already been claimed by governments and jurisdictions are difficult to privatise, which prevents entry by new competitors. Besides, it is very costly to switch governments – Moving to another country usually requires giving up many things. It is therefore difficult to successfully compete with the world's current governance cooperatives.

As with other cooperatives, the managers of representative governments have little interest in changing their institutional forms. They do not stand to gain from privatising their jurisdictions. However, their support can perhaps be won with financial incentives or by presenting the privatisation of jurisdictions as a solution to their most pressing problems. Besides these, more ways out of the

164 As explained in Chapter 9.

165 As explained in Chapter 11.

166 As explained in Section 11.5.

lock-in could perhaps be found. Considering the potential benefits of proprietary governance for human prosperity, there is much reason to look for them.

## CHANGING CIRCUMSTANCES

Over the last three millennia, governance cooperatives have existed in many varieties, from the Greek poleis and the Roman Republic to the Florentine Republic and the Dutch Republic. The governance cooperative is therefore not exclusive to any period in history. Different forms of government come and go, as they become more expedient for incumbent rulers and better suited for new circumstances. Various circumstances determine whether a cooperative or a proprietary firm is more efficient and durable, and these change over time. This applies to all types of entrepreneurial endeavours. Cooperatives or proprietary firms that were once successful because of their cooperative or proprietary nature can later be outcompeted for it. This also applies to governments. The hereditary monarchical system was under serious strain in the nineteenth century, prompting a transformation of hereditary monarchical governments into cooperatives. Initially, these cooperatives only included landowners and wealthy men. Over time, mass democracy emerged because elected representatives found expanding the franchise to be in their interests at each increment. As circumstances change, governments are not unlikely to change their institutional form again in the future, or to be replaced by proprietary governments.

The internet and the drastic decrease in travel costs have made exit less costly and people can inform themselves better of political affairs than ever. The proprietary system has therefore become more suitable. Conversely, if proprietary governments cannot be prevented from exploiting advantages at the expense of subjects, which could occur in the future as the means of governments improve, the cooperative may be better. Then, new technology could perhaps be used to transform proprietary systems into cooperatives – Decentralised Autonomous Organisations (DAO) can buy shares in proprietary organisations and institute themselves as cooperatives. New technologies like AI agents could then perhaps reduce or even eliminate the problems of rational ignorance and rational irrationality among voters, making the cooperative more functional.

PART IV

# THE PROPRIETARY JURISDICTION IN PRACTICE

CHAPTER 12.

# PRIVATISING JURISDICTIONS

## 12.1 VARIANTS OF THE PROPRIETARY JURISDICTION

### THE SEMI-PROPRIETARY JURISDICTION

A government can be proprietary to a degree, depending on how large a part of its shares or voting rights is alienable. If only a part of a government's shares or voting rights is alienable, it is *semi-proprietary*. There are various ways to make a government and its jurisdiction semi-proprietary, each with its own advantages and disadvantages.

The simplest way for a government to be semi-proprietary is for only a part of its voting rights or shares to be alienable. For instance, a non-proprietary electorate can have 70% of the voting rights, distributed according to the 'one man, one vote' rule, while the remaining 30% of the voting rights form a separate class of proprietary (i.e. freely alienable) shares that include some right to dividends. Voters would then elect representatives to a legislative council. Some representatives would serve the interests of the representative voters while others would serve the interests of the proprietors. In this system, the representatives of the proprietors need some popular support for the laws they want to pass and the ministers they want to appoint. The ratio of proprietary to non-proprietary voting rights can vary, such that the system tends towards either representative or proprietary governance. In a semi-proprietary system, a majority of votes must be non-proprietary if the government is not to be effectively proprietary, because a majority of voting rights is enough for proprietary voters to disempower non-proprietary voters.

In a semi-proprietary system, the non-proprietary electorate may include various groups of people. Universal suffrage for adults is one possibility. Non-proprietary voting rights can also be assigned exclusively to property owners, possibly weighted by the value or size of their properties. Such an arrangement currently exists in the

Próspera ZEDE, the semi-proprietary jurisdiction in Honduras operated by Honduras Próspera.[167]

In a hybrid system with a representative higher-level government, there is another way for a lower-level government to be semi-proprietary. In this variant, some or all of the non-proprietary voting rights in the lower-level government are held in trust by officials of the higher-level government on behalf of their voters, while the other voting rights in the lower-level government are proprietary. The non-proprietary voting rights in the semi-proprietary government are then not directly controlled by their non-proprietary owners, but by the representative system's parliamentarians they elect.

Within this category, different variants are available. For example, it could be arranged that the parliamentarians controlling the non-proprietary voting rights on behalf of their voters decide on the use of these voting rights by majority vote. They then vote as one in the semi-proprietary government. Or they can each individually be given a part of the non-proprietary voting rights in trust, such that they can each vote differently and each of them is represented in the semi-proprietary government. The difference between these two arrangements is substantial, because if a majority of the voting rights in the lower-level government are non-proprietary and the representatives entrusted with them vote as one, the proprietary voters need majority support from the voting representatives for the laws they want to pass and administrators they want to appoint. But if the entrusted representatives vote individually, the proprietary voters need much less support. For example, if 55% of voting rights are non-proprietary and the entrusted representatives vote as one, the proprietary voters need majority support among the entrusted representatives. But if the entrusted representatives vote individually, the proprietary voters only need the support of 6/55 of them.

Another way to make a jurisdiction semi-proprietary is the idea of 'double democracy' by Tom W. Bell.[168] This system lets the electorate veto some or all new laws and policies, and appointments of some

[167] For an informative article about Próspera, see Scott Alexander (2013).

[168] See Double Democracy, in Bell (2017), pp. 157-168.

administrators. A new law, policy or appointment of an executive would then be proposed by the proprietary government and subsequently approved or declined by the electorate.

A proprietary government and thereby its jurisdiction can be either partly or fully proprietary. When the rights of government over a jurisdiction are fully alienable in every way, it is fully proprietary. But the proprietary nature of a jurisdiction can be limited in different ways. When only some of the rights of government over the jurisdiction are proprietary in the sense that the rights of government over only some policy domains take the form of freely alienable voting rights, it is part of a hybrid system. When only some of the voting rights that make up rights of government are proprietary, the government and its jurisdiction become semi-proprietary. Both fully proprietary and semi-proprietary governments can thus be part of a hybrid system, as a fully non-proprietary government can still possess rights of government over the same jurisdiction. The possible variants can thus be categorised as fully proprietary jurisdictions, semi-proprietary jurisdictions, fully proprietary jurisdictions as part of a hybrid system and semi-proprietary jurisdictions as part of a hybrid system.[169]

[169] In reality, countless shades on the spectrum between fully proprietary and non-proprietary rights of government are possible, in the form of different restrictions on their alienability. For the purposes of this chapter, it is most appropriate to divide the countless possibilities into these four categories.

As explained in Section 11.1, some restrictions on the alienability of the rights of government can be beneficial by ensuring that they do not end up in the hands of people with bad intentions. The proprietary nature of the rights of government is then limited, but this could be benign in that it does not prevent a highly efficient allocation of them. When only such restrictions are put on their alienability, it is therefore quite accurate to refer to the government and its jurisdiction as proprietary or semi-proprietary while mentioning the exact restrictions.

### DIFFERENT KINDS OF HYBRID SYSTEMS

In a hybrid system, governments of different levels can take different forms. Since the representative system has unique benefits and many current political systems are representative, a hybrid system is likely to consist of a fully representative higher-level government and proprietary or semi-proprietary lower-level governments. However, this may not be feasible in all countries. Some states are hereditary monarchic and some have a theocratic element. In these countries, the theocratic and hereditary monarchic governments can keep their rights of government in relevant policy domains while transferring other rights of government to lower-level proprietary governments. Existing theocratic and hereditary monarchic states can thus also be transformed into hybrid systems, enabling such countries to obtain the benefits of proprietary governance while their rulers keep their relevant policy domains and their military supremacy.

## 12.2 WAYS TO PRIVATISE JURISDICTIONS

As explained in the previous section, different variants of the proprietary jurisdiction can be created. For convenience and because they are all proprietary to some extent, I will from now on refer to them all as proprietary. There are at least three ways to create proprietary jurisdictions.

### PRIVATISING VOTING RIGHTS

The simplest way to privatise a jurisdiction is by making a government's rights of government, such as voting rights, alienable and accumulable. Thereby, a non-proprietary government of any level can be made proprietary. Forming new proprietary governments is therefore unnecessary. The advantage of this method of privatisation is that start-up costs are lower – Many civil servants can keep their jobs, and the proprietary government does not need to build its own organisation but can simply improve that which it has.

## GOVERNMENT CHARTERS

Another way to privatise a jurisdiction is to give companies or individuals an alienable charter to rule with certain policy discretion. This policy discretion can include all rights of government including the right to superior force, in which case the jurisdiction is privatised completely, or only some rights of government, in which case a hybrid system is created.

The proprietary governments thereby created can be given rights of government over predetermined territories without the possibility of expansion, or the possibility to expand their jurisdictions subject to approval by the higher-level government[170], or the right to expand by acquiring properties or approval from property owners.[171]

The charter method has thus far been used for colonial proprietary jurisdictions[172] and the Honduran ZEDE[173] system. Under

[170] When a government administration grants rights of government over a territory it chooses, or when the expansion of a jurisdiction requires its approval, this can involve knowledge and incentive problems. That is, those who get to designate or approve the territorial boundaries of the proprietary jurisdiction do not know which areas are best privatised and may privatise the wrong parts of their jurisdictions for political or personal gain even if they do know. In particular, they can abuse this authority to extract rents or to favour their own voter base. See Knowledge and incentive problems with SEZs, in Chapter 2: Are SEZs better than the status quo?, in Moberg (2017). See pp. 35-41 for an explanation of the knowledge problem and pp. 45-57 for an explanation of the incentive problem.

[171] The latter currently exists in the Honduran ZEDE system. See the ZEDE Organic Law, Source included in the reference section.

[172] See Chapter 13 for more information about the proprietary colonies.

[173] Zonas de Empleo y Desarrollo Económico or Zones for Employment and Economic Development. For information on the ZEDE, see

the ZEDE Organic Law, companies could become proprietary governments by receiving a charter from the CAMP[174], a commission initially appointed by the president. Until the enabling legislation for the ZEDE was repealed[175], proprietary governments could obtain voting rights in the legislative councils of the ZEDE jurisdictions to be established. Honduras Próspera Inc. is one of these proprietary governments. As per the Próspera charter, Honduras Próspera Inc. has the right to appoint four of the nine council members that form the legislative body of its jurisdiction. Another four members are appointed by residents, and the ninth member is the Technical Secretary who oversees the day-to-day governance of the zone. The technical secretary is appointed by CAMP after being proposed by the residents, organisers or promoters of the ZEDE.[176] Until the Próspera ZEDE reaches urban population density, two of the four members to be appointed by residents are appointed by landowners instead. A ZEDE can be expanded by acquiring permission from the landowner whose lands are to be incorporated.

## DEVOLUTION TO LANDOWNERS

Another possibility is to devolve rights of government to landowners. The higher-level government then designates a zone over which it deregulates some policy domains and limits its right to levy taxes, while giving up the right to regulate these policy domains without the consent of the landowners in the zone. Rights of government over the devolved policy domains are thereby effectively transferred to the

---

Wikipedia.org, Zone for Employment and Economic Development, or Archive.org: zede.hn. Sources included in the reference section.

174 Comité Para la Adopción de Mejores Prácticas or Committee for the Adoption of Best Practices.

175 For more information, see Reuters (2022).

176 Section 3.08 of the Próspera Charter, p. 22

landowners, as they can make presence on their lands conditional on their right to impose penalties on those who do not comply with their rules. These rules could for example include to pay them certain taxes. Deregulating policy domains allows landowners to fill the void with their own rules instead. Crucially, the devolving government gives up the right to regulate the deregulated policy domains without the consent of the landowners. Otherwise, it would merely make laissez-faire policies, not privatise its jurisdiction. It then effectively grants the landowners the right to govern these policy domains, which they can then transfer to others. Landowners are thus made proprietary governments. To separate proprietary governance from landownership, they can subsequently sell their rights of government to specialised proprietary governments. Alternatively, they can sell their lands while keeping their rights of government.

If the devolving government allows it, landowners can also make use of their lands conditional on granting them a right to superior force, as well as granting their judiciary the right to adjudicate and their police the right to enforce. Without these rights, the benefits of proprietary governance are smaller because adjudication and enforcement would still be provided by a non-proprietary government.

If a government gives up all its rights of government over a territory, i.e. if it gives up its right to superior force over the territory, completely eliminates its regulations and makes itself unable to reimpose governance without the consent of the landowners, it thereby makes the landowners sovereign in its own stead. If it only gives up some of its rights of government, it becomes part of a hybrid system.

This method creates proprietary jurisdictions without any official status as such, which has benefits in the privatisation process that granting charters does not. The official status of proprietary governments and jurisdictions as such makes the privatisation of jurisdictions obvious and can thereby make it vulnerable to political opposition. This risk is smaller with devolution, although a proper devolution does require extensive deregulation, which can also attract political opposition.

Devolution has some disadvantages. For example, institutional arrangements for proprietary democracy are less easily made. Small landowners that become proprietary governments do not have the scale to make a separation of powers work and it may be difficult for a higher-level government to keep oversight over the many proprietary governments that may emerge. Besides, the relationship between the higher-level government and the lower-level proprietary government involves contracting over taxation rights and other matters. The more lower-level proprietary governments there are, the higher the total costs of contracting. However, these problems can be solved by only devolving rights of government to landowners with sufficiently large plots.

One last difficulty with devolution is that it conflicts with the principle of parliamentary sovereignty, which holds that the parliament of a representative government may repeal any change in law. Because of this principle, a government may not be able to give up the right to regulate certain policy domains. Parliamentary sovereignty is embedded in some constitutions, which makes it difficult or even impossible in some countries to devolve rights of government to landowners.

## RESCINDING RIGHTS OF GOVERNMENT

When a proprietary government is granted rights of government, they must be in its ownership, meaning that they cannot be rescinded without its consent. Otherwise, they are *de facto* still held by the former government. By rescinding them, the former government can then extend its regulatory scope as it wishes, which undermines the purpose of privatisation. Rights of government that can be rescinded under any condition by the government that has granted them are no meaningful rights.

A government could keep call options on the rights of government it grants. Call options give it the right to purchase the rights of government at a predetermined price under predetermined conditions. This limits the proprietary government's ownership of its rights of government, but it is still the owner. However, the weaknesses of such an arrangement are obvious – The proprietary government can be less confident in using its rights of government and people may be led to invest less in its jurisdiction.

Instead of not permanently giving up rights of government, a government can also privatise them for a limited time. For example, if rights of government are privatised for a period of only 40 years, proprietary governments can prove their worth such that more permanent decisions can subsequently be made based on actual results.

## 12.3 FINDING SUPPORT AND AVOIDING OPPOSITION

Privatising jurisdictions can drastically decrease government corruption and dysfunction. Instead of an anti-corruption drive, politicians may want to privatise their jurisdictions because they can thereby virtually eliminate corruption without being opposed by those who benefit from it. Besides, because proprietary jurisdictions can be expected to have better institutions for economic development, this may attract the interest of politicians who care about the prosperity of their country. But this requires incumbents to pursue the interests of their countries instead of their own material self-interest. If politicians are like most people, we cannot assume them to do so.

It is also unlikely that electorates, their representatives or civil servants will support the privatisation of jurisdictions. Electorates can be expected to be distrustful of it, because they are unlikely to understand that it will result in another form of democracy rather than its abolition. It therefore seems difficult to create broad support for the privatisation of jurisdictions, at least until it has proven its worth by making people more prosperous. Civil servants and elected politicians in principle have little reason to limit the scope of their authority.[177] Especially politicians and bureaucrats in corrupt governmental organisations can be expected to object, while it is those states that need proprietary governance the most. However, there are ways to give a government and its agents an interest in privatising rights of government and upholding these rights.

[177] The incumbent managers of organisations can generally be expected to oppose changes to their organisations' institutions. They have self-selected into the system and therefore often believe in its merits, and they benefit from its preservation as they can best navigate its institutions to obtain positions of power. If the institutions change, they may not be able to keep their positions. I am not the first to see this problem. See for example Weber (1947), pp. 318-319.

Generally, those whose incomes depend on the representative system, including bureaucrats and politicians, as well as other beneficiaries, will be critical of proprietary democracy. They both support the representative system ideologically and depend on it for their incomes.

For instance, proprietary governments with limited policy discretion can be presented as a solution to the problems they want to solve. In representative systems, these are often pressing problems of electoral importance in the near future, because incumbent politicians tend to prioritise re-election. Pressing problems can for instance be the need for a crucial piece of infrastructure, like a road or a bridge. The rate of unemployment may also be high. Granting rights of government to corporations in exchange for building new infrastructure and giving people employment opportunities could win an incumbent the next election.

Another way to align the interests could be a profit-sharing arrangement between the privatising government and the proprietary government. Even if the privatisation of a jurisdiction does not make its population more productive, it can be lucrative to a host government by attracting people from elsewhere.

Host governments and competing governments can become hostile to a proprietary government. Many factors can make them hostile, ranging from ideological opposition to geopolitical interests. It is important to know under what conditions they and their agents have an interest in becoming hostile and how this can be solved or mitigated.

One way to prevent a host government from violating the rights of a proprietary government is to make the host government agree to pay large penalties in case it does. Subsequent administrations must then choose between letting the proprietary government operate freely or closing it down at the cost of large penalties. In the representative system, incumbent politicians tend to have high time preferences due to their focus on re-election and because they are allows to serve a limited number of terms. Significant short-term penalties can therefore serve as strong incentives to uphold the rights of proprietary governments. The high time preference of incumbent politicians can be used against them.

Foreign governments and their representatives, which compete with a proprietary government, also have an interest in becoming hostile to it. Proprietary jurisdictions, by being governed more efficiently at lower tax rates, are likely to attract many subjects from countries with representative systems. As a result, representative governments, their agents and their beneficiaries have an interest in acting anticompetitively and harming the reputations of proprietary governments. But incumbent politicians in representative systems are, by the design of their system, oriented on the short term. They can therefore be expected not to care much if competition from proprietary jurisdictions only harms their tax bases in the long term. To prevent these states from becoming hostile, a proprietary government can limit immigration from their jurisdictions, such that the short-term decreases in their tax bases are not so large that they elicit hostile action from them. If only small percentages of their subjects leave to proprietary jurisdictions every year, incumbent politicians do not suffer much from the consequences during their own rule. Little opposition can then be expected from them. Besides, if host governments and their agents are made to benefit from proprietary jurisdictions, they will try to counteract hostility from competing governments.

There is also likely to be ideological opposition. The privatisation of a jurisdiction is likely to be seen as a limitation to democracy, instead of an expansion of it or the substitution of one form of democracy by another. Those who see the viability and benefits of proprietary democracy are not likely to come with this criticism, but the representative system has staunch believers who are unwilling and unable to see any better alternative.

One type of private jurisdiction that may receive their support, however, is the *refugee zone* or *refugee city* – A zone specially developed and governed to provide a haven for refugees, where they are given employment opportunities and the choice between staying or moving on to other places. These zones are best created as proprietary jurisdictions, and are likely to be very profitable while greatly improving living conditions for the refugees they accommodate. This may make privatising jurisdictions more attractive to both governments and their subjects, as well as reduce hostility to refugees. The refugee zone will be addressed in more detail in Section 15.1.

## ALIGNING ENTRENCHED INTERESTS

As explained in Section 9.4, a proprietary government can be expected to eliminate corruption and regulate competition such that its subjects obtain the best possible terms from entrepreneurs. Those who benefit from corruption can therefore be expected to oppose the privatisation of jurisdictions. However, a proprietary government can win their support. It can do this by buying the enterprises that benefit from corruption at a price that reflects the extra profits it yields them, possibly in exchange for a corresponding share in the proprietary government. Without harming anybody, special interests are thereby aligned with those of the proprietary government, giving it the support from powerful elites. The enterprises bought can subsequently be sold without the privileges they previously received, or they can stay in the proprietary government's ownership and charge their customers at competitive prices. The deadweight losses eliminated by reducing corruption and regulating competition accrue to the proprietary government's tax base.

Besides, proprietary jurisdictions can initially be small, such that rent-seeking elites who do not participate in the proprietary government are not harmed much in their incomes. In fact, because of the economic development that the presence of proprietary jurisdictions will foster, rent-seeking elites even stand to benefit from the presence of proprietary jurisdictions. To win their support, it can be beneficial to point them to examples of such *backward linkages*.

## EXTERNAL SUPPORT

Hegemons can also benefit from the privatisation of jurisdictions and can therefore perhaps be moved to support it. Proprietary jurisdictions can serve geopolitical ends by enabling people to emigrate from the jurisdictions of geopolitical adversaries without giving them political power at home. A hegemon can thereby reduce the tax bases of geopolitical adversaries and grow those of its allies.

They can also make more stable regimes in unstable regions, such as the Middle East. Contrary to democratic peace theory, the military allegiance of Middle Eastern hereditary monarchies to the United States shows that democracies are not necessarily less violent than other types of government. Democracy can be a more unstable and violent form of government by allowing radicals and demagogues to come to power.

Furthermore, proprietary democracy, as opposed to representative democracy, can succeed in any culture. To function well, representative democracy requires subjects to be sufficiently educated, generally accept different viewpoints and politically participate by informing themselves of political matters and voting. Representative democracy is therefore only suitable for some populations. Proprietary democracy, on the other hand, can succeed with any population.

Only the proprietary government, which can even take the form of shareholders that are the direct subjects of a hegemon, promises to be a reliable partner to hegemons. Democracy, hereditary monarchy and dictatorship can lead to rulers who are unreliable partners for electoral reasons, because of ethnic loyalty or because of plain incompetence and irrationality. The Middle East is a good example. Instead of installing democratic and hereditary monarchic systems, the western hegemonic powers should have installed proprietary governments with western shareholders. Instead, the Arab hereditary monarchies have used much of their capital to fund radical Islamic clerics, which has radicalised Muslims worldwide and made Muslim minorities in the west hostile to their host societies. In some countries, like Iraq and Syria, democracy ended in dictatorships with unreliable partners at the helm. In other countries, like Lebanon, democracy has set the stage for civil war between its ethnic and religious groups. The hegemonic strategy of installing democracies, hereditary monarchies and dictatorships has been an abject failure. It has caused much unnecessary suffering and has led to unnecessarily failures of the Unites States in many parts of the globe. When hegemonic powers see the relative benefits of having proprietary governments as partners, they can be expected to support the privatisation of jurisdictions.

In short, promoting proprietary democracy in the developing world could thus form part of a foreign policy that seeks to weaken opponents while fostering peace and prosperity.

CHAPTER 13.

# THE PROPRIETARY GOVERNMENT IN HISTORY

## 13.1 THE PROPRIETARY COLONIES AND THE TRADING COMPANIES

Although most governments have been hereditary or democratic, proprietary governments have existed in various forms. This chapter contains multiple examples of these.

Proprietary governments played a large role in European colonisations, including the colonisation of America. Rights of government over the colonies, including the French, English, Spanish and Dutch colonies, were not only held by the home state or granted in hereditary form as part of a feudal relationship – The institutional arrangements to create colonial governments also took other forms. Individuals and incorporated groups were often given jurisdictions by state charter.

Concentrating on the English colonies in particular, I divide the colonies and their governments into three categories – the corporate, the proprietary and the royal. This contrasts with the more common classification introduced by William Blackstone, which divides the colonies into the provincial establishments, proprietary governments and charter governments. Historian of American colonial history Herbert Osgood correctly rejected Blackstone's classification.[178] Charters are granted in many contexts, not only when rights of government are bestowed, so the charter does not distinguish governments as such. Charter governments can take any form

[178] Osgood (1896a), pp. 259-263

as any right can be bestowed by charter. Instead, Osgood only distinguished two types of colonies – the corporation and the province. But in this categorisation, the proprietary and royal provinces are grouped together. This is not incorrect, but we are interested in the proprietary government as distinguished from other types. I have therefore chosen to narrow down Osgood's classification by dividing the provinces into the proprietary and the royal provinces, according to the distinction he makes between them.

The proprietary governments differed from both the Crown and the so-called corporations in important ways. The rights of government of the king are inherited, not traded freely. As a result, they are not allocated to those who will use it best. And in the corporate system, not to be confused with the modern-day corporation, rights could not be accumulated. Shares were divided according to the one man, one vote rule. The corporate government was therefore a cooperative rather than a proprietary company. As the participants, the *patentees*, in a corporate system moved to their colonies and increased in number, the corporation thus became a representative system.[179] The proprietary governments, on the other hand, were characterised by the free alienability of the rights of their patentees, which allowed patentees to accumulate them. Proprietary governments could take the form of individuals and of companies. By dividing the colonial governments into the corporate, the proprietary and the royal we thus obtain three categories that differ importantly in the inalienability of their rights of government, while only narrowing down Osgood's classification rather than contradicting it.

179 As happened in Massachusetts under governor Winthrop between 1632 and 1644, the necessity of which he explained as follows: 'When the patent was granted, the number of freemen was supposed to be (as in like corporations) so few, as they might well join in making laws; but now they were grown to so great a body, as it was not possible for them to make or execute laws, but they must choose others for that purpose.' From Osgood (1896b). See in particular pp. 514-517.

Other factors also contributed to the transformation of the Massachusetts Bay Company into a representative system. See also Osgood (1896c).

In historical literature, the definition of the proprietary colonial government accords with the definition of the proprietary government given in this book. In its various forms, the proprietary government has been referred to under different names, including proprietor, lord proprietor and the proprietary company. As defined in one paper:

> Proprietary companies are historically enterprises owned by a private person or persons that receive the right of colonizing, including the right to create its own governance, alienation of overseas land, the power to wage war and engage in binding treaties with indigenous peoples or European competitors, and develop unique social institutions. In an important sense they are a leap of faith by the royal sovereign that their delegated authority would be respected and upheld in new lands.'[180]

The features of proprietary governments and representative systems explained in Part II were also observed in the proprietary colonies. For example, possessions of the proprietary governments were more likely to be sold or leased than those of corporations.[181] And as the members in a corporate colonial government decreased in number, they behaved more like proprietors.[182] Since the rational ignorance

[180] Banks (2007), pp. 80-81.

[181] See Osgood (1897), pp. 655-656: 'But the proprietary province was subject to the conditions of natural inheritance, testate and intestate, and to all the possibilities of change and multiplication of owners involved therein. Moreover the possessions of proprietors were more likely to be sold or leased than were those held by corporations. In other words the proprietary province was treated as an estate of land. It was a vast tenement which the grantee did or might sell, mortgage, lease, devise, or convey in trust, as he would a farm or a homestead.'

[182] See Osgood (1896a), p. 275: 'As the attendance and membership fell off, the council became more and more like a board of proprietors. Because its membership was limited to forty, and none of those intended ever to settle in New England, all the colonists under this system must be

and rational irrationality of participants in such systems increases in the number of participants, this can be expected *a priori*.[183]

The Dutch proprietary companies, the trading companies, took the form of joint-stock corporations. The *West-Indische Compagnie*, the Dutch West India Company, was subject to more government involvement because it had a relatively important role in the Dutch war of independence against Spain, the Eighty Years War. It served both commercial and geopolitical ends in the Western Hemisphere. In North America, it founded New Amsterdam, which later became New York after the WIC had to yield it to the English.

In its American colonisation, the WIC did not only establish its own settlements but also allowed for the establishment of lower-level proprietary jurisdictions, called *patroonschappen*.[184] These were granted to merchants who participated in the WIC. Their rights of government were extensive, including rights to the natural resources as well as high, middle and low jurisdiction. As per article VII of the 1629 charter of Freedoms and Exemptions and later repeated in the 1640 and 1650 charters, owners of these jurisdictions could apply for *venia testandi* – the right to grant their jurisdictions to others.[185] This gave their jurisdictions alienability, but only with approval from higher authorities. Dutch proprietary jurisdictions were not new at the time, as they already existed in the Dutch Republic in the form of the *heerlijkheden*. By the proprietary, i.e. alienable, nature of rights

tenants or simply inhabitants. They could never become members of the governing body. The council, in other words, could never expand into a commonwealth. On the other hand, year by year it degenerated toward a proprietorship; and in fact that was the governmental form which it most resembled, and toward which the inclinations of its members naturally gravitated.'

183 See Section 5.1.

184 See Jacobs (2007).

185 See Fabius (1915), p. 563. For the 1650 charter, see Brodhead (1856), p. 402.

of government over the *heerlijkheden*, local governance was in much of the Republic proprietary.

The *Vereenigde Oostindische Compagnie*, also known as the Dutch East India Company, also had sovereign powers. As its name suggests, it operated in a different arena, which it dominated. While not given free reign, the VOC was spared from the extent of involvement by the Republic that the WIC was subject to. This was partly because it was less important in its area of operation, as the Dutch Republic's adversaries had a smaller presence there. What also played a role was its distance from home, which made communication more difficult as it took more time for messages to go back and forth. The VOC was much more profitable than the WIC. After ousting the Portuguese from the East Indies, it was able to monopolise the East Indian spice trade by force. Its monopoly was never absolute, but allowed it to make enormous profits. As Jan Pieterszoon Coen, the governor-general of the VOC who directed the company in its rise to dominance, wrote to his directors in Amsterdam:

> Your Honours know by experience that trade in Asia must be driven and maintained under the protection and favour of Your Honours' own weapons, and that the weapons must be paid for by the profits from the trade; so that we cannot carry on trade without war nor war without trade.'[186]

The French proprietary companies relied heavily on investment and involvement from the French state and were therefore significantly less proprietary than their Dutch and English counterparts.[187] Two of these companies, the *Compagnie des Indes Orientales* and *Compagnie des Indes Occidentales*, respectively Company of the East Indies and Company of the West Indies, are good examples of this. They were established at the behest of king Louis XIV's mercantilist minister, Jean-Baptiste Colbert, and were used as geopolitical tools to em-

186 Phillips & Sharman (2015), p. 109

187 Banks (2007), pp. 80-81

ulate and compete with their Dutch competitors.[188] To this end they were given the usual governmental rights and privileges, including the rights to arm ships, raise armies and manufacture armaments. In particular the *Compagnie des Indes Occidentales*, like the Dutch West India Company, was subject to extensive state involvement, which is understandable considering the intensity of military competition between trading companies in the Western hemisphere. It was established and used as a government-led military and commercial organisation in the form of a semi-proprietary government.[189] Other examples of French proprietary governments overseas can be found in both the Caribbean and in North America.[190]

The English proprietary companies were, more so than their Dutch and French counterparts, established for the purpose of colonisation. They were therefore given rights of government, which they needed to make their colonies succeed. While the French and Dutch companies were intended primarily as trading companies and military enterprises to undermine the overseas endeavours of rival states, the English proprietary companies prioritised colonisation in North America. By a 1609 royal charter, the first English proprietary company with jurisdiction in America was incorporated as a joint-stock company called 'The Treasurer and Company of Adventurers and Planters of the City of London for the First Colony in Virginia'. Originally, the group of patentees was granted a royal charter in 1606 to colonise Virginia, but not as a fully proprietary venture. It was originally thought to be more successful as a royal colony, because state support and the resulting prestige of the project would encourage contributions to it and make foreign nations less likely to harm it. Initially, the rights of government were therefore still in hands of the Crown, by its right to appoint the members of the

188 Ibid. p. 88

189 Ibid. p. 89

190 For an account of French colonisation efforts in the Caribbean, see Boucher (2007). For accounts of French proprietary governance in North America, see Choquette (2007) and Vidal (2007).

council that governed the colony. Members were partly chosen from the patentees.[191] However, after failing to successfully establish a colony, the company secured a new charter in 1609 which granted it governmental powers and another charter in 1612 which confirmed the company's rights of government. Thereby, it obtained substantial independence from the Crown and became a true proprietary company. The company existed for fifteen years and for a brief period also governed the Bermuda Islands, but these were soon brought under the rule of a separate corporation, the members of which largely came from the London company.[192]

Later proprietary companies took inspiration from the London company in organising themselves. One example is the company that colonised New England. It was bestowed powers of government by royal charter and was called the 'Council established at Plymouth in the County of Devon of the Planting, Ruling, and Governing of New England in America.'

The trading companies were primarily proprietary governments to fend for themselves and obtain trade monopolies, not to govern their jurisdictions. In Africa and the East Indies, governance was left to local rulers because the companies only sought to monopolise markets by force and survive militarily. In the West Indies, they also served a military and geostrategic role for their countries and engaged in colonisation, which is why they were respectively under larger state involvement and given rights to govern their colonies.

The trading companies were simultaneously proprietary governments because their business moved them into an anarchic realm. They acquired their goods in areas where no government effectively enforced rights and did so in competition with trading companies from other countries. While they were protected from domestic competition by the monopolies they were granted, they were not protected from international competition, which was not overseen by any government. There was no government oversight on the seas, nor any treaties, trade agreements, or any other effective interna-

191 Osgood (1904), pp. 25-31

192 Ibid. pp. 55-58

tional mechanism to ensure peaceful competition. The trading companies were therefore given rights of government to fend for themselves and monopolise the supply of their goods.

The purely colonial companies, on the other hand, which came mostly from England and France, were granted rights of government for the purpose of governing their colonies.

The account of the proprietary colonial governments and trading companies in this section is far from exhaustive. Entire books have been written about their history and this section does not address their role in the later African colonies, for which I currently do not have the time. These examples are only meant to explain the origins of proprietary governance in the New World and Asia, and the purposes for which proprietary governments were established at the time.

## SIMILAR TYPES

Various forms of government similar to the proprietary government can be found in colonial history, but these were not truly proprietary nor are they referred to as such. For example, for the colonisation of Brazil, the Portuguese crown instituted 'donatary captaincies' by royal charter. The relationship between the king and the donatary captain was essentially feudal, not proprietary. The donatary captaincies were granted to men close to the king and were heritable, but inalienable except in a few exceptional cases with explicit royal permission.[193] Whether this system is to be seen as 'capitalist' or feudal is contested, since the domains of the donatary captaincies were at first governed with the profit motive.[194] Despite the profit-oriented governance by the initial captains, the system was still feudal and the alienability of the jurisdictions was severely limited. They were in principle only heritable, so whereas the original grantees governed their domains to earn a profit, their

[193] Augeron & Vidal (2007), pp. 26 and 49

[194] Ibid. pp. 28-29

successors were not necessarily most competent or motivated at doing so.

In the English 'corporate' colonial governments, participatory rights were not freely alienable and therefore could not be accumulated. Initially, these governments behaved much like the proprietary companies because they had few participants and were not their own subjects.[195] They were cooperatives and therefore more like clubs or associations. When the number of their patentees increased, they were transformed into representative systems[196] and their behaviour started to deviate from that of the proprietary companies.

## THREE CATEGORIES OF COLONIAL GOVERNMENT

As explained in Section 4.6, governments are characterised by their rights of government. The charters that were granted to colonial governments bestowed on them extensive rights of government over their colonies, including rights to assemble armies, establish courts, appoint governors and impose capital punishments. What distinguishes the different types of governments are the specific limitations to the alienability of their rights of government. In the feudal system, which includes the royal colonies and the donatary captaincies, the rights of government were in principle heritable but not alienable. In the proprietary and corporate colonies, the rights of government took the form of voting rights held by the participants, who were called 'freemen', 'adventurers' or 'patentees'. The corporate colonial government took the form of a cooperative. The alienability of its voting rights was limited such that they could not be accumulated. After growing in membership and moving into the colony, a corporate colonial government therefore developed a representative system. In the proprietary system, the alienability of voting rights was unlimited or as good as unlimited, such

[195] For an example of this relationship, see footnote 181.

[196] See footnote 178.

that they could be transferred to others more suited for the roles that they bestow on their holders. In colonial history, the feudal, the cooperative and the proprietary government can all be found.

The proprietary government therefore does not relate to colonialism more than other types of government do. Contrary to what some detractors of proprietary governance may assert, history does not point to any special relationship between proprietary governance and colonialism.

## 13.2 LORDSHIPS

Outside the colonies, proprietary jurisdictions already existed at the local level in the form of alienable lordships. Lordships were lower-level jurisdictions that first emerged in feudalism and endured until after the Middle Ages. In some countries they were proprietary, while in others they were not.

In England, the lordships were mostly alienable throughout their history. Their proprietors, the 'lords of the manor', initially held extensive 'manorial rights' – their rights of government. This made the lordship an important level of government in medieval society. The lord of the manor administered justice, provided arbitration in disputes, facilitated trade, fulfilled other governmental roles and possessed rights to extract natural resources.[197] Thereby, lordships were a source of considerable income for those who held them. A lord's role was essentially governmental, because he did not necessarily own the lands over which he ruled. Many of these lands were sold to third parties, leaving him only *seignory* over them – the rights of government a lord keeps after he grants an estate.[198] Lords could possess manorial rights over many manors at once, which was also a source of prestige at the time. Over the centuries, mano-

[197] See Lord of the Manor – Lordship Rights in Law, in the reference section.

[198] See Seignory, in the reference section.

rial rights diminished. By the end of the Middle Ages, the lordships had significantly less autonomy.

Elsewhere in Europe, lordships included similar rights of government. In the Netherlands, nobles started to sell their lordships, called *heerlijkheden*, around 1500. Buyers were mainly wealthy merchants and a class of rulers known as regents.[199] As in other countries, lordships were the lower-level jurisdictions of the Netherlands. Lords provided policing, courts, basic infrastructure and other government goods and services. The heerlijkheden, as proprietary jurisdictions, changed hands among burghers. By acquiring a heerlijkheid, a wealthy burgher such as a merchant or regent could add the title of 'heer' (lord) to his name and obtained hunting rights, which were valued status symbols. After the revolt of 1579, which resulted in the Republic of the Seven United Provinces, the ruling class consisted mostly of a non-noble elite of merchants and regents, whose surnames nonetheless often resembled those of noble families. By acquiring a lordship, a burgher could add the name of his lordship to his surname. A merchant bearing the surname Deutz, for example, could use the name 'Deutz van Assendelft' after acquiring the lordship of Assendelft.

The heerlijkheden were abolished in the 1790s, after the French invasion of 1795 and the founding of the Batavian Republic. The last remnants of the heerlijkheden disappeared in Belgium in 1830 and in the Netherlands in 1848. The heerlijkheden were replaced by the municipalities in their administrative functions and by the national government in their arbitrational and judicial functions.

Like the Dutch heerlijkheden, the French lordships, called *seigneuries*, became alienable after the feudal era. Rich commoners started to acquire seigneuries, which was a requirement for ascendance into the nobility. The German lordships of the Holy Roman Empire, called *herrschaften,* were similar to those in other countries, except for the existence of immediate herrschaften. An immediate herrschaft, as opposed to a mediate one, did not fall under the higher-level jurisdiction of a duke, margrave, count, prince or similar authority. Instead, they were only subject to the emperor's higher-level jurisdiction.

[199] Janse (2002)

## WHY LORDSHIPS BECAME ALIENABLE

Lordships were originally inalienable because higher-level rulers needed the loyalty of lower-level rulers to fend off hostile lower-level rulers and outside threats. To wage war, a king needed the knights and soldiers sent by his nobles. Intergovernmental relationships were personal and mostly based on loyalty. To align the interests, families often married off their children to each other. These relationships would be impossible if rights of government were alienable. If rights of government could be alienated, governments would have to reestablish new personal relationships with new governments and find out whether a new government could be trusted. Arranged marriages would not work because one could not trust that the other side would keep their rights of government. Loyalty and personal relationships required lasting relationships between families and thus required inalienability in the rights of government.

Later, when states were centralised, populations urbanised and wars were fought by mercenaries, lower-level rights of government became alienable. The loyalty of lower-level lords became less important for several reasons. First, the king could amass an army with his own money, one that could overpower any lord's defences. At the end of the Dark Ages, the invention of gunpowder improved offensive capabilities. This weakened lower-level governments while strengthening higher-level governments, obviating the loyalty of the former to the latter. Lower-level lords also no longer needed each other's loyalty, as higher-level governments could use their superior military power to keep lower-level lords at peace with each other. Second, state formation, i.e. the development of effective administrative apparatuses, made governments better at enforcing their own rights. Third, urbanisation made local lords less significant economically and less powerful militarily. The loyalty of local lords therefore became relatively less important. As a result of these factors, relationships between feudal rulers did not need to be personal anymore, as loyalty lost its value. Lordships could thus finally become alienable.

## 13.3 THE FEUDAL SYSTEM VERSUS THE PROPRIETARY SYSTEM

In much of the history of commerce, enterprise was almost exclusively a family affair. Before the advent of the joint-stock corporation, the number of participants in an enterprise was limited because that institutional innovation enabled large numbers of people to participate. In the feudal system, the enterprise of government was also a family affair. Rights of government were held by families and were obtained by inheritance. When rights of government were bestowed, their recipients could only leave them to their heirs. Although there were exceptions to this in the form of lordships, these only existed at lower levels. Centuries later, in the age of the trading companies, proprietary governments emerged with complete rights of government overseas. However, most European governments were still feudal, with some exceptions in the form of cooperatives and theocratic organisations.

Governance has in many ways evolved in lockstep with other types of endeavours – Small firms were replaced by large firms and personal relationships by impersonal relationships. In the feudal system, many people knew and interacted with their lords personally, but the expansion of state apparatuses replaced this with interaction between civil servants and citizens. Like other enterprises, government has become systematized. But while property rights have become well-defined and tradeable in almost all sectors, this does not apply to governance. Instead of proprietary governments taking their place, feudal governments have been replaced by cooperatives in the form of representative systems. As explained in chapters 10 and 11, governance cooperatives have some unique benefits, but also great costs. Their creation was not without reason, but they did not need to replace other systems at all government levels.

Instead of being replaced by representative systems, feudal governments could have evolved into proprietary governments. Especially at lower levels, that is, at the levels of dukes, counts, barons, lords and so on, they did not have to be replaced by representative municipalities. Had they evolved into proprietary systems at lower levels, people could have enjoyed the benefits of both proprietary and representative governance. Besides, the centralisation of governance would not have been necessary. Proprietary governments could have had extensive autonomy on regional and local levels because they could have been functional at these levels and contracted with each other for shared interests.

Most feudal governments could thus have been the precursors to proprietary governments. Perhaps, one day, we will see how good their governance would have been.

CHAPTER 14.

# THE FUTURE OF THE PROPRIETARY JURISDICTION

## 14.1 POTENTIAL FOR IMPLEMENTATION

### DEVELOPING COUNTRIES

Many poor countries are held back by failing institutions. Their politicians and civil servants do not act in ways conducive to economic prosperity, but instead engage in rent-seeking and inefficient policy making, thereby keeping the country in its underdeveloped state. The solution to their woes is therefore institutional – Their government systems must be improved. Besides, poor countries will probably be more open to privatising jurisdictions as they have more to gain and are more desperate for solutions to their problems. Whereas rich countries have more to lose and less to gain from trying out new forms of government, the opposite holds for poor countries.

In poor countries, it is often the interests of rent-seeking elites that keep them from liberalising the economy and improving government systems for economic development. However, as explained in Section 12.3, it can be made in the interest of a rent-seeking elite to support the privatisation of a jurisdiction by giving them stakes in the proprietary government. Besides, proprietary jurisdictions can start small, such that rent-seeking elites who do not participate in the proprietary government are not harmed much in their incomes. In fact, because of backward linkages, these elites even stand to benefit as well.

To convince rulers and elites in poor countries of the benefits of privatising their jurisdictions, it is also important that the first proprietary jurisdictions clearly fulfil their promises. Rulers, elites and electorates, who are unlikely to be familiar with the theory of proprietary governance and are therefore more likely to be convinced by empirical cases, will then be more supportive of privatising their own jurisdictions. To make states open their doors for proprietary governance, it is thus important that the first projects succeed and that their benefits are publicised well. The Honduran ZEDEs could fulfil this role.

This could also widen perspectives in the international development community. Western elites, firmly educated to believe that representative democracy is optimal for the entire world, must realise that imposing this system has done much harm to the economies of developing countries. Furthermore, the efforts of development economists, international development agencies, charities and NGOs have been fruitless with few exceptions. Many countries in the third world would be better off if they were ruled by proprietary governments. Opposition to proprietary governance could condemn a great number of people to a life of poverty.

## REFUGEE CITIES

As briefly explained in Section 12.3, one type of proprietary jurisdiction that may receive much support is the 'refugee city' or the 'refugee zone' – A zone specially built and governed to provide a haven for refugees, where they are given employment opportunities, education, and the possibility of staying or arranging their move on to other places. These zones are best created as proprietary jurisdictions and are likely to be very profitable while greatly improving the lives of the refugees they accommodate. This may make privatising jurisdictions more attractive to both governments and their subjects, as well as reduce hostility to refugees.

Governments collectively spend billions to limit the influx of asylum seekers, among whom are both refugees and illegal migrants. Instead of keeping these migrants in camps, where they are mostly idle, they can be accommodated in proprietary jurisdictions. There, they can work and receive education, and are likely to be governed much better. These settlements can be self-sustaining and profitable for the host country. Refugee cities could therefore receive strong support from governments in both the developing and the developed world. Perhaps the governments of immigration countries will be willing to finance refugee cities and support efforts for enabling legislation in potential host countries.

As Michael Castle-Miller, a consultant in the special economic zone sector, explains:

> For countries hosting large numbers of refugees, refugee cities convert a perceived problem into an economic growth opportunity. Since these countries cannot keep migrants outside their borders for both practical and political reasons, they must decide how they will handle migrants. If they house migrants in typical camps without economic opportunities, the migrants will tend to drain public resources and possibly become more prone to radicalization and violence. The migrants will also tend to find ways to leave or avoid the camps and instead work in the informal sector "where they have less of a positive impact on the economy than if they were allowed to work legally." On the other hand, efforts to allow refugees to work anywhere in the country face overwhelming political resistance, especially due to the fear that they will take away employment opportunities from citizens.
>
> Refugee cities would help countries realize some of the potential benefits of refugees by designating new spaces where refugees can work and start businesses, and where new foreign investment can be brought in, without competing for existing resources in existing spaces. Host populations could also live and work in the new spaces and benefit from the opportunities and infrastructure developed there.
>
> Refugee cities are better tools for accomplishing the goals of refugee camps. Host countries often use refugee camps to cluster refugees to facilitate aid distribution, avoid competition for jobs, and more easily locate and, eventually, repatriate them. Camps often do not accomplish this goal well, however, since refugees often avoid them because of the few economic opportunities there. Refugee cities can reverse this trend by attracting migrants rather than repelling them.
>
> ...

Refugee cities can also offer the international community a more cost-effective response to refugee crises than existing humanitarian methods. International organizations traditionally respond to mass migration with food aid, tents, water, basic security, and emergency medical care. Refugee cities would offer these services, while also creating a platform for migrants to become self-supporting. Private capital can be invested in real estate, businesses, and infrastructure and can generate returns from these productive assets. Donor institutions can simply facilitate and abet this investment through technical support, investment guarantees, and monitoring and evaluation.

For developed countries, such as in Europe, that are weary or fearful of migrants passing through refugee hosting countries and entering their territory, refugee cities could provide refugees with other attractive areas for settling. Rather than attempting to find opportunities in an advanced economy, they can find opportunities in the countries hosting them.

...

Refugee cities can also open up new markets and underutilized talent pools for foreign and domestic investors. Refugees and other migrants are perhaps often among the most motivated and enterprising workers, and yet their abilities are normally withheld from the labor force. Businesses in a refugee city could benefit from their abilities, as well as from other regulatory and business environment reforms introduced from the SEZ concept.

...

Most importantly, refugee cities allow migrants themselves an often-rare opportunity to benefit themselves and their families through their own work. They can earn income, experience the psychological benefits of meaningful work, and, perhaps, help rebuild their home countries from a better position than if they had lived in a refugee camp.[200]

## SPECIAL ECONOMIC ZONES

So-called 'special economic zones' are zones specially designated for different legislation and administration. They enable governments to test new policies and make reforms without having to do so in their entire jurisdictions. Many special economic zones, however, have failed. They are often too small, poorly located or subject to the same governance problems as the rest of the countries they are located in. Non-private special economic zones can also be subject to rent-seeking and are often poorly invested in.[201] By turning special economic zones into proprietary jurisdictions and by promoting new proprietary zones, they can be made more successful. Countries that have already made large investments into special economic zones that are at risk of being wasted if these zones do not become successful, have a strong interest in allowing these zones to become proprietarily governed.

This can easily be done through devolution, possibly combined with further deregulation. Special economic zones are then turned into proprietary jurisdictions by simply giving up the right to regulate the devolved policy domains.

## REPLACING DYSFUNCTIONAL REPRESENTATIVE SYSTEMS WITH BETTER ONES

Many poor countries in the world are governed by representative systems, which are often corrupt and inefficient. A way to replace such a dysfunctional representative system by a better one, which can

200 Castle-Miller (2018). For two more articles on refugee cities, see Cleppe (2016) and Smith & Cleppe (2015).

201 See Part I The Theory of Zone Politics, in Moberg (2017), pp. 21-103.

be done with both higher-level and lower-level governments, is the following.

First, parts of a jurisdictions are privatised. To ensure that corrupt politicians will not seek to counter their privatisation, these parts are made small enough and expanded incrementally until the entire jurisdiction is privatised. A 'salami tactic' is thereby used against rent-seeking elites. To buy their support, corrupt elites can also be given stakes in the proprietary jurisdiction. Meanwhile, the proprietary governments are bound to agreements that force them to establish a rule of law and to transfer their rights of government, either at one point in the future or gradually, to subjects in the form of inalienable voting rights.

For example, every election cycle the proprietary government could issue voting rights at random to 1/20th of its eligible electorate. The weighting of these votes are then made to be 1/20th of the total weighting of all voting rights, including alienable shares. These newly issued voting rights are then inalienable and distributed randomly to 1/20th of the eligible electorate. Every election cycle, the voting rights randomly distributed among the eligible electorate grows by 1/20th of the electorate. 1/20th of the eligible electorate then votes in the first election cycle, 2/20th of them vote in the second cycle, and so on. After twenty election cycles, the complete rights of government over the jurisdiction take the form of non-proprietary voting rights distributed to the entire eligible electorate according to the one man, one vote rule.

Alternatively, the entire eligible electorate can also be given voting rights first, of which the weighting is then gradually increased at the expense of the weightings of the proprietary shares. This has the advantage that no unfair random distribution of voting rights can take place, nor any meddling in their distribution, but may at first lead to low voter turnout.

In either case, the government has then fostered economic growth and built up a civil service when it was proprietary, and has subsequently become a functional, non-corrupt representative system. Its institutional integrity results from the incentive systems that the initial owners created to combat corruption and protect their rights. A constrained proprietary system is better for prosperity than a corrupt representative system is, which is only representative in name. Both before and after the system becomes representative again, the subject therefore stand to benefit.

It is difficult to transform a corrupt representative system into a functional one, because it is against the interests of the corrupt elite to allow this. The winners of the game are generally against changing the rules, because the rules work in their favour. But it is possible to align their interests with privatising their jurisdiction or parts of it, and a proprietary system can be designed such that it is subsequently transformed into a functional representative system and fosters prosperity in the meantime.

## 14.2 INSTITUTIONAL FAILURE IN THE AGE OF THE SOVEREIGN INDIVIDUAL

As Hansmann explained in his book, cooperatives tend to become more like nonprofits as their members become more transitory, numerous or dispersed. Their members then become more passive, which allows their administrators to act without effective oversight over them. Besides, their administrators are then elected more frivolously because of rational ignorance and rational irrationality on the part of their members. As members become more transitory, numerous and dispersed, cooperatives thus become more vulnerable to institutional capture and corruption.

As explained in Section 11.7, the representative system is in fact a 'governance cooperative'. It is a consumer cooperative that fulfils the role of government, and therein delivers the benefits of the consumer cooperative that other forms of government do not. The members of governance cooperatives have always been numerous, but they are now also becoming increasingly transitory and dispersed. Rational ignorance and rational irrationality can therefore be expected to increase. Furthermore, as many immigrants at least initially speak their new country's language poorly, their voting behaviour is less likely to be based on any political viewpoints and more likely on ethnic and religious identity. As immigrants tend to stick to their own ethnic and religious communities, particularism can also be expected to increase.

Besides voter passivity, tribalistic politics and particularism, there are more reasons why representative systems can be expected to become more dysfunctional. Migration has become much less costly, and people tend to go where they are treated best. As language barriers and travel costs become smaller, governments will have to keep their tax rates competitively low to keep their most productive taxpayers. Tax competition has already limited government revenues from certain sources, such as corporate taxation, and can be expected to increase even further, especially in the domain of income taxation. This will inevitably result in smaller welfare states, causing increasing polarisation, social unrest and political radicalism.

Meanwhile, the institutional arrangements that maintain the integrity of the representative system tend to erode over time. The winners of the game get to change the rules. As any student of the United States' constitutional and legal history knows, restrictions of a government's rights to govern and tax are by no means permanent. When it suits the incumbent administrators, these restrictions can often be removed or outright ignored.

Representative systems can therefore be expected to become more dysfunctional over time. As people and legal entities become more mobile and as the institutional integrity of cooperative systems erodes further, the institutional conditions for prosperity can be expected to worsen. More countries will need better political institutions and this cannot always be done by improving the systems that already exist. Sometimes, new systems are necessary. The proprietary system can fulfil that role. As explained in Chapter 12, different variants of the proprietary jurisdiction can be created in different ways for different political contexts. As opposed to improving existing institutions, privatising jurisdictions can be made in the interests of incumbent elites and is therefore more viable. And as explained in Section 14.1, it can also replace failing representative systems with better ones. The benefits of representative governance therefore do not need to be sacrificed.

CHAPTER 15.

# PROPRIETARIANISM IN COMPARISON

## 15.1 THE PROPRIETARY STATE VERSUS SIMILAR IDEAS AND ALTERNATIVE TERMINOLOGY

After its limited existence in history and after receiving some attention from historians, the proprietary jurisdiction has gained increasing attention in recent years. This attention has come from four writers in particular. One is Curtis Yarvin, under the alias Mencius Moldbug, who described his own vision for the proprietary government in his article series titled 'Patchwork: A Political System for the 21st Century'.[202] More recently, books have been written about different variants of the proprietary jurisdiction by Titus Gebel, Tom W. Bell and a writer using the alias Calvin Duke.[203] These four writers seem to have been the first to address the idea of proprietary governance, but a rigorous theory of proprietary governance has not yet emerged. Besides, theorists in this field have been using different terms to describe roughly the same idea, i.e. a territory governed by a private corporation with a profit motive. These terms include the term 'free private city' coined by Titus Gebel and 'entrepreneurial community' as used by Calvin Duke. Each writer, myself included, has used his own unique terminology, perhaps because this subject has scarcely been explored until recently.

[202] Mencius Moldbug (2008)

[203] Gebel (2018), Bell (2017), Calvin Duke (2020)

In this section, I will first explain some problems with the terminology used by writers other than myself, as well as the differences between their ideas and the idea of the proprietary jurisdiction. I will explain why the terms 'proprietary jurisdiction' and 'proprietary government', both semantically and historically correct, are most suitable for referring to such a jurisdiction and its government. Lastly, I will compare the idea of the charter city with that of the proprietary jurisdiction. It is important not to confuse the two.

## THE FREE PRIVATE CITY

In his book, 'Free Private Cities: Making Governments Compete for You', Titus Gebel conceives his idea of the 'free private city' as a place governed by a for-profit company acting as a 'government service provider'. This roughly corresponds with the idea of the proprietary jurisdiction. However, if 'free private city' is to refer to a liberal, urbanised jurisdiction as the name suggests, it cannot refer to every proprietary jurisdiction. A proprietary jurisdiction is not necessarily 'free'. Proprietary governance can be as invasive as the proprietary government wants. A proprietary government may for example prefer to impose Islamic law instead of liberal policies. There are millions of people globally who do not mind living in such a jurisdiction. Or it can be a night's watchman state, in which the government only enforces rights and does nothing else. Surely, there are also some who would prefer to live in such a jurisdiction. Proprietary jurisdictions are thus not necessarily 'free', but some of them probably will be.

The last word, 'city', also narrows the term by making it refer exclusively to urbanised areas. But not all proprietary jurisdictions have to be urbanised. Some may for example be established for agricultural purposes, while others may have both high-density and low-density settlements.

The term 'free private city' refers, if used in a semantically correct way, to a narrower category of jurisdictions than 'proprietary jurisdiction'. It must be said, however, that Gebel did not exclude the possibility of illiberal free private cities, nor did he restrict the category to urban jurisdictions. But then the term is unfit for his purpose.

Gebel also includes the possibility of free private cities governed by representative systems, which he correctly calls cooperatives.[204] But this also leads to a problem. If 'private' is to mean 'non-governmental', as it commonly does, and a free private city is to be governed by a cooperative, then the cooperative cannot be a government. That is, it cannot have rights of government, including a right to superior force. But how can such a jurisdiction then prosper? The functions that a government fulfils are crucial for human prosperity and require corresponding rights of government. Alternatively, if private is not to mean 'non-governmental' and the private nature of a free private city lies in the alienability of the rights of government over it, it cannot be a cooperative. In either case, the idea that a free private city can be governed by a cooperative is incorrect.

Moreover, as explained in this book, because of the inalienability and dispersion of voting rights that it requires, a governance cooperative has the problems that are endemic in all representative systems. That is, corruption, bureaucracy, inefficiency, incompetence, irrational and ideological policy making and so on. If the free private city is to deliver the benefits promised by Gebel, it cannot be governed by a cooperative, i.e. by a representative system.

The free private city as conceived by Titus Gebel and the proprietary jurisdiction thus differ in crucial respects, and the terms refer to different categories of jurisdictions. The term 'proprietary jurisdiction' as defined in this book is not subject to the other restrictions in the term 'free private city'. It is then either a more suitable term or it is a broader category of jurisdictions bound together by their proprietary nature, i.e. the alienability of the rights of government over them.

## THE CITIZEN'S CONTRACT

As Gebel explains, presence in a free private city is voluntary and the government is bound by what he calls the 'citizen's contract'. This contract is an equivalent of the social contract that according to

204 Gebel (2023)

some theorists, starting with Rousseau, underlies our relationships with our governments. The citizen's contract, as explained by Gebel, is an explicit contract between the government and its subjects that is agreed to by both parties. Like any other contract, it cannot be changed unilaterally by either party. Any change to it requires the consent of all parties involved, in contrast to the unilateral changes to the law that are made by the world's current non-proprietary governments.

As conceived in this book, the government sets the terms of the government-subject relationship and the subject agrees to those terms by choosing to be subordinated to it. If the subject is free to leave, unless he has given up the right to do so, this arrangement of rights is to count as contract. It is as legitimate and consensual as the citizen's contract conceived by Gebel. Every moment the subject decides to stay, he re-enters the government-subject relationship according to the laws made by the government. An explicit citizen's contract as conceived by Gebel is not necessary for the subordination to be consensual, and thus for proprietary democracy, in which people 'vote with their feet'. Governance is a club good, and like any other club the government should in principle be allowed to change its rules unilaterally. Subjects should then in principle be free to end their 'membership'. No subject is then forced to accept any terms. If the government and a subject then wish to enter into a contract that gives the subject special terms to subordination, this is still possible. But non-proprietary governments, including the world's present governments, can already do this. The citizen's contract is then not a unique feature of a free private city. It is possible in all government-subject relationships, regardless of the form of government.

Moreover, what if the citizen's contract gives the government the right to unilaterally change some of its laws? Some of the subject's rights may then not require his consent to be withdrawn. This governmental discretion is then consented to by the subject while specific unilateral changes to the law do not require the subject's consent. If a citizen's contract as defined by Gebel cannot allow for this, the government and its subjects must be constrained in their freedom of contract. They cannot then enter into a government-subject relationship, however consensual, in which the government can unilaterally change some of its laws. This can only prevent mutually preferred government-subject relationships.

Finally, the citizen's contract refers to a class of people other than subjects, even though the two groups overlap. If it were semantically correct, it would therefore not apply to subjects who do not possess citizenship, but this is a benign inaccuracy.

## THE ENTREPRENEURIAL COMMUNITY

In his eponymous book[205], Calvin Duke uses the term 'entrepreneurial community' to refer to the proprietary jurisdiction, thereby following the terminology used by Spencer Heath MacCallum.[206] I have chosen not to use the term first because of its ambiguity, as many different things can be called 'entrepreneurial communities'. For example, it could refer to social clubs for entrepreneurs, to particular ethnic groups, or to towns with many entrepreneurs. It is easy to see what 'representative democracy' refers to, because its defining characteristics are reflected by its name. The same holds for 'dictatorship', 'hereditary monarchy' and the terms 'proprietary jurisdiction' and 'proprietary government', but not 'entrepreneurial community'. Second, if it includes non-governmental communities based on real estate ownership, as originally conceived by Spencer Heath, it cannot fulfil the roles of the state. This has been explained in Section 5.4.

## THE CHARTER CITY

Charter cities, broadly defined, are cities that have been granted special jurisdictions to create new systems of governance.[207] The Charter Cities Institute defines them as 'new cities with new rules'.

[205] Calvin Duke (2020)

[206] For example in MacCallum (2003). See also MacCallum (1997).

[207] See An Introduction to Charter Cities, referred to in the reference section.

According to this definition, a charter city may or may not be governed by a proprietary government. Nor does it have to be governed by another specific type of government. The original definition given by its most prominent proponent, Paul Romer, is different. He conceived the charter city as a special jurisdiction in a developing country, but governed by a country with better institutions. Such a charter city could be in Africa, for example, but governed by the government of Denmark. Not long after its introduction by Romer, the idea was be branded as 'neo-colonial' because of its obvious similarities to the colonies. Both the definition used by the Charter Cities Institute and that of Paul Romer refer to an urban jurisdiction that is different from a proprietary jurisdiction. A proprietary jurisdiction is governed by a proprietary government and need not be urban.

## THE PROPRIETARY JURISDICTION AND THE PROPRIETARY GOVERNMENT

'Proprietary jurisdiction', on the other hand, refers to the distinctive feature of the rights of government over it – They are proprietary, i.e. alienable. The term 'proprietary government' is appropriate for the same reason. These terms are unlikely to be misunderstood, are not already used to refer to other ideas and do not suffer from the problems that the terms addressed above suffer from.

Moreover, as explained in Section 5.3, the terms 'proprietary government' and 'proprietary jurisdiction' accord with the terms that have been used to refer to historical proprietary governments. Some of the world's first proprietary jurisdictions, the seventeenth-century 'proprietary colonies', were governed by 'proprietary governors'. In eighteenth-century discourse and later historical literature on these jurisdictions, the term 'proprietary government' has been used to refer to their governments, which included both individuals and companies. The terminology I use therefore continues and conforms to historical terminology.

Besides, using the word 'proprietary' avoids a semantic controversy that could arise from using 'private' instead, because using the latter relies on a definition of private property that conflicts with common doctrine. 'Proprietary' here refers to the completeness of property in the rights of government that stems from their alienability, not necessarily to its thereby private nature. The terms 'proprietary jurisdiction' and 'proprietary government', as well as their conjugations, therefore seem to be the most appropriate and most likely to be accepted by economists.

As explained in Part III, proprietary governance does not necessarily deliver all its potential benefits. For it to do so, a number of conditions must be met, including at least those discussed in Chapter 8. Governments differ in important respects from all other groups of people. Most entrepreneurs and producers are subject to an arbiter, in the form of a government, that enforces rights and regulates entrepreneurs and producers as it sees fit. But governments are, in principle, not subject to such an arbiter. Institutional arrangements, such as those discussed in Chapter 10, must therefore be made to ensure that these conditions are satisfied as much as they can be, such that a proprietary jurisdiction delivers as much value to its subjects as possible and does not descend into tyranny instead. For the ideal thereby aimed for, under which the interests of a government are aligned with those of its subjects, the term 'proprietary democracy' is well suited. As this book argues, proprietary democracy is of paramount importance and measures must therefore be taken to promote it.

Moreover, it must be recognised that the now emerging proprietary governance sector cannot develop without the permission of non-proprietary governments. All of the world's habitable land is ruled by representative systems, dictatorships and hereditary monarchies. For proprietary governance to prove its potential by improving the lives of millions, the approval of such governments is necessary. These governments are all, to various extents, constrained by the whims of the public. Meanwhile, the idea of privatising the rights of government in representative systems, which would require the abolition or restriction of representative democracy in some places, is unlikely to appeal to anyone except perhaps libertarians. As a result, the permission of host governments will likely be difficult to obtain. So, to indicate that there can certainly be a form of democracy under a proprietary government, a democracy in which people 'vote with their feet', proprietary democracy can be a useful term. Using this term is in the interests of the entire sector and is more strategic than using the terms entrepreneurial community, charter city or free private city.

## CHARTER CITIES VERSUS PROPRIETARY JURISDICTIONS

Of the various types of new jurisdictions, the idea of the charter city has thus far received the most attention. But as explained above, the term now usually refers to an idea that is different from what Paul Romer, who conceived the term, originally meant. Originally, it referred to special jurisdictions in developing countries, governed by the governments of developed countries with better institutions. The Charter Cities Institute now defines it differently, namely as a 'new city with new rules'. The particular model advocated by the CCI takes the form of a public-private partnership in which private city developers are given seats on the governing council. This would not involve fully proprietary governance, but only some proprietary element.

Thus, neither the original idea of the charter city nor the CCI's definition of it concerns a proprietary jurisdiction. The problems of representative governance therefore also affect a charter city, although perhaps to a lesser extent. The proprietary government is the best form of government that can eliminate or mitigate the problems of representative governance that afflict developing countries. While charter cities allow countries with poor institutional environments to be governed by better governments, they do not solve the problems endemic to representative democracy. All representative systems, by their design, inevitably suffer from more corruption, more inefficiency, more ideological and incompetent policy making, and other problems. Proprietary jurisdictions are a solution to these problems, whereas charter cities can only mitigate them.

The CCI proposes to create charter cities on 'greenfield sites'. Existing government systems are often a source of rents for powerful elites, so turning existing settlements into charter cities can encounter their resistance. In the CCI's words:

> While economists largely agree on the importance of institutions for economic growth, reforms that change long-run growth rates are rarely implemented for public choice reasons. In existing jurisdictions, would-be improvements in governance are too often stifled by entrenched interests and ineffective bureaucracies. By creating a special jurisdiction in a new city built on

> greenfield land, charter cities avoid these public choice problems that often stymie reforms in existing jurisdictions without radically changing the rents enjoyed by elites in existing cities. Greenfield sites therefore allow for deeper institutional change than would otherwise be politically feasible.[208]

Unlike a charter city, a proprietary jurisdiction does not need a greenfield site because it can be organised to align entrenched interests. By giving entrenched elites shares in the proprietary government to compensate them for the rents they stand to lose from the privatisation of the jurisdiction, their interests are aligned with privatisation. Their support can thus be bought. In this way, proprietary governance can be introduced to existing settlements. Thus, a proprietary jurisdiction does not need a greenfield site and large development costs to be successful, whereas a charter city does.

A charter city, whether as originally defined or as defined by the CCI, thus differs from a proprietary jurisdiction in important ways. Unlike a proprietary jurisdiction, a charter city does not completely eliminate the problems of representative governance and needs much more capital to succeed, whereas a proprietary jurisdiction needs less capital and can align the entrenched interests in existing representative governments to subsequently remove them.

## THE NETWORK STATE

Finally, Balaji Srinivasan's idea of the 'network state' must be addressed, since it has become very popular in some circles.[209] According to Srinivasan, an online community could obtain permission to start their own jurisdiction somewhere once it has amassed enough members on the internet. However, a network state cannot

[208] See 'An Introduction to Charter Cities', Charter Cities Institute. Referred to in the reference section.

[209] Srinivasan (2022)

be proprietary. A proprietary network state would not be a network state for long. As in any proprietary system, voting rights would be accumulated by profit-oriented investors. Except any constitutional limitations, nothing will then keep them from catering to other groups than the network. Accordingly, the network state is conceived as some kind of representative system. In a network state, all the problems of representative systems are therefore bound to emerge. A network state is thus unlikely to be better than the states we are already familiar with. A network state may allow people to move to jurisdictions where people have more aligned preferences, but a proprietary government has an interest in catering to the preferences of every potential taxpayer. Proprietary governments will tailor their offerings to different segments of taxpayers insofar it is efficient to do so, so in that respect the proprietary state obviates the network state.

## 15.2 PROPRIETARIANISM VERSUS LIBERTARIANISM AND ANARCHO-CAPITALISM

The theory in this book, which is fully 'Austrian' by its method, challenges ideas commonly held by economists of the Austrian School. In particular, it contradicts libertarian and anarcho-capitalist ideas. Part II argues that governments can rule with the consent of their subjects and perform important functions for society, and challenges the anarcho-capitalist ideas that the state can be replaced by private protection agencies and that the very existence of a state is bad for society. Moreover, it explains that it is economic for the state to provide more than only the enforcement of rights. The theory in Chapter 7 challenges the idea of consumer sovereignty and concludes that governmental intervention can increase consumer sovereignty rather than decrease it. This book thus contradicts libertarian and anarcho-capitalist ideas by the same method that is commonly used to defend them.

The theory of the proprietary government not only refutes important ideas in libertarian and anarcho-capitalist ideology, but also points in the right direction. Whereas an anarcho-capitalist supports the abolition of the state and a libertarian supports its limitation, a proprietarian supports its privatisation.

## THE INEVITABILITY AND IMPORTANCE OF THE STATE

The state does not exist for no reason. Rights must be enforced, and providing enforcement requires the right to superior force. As explained in Sections 4.4 and 4.5, some people must have the supreme power to direct force over a territory in order to prevent violations of rights. In defence against this, anarcho-capitalists typically resort to two arguments – the alleged possibility of non-governmental enforcement, and examples of 'stateless' societies in the past.

One proponent of non-governmental enforcement is David Friedman. He argues that rights should be enforced by private protection agencies rather than by governments. The idea that this is a non-governmental solution is easily punctured. Any protection agency relies on a capacity to use force that is superior to that of the people it protects against. To be effective, it requires a superior capacity to direct the use of force, which it must maintain. This requires the right to superior force, and thus statehood. The protection agency's superior power to coerce would be unnecessary if its customers would already have this capacity. Therefore, if a protection agency is hired in the further absence of a state, such a protection agency can easily coerce the people it 'protects' into paying more than the value of their protection. As a result, their victims, or 'clients', then cannot hire other protection agencies to liberate them. This logically follows from the superior power to direct force that protection agencies need. And if clients could hire other protection agencies that have the power to liberate them from their current ones, why would their new agencies not, after 'liberating' them, coerce them instead? This has not been uncommon, when one ruler uses force against another to expand his rule. He may liberate the people from their present ruler, but only by replacing him with another one, viz., himself. The ability to use force is inevitable, as is the fact that one can benefit from using this ability violatively. Therefore, protection agencies would not necessarily be any different from governments as we know them.

Friedman also claims that competing private security companies would peacefully resolve all conflicts between themselves and their clients. But if this is to be expected of them, why are areas where the state is absent so underdeveloped and violent? Why are favelas so much more violent and unsafe than government-policed areas? Would competing gangs not resolve their conflicts peacefully?

If Friedman's expectations are realistic, then where are Biggie and Tupac?

He also claims that successful stateless societies have existed in the past. However, all examples of such 'anarchic societies' he and other point towards were primitive, small-scale societies that have no counterpart today. As Friedman recognised, their ways of resolving and preventing conflicts are not necessarily applicable in our world.[210]

## CONSENSUAL SUBORDINATION

As explained in Part II, voluntariness as a condition for human interaction is neither feasible nor desirable, however appealing it may sound. Instead, the efficient allocation of rights and the resulting cooperations that all contracting parties prefer to take place requires the congruity of actions with the rights that have been granted. The enforcement of rights can conflict with someone's will but is not necessarily wrong. Coercion is often congruous with rights and can therefore be based on consent.

Subordination to a government, however coercive, can be voluntarily agreed to. The government-subject relationship can be consensual and congruous. In this relationship, the subject grants the government its rights of government by choosing to be present within its jurisdiction.

One could contend that not everyone can make voluntary choices or that people should be restricted in their freedom even if they can. Consent is therefore not always possible or desirable. But this applies to everything that people in this category do. Children and the mentally impaired do not choose what they eat, where they live, or whether or not they are in subordination to a state. Children who are in subordination to governments have not chosen to be, but neither have children who are not. Consent is not always possible and neither is unconsent. Moreover, even if it were possible, restrictions on the freedom to consent are not necessarily wrong, as when par-

210 Friedman (1979)

ents restrict the freedom of their children. Parental restrictions on the freedom of children are not generally seen in a negative light – They are an essential part of responsible parenting.

One could also contend that the current arrangement of rights is illegitimate, since they do not originate exclusively from voluntarily established rights. Even though we are voluntarily subordinated, the state may have come into being without the consent of the governed. This may be true, but it is equally true in anarchy and applies to all rights. Even if all transfers of rights for the last thousands of years were voluntary, the properties to which they refer may originally have been acquired by conquest. In fact, all land was once first claimed without the consent of others. If this were to make current rights illegitimate, all rights would have to be rearranged in the transition to anarchy. Even if this were possible, would it be legitimate if most people alive today were only involved in voluntary transfers of rights? Moreover, the rights that have emerged are the result of deliberate, optimising decisions to eliminate Pareto inefficient courses of action. It would not be efficient to redistribute property in a transition to anarchy.

Thus, the rights of government are not any less legitimate than other rights and the subordination of people to governments is at least as legitimate as anarchy would be.

## GOVERNMENTAL ADMINISTRATIVE ENTREPRENEURSHIP

Anarchists and libertarians fail to see that administrative entrepreneurship by a state can create more value than it costs. The value of government regulation and intervention cannot be ignored. It is not without reason that the rights of government take the form they do.

Although some of the ideas of Spencer Heath MacCallum are contradicted in this book, he was right to point out the value of administrative entrepreneurship and that it is also provided by non-governmental entities. For example, non-governmental entities themselves have shown that zoning, much criticised by libertarians, can indeed add value:

> Shortly after the turn of the century, a handful of land developers including, among others, Edward

> H. Bouton of Baltimore, Jesse Clyde Nichols of Kansas City, Hugh Potter of Houston, and Hugh Prather of Dallas, found a common accord in their enthusiasm for the profit opportunities afforded by good land planning in subdivisions. Among the principles developed by these men was the thought that, if commercial land uses could be clustered and provided with a degree of orderly development instead of being strung out haphazardly, the value of both residential and commercial property would be protected, and blight and eventual deterioration of the whole area might be avoided. Convenient and attractive shopping facilities would enhance residential values, while good residential development nearby would boost commercial values.[211]

The rights of the government to govern its jurisdiction with such policies can result from consensual government-subject contracting. Governmental actions that are typically seen as coercive are in fact often efficient, and mostly rely on the consent of the governed. This is also true of many other government policies that are much criticised by libertarians and anarchists.

Take expropriation, for example. Suppose a property owner fully owns his property and makes the use of it conditional on consent to his right to regulate its use in certain ways. Since it is his own property, he is free to make its use conditional on these terms. Suppose he then sells a bundle of rights over his property. For instance, a limited right to use it, as well as the right to keep most of the income thereby generated and the right to transfer these rights to others. He keeps a purchasing option on this property, which he calls 'the right of expropriation' or, if he is an American, 'the right of eminent domain'. The right of expropriation is therefore granted voluntarily. How is this voluntary arrangement of rights, which should be possible and perfectly permissible in an anarcho-capitalist society, any different from that which property owners are currently subject to in subordination to the state?

[211] MacCallum (1970), p. 16

## PROPRIETARY GOVERNANCE AND NON-GOVERNMENTAL SOLUTIONS

Without a government, people still cooperate with others. Many relationships, including business relationships, can endure in anarchy. For this, mechanisms other than governmental solutions are possible. Think for example of reputation mechanisms and community membership conditional on conduct, such as in religious communities and guilds. Since we are evolved to care about our families, cooperating with family members can solve principal-agent problems without allocating rights, which need enforcement. And even friendship and the fear of retribution from a god can facilitate cooperation. Clearly, there are many mechanisms other than enforcement to encourage congruous action. Moreover, non-governmental administrative entrepreneurship has also has been shown to be effective in regulating human behaviour. However, this does not mean that these mechanisms together are better for prosperity than an arrangement wherein a government enforces rights and regulates society.

Under some degree of proprietary democracy, a proprietary government obtains the best terms it can get by allowing and facilitating non-governmental regulation when this best satisfies the preferences of its subjects.[212] If non-governmental security agencies are better at providing enforcement, it will be most gainful for a proprietary government to allow them to do so. If non-governmental administrative entrepreneurship, as described by Stringham and others[213], better facilitates economic cooperation, it will be most gainful for a proprietary government not to crowd it out. To the extent that government regulation and enforcement creates results in more prosperity than anarchy does, the government maximises profits by fulfilling its roles. Insofar as anarchy results in more prosperity, the government gains by withdrawing from its role as regulator and enforcer. Proprietary governance thus embraces non-gov-

[212] This was explained in Section 9.3.

[213] Stringham (2015). And see for example Leeson, (2014).

ernmental solutions when they are superior. When put into practice, proprietary governance will show the extent to which government involvement is efficient.

## PROPRIETARIANISM IS POLICY AGNOSTIC

Proprietarianism is not a political ideology, or at least not one like any other, because it does not involve any policy positions. Just as a phone buyer typically has no opinion on how phones should be made and a shopper has no opinion on how a shopping centre should be built, a proprietarian has no opinion on what laws and policies a government should have. How governments should govern is up to themselves. A proprietarian seeks to improve institutions at the margin, not to change policies by winning elections or conducting political campaigns. What matters is that private enterprise is free to compete with public enterprise, because private enterprise results in the most efficiently produced goods and services best adapted to our preferences. Proprietarians apply that truth to governance, and seek to give private enterprise a chance to compete in that field as well. In that sense, the proprietary state is the ultimate form of capitalism. Proprietarianism takes capitalism to its extreme not by abolishing the state, but by privatising it.

Moreover, proprietarians do not need to win any elections. Incumbent politicians can be mobilised in favour of privatisation. There should therefore be no proprietarian political parties or campaigns. In fact, proprietarian campaigns can draw unwanted attention to the privatisation of jurisdictions, which could frustrate the privatisation effort.

## CONCLUSION

I hope to have convinced anarcho-capitalists and libertarians that governance, possibly involving coercion and based on rights of government that can include a right to superior force, is something that people consent to. It is a legitimate business essential to modern prosperity. Governance involves enforcement as well as other tasks, including possibly invasive regulation. The criticism of governments that has come from anarchists and libertarians is often well-founded. However, as this book has explained, virtually all the problems that libertarians and anarcho-capitalists claim are inherent in any government are only inherent in the representative system. A proprietary government, on the other hand, will be careful to operate efficiently and not to over-regulate. Unless proprietary democracy is completely absent, which it is unlikely to ever be, privatising jurisdictions will solve many of the problems that libertarians and anarcho-capitalists have addressed. With this book, I hope to have convinced many of them to no longer consider themselves as libertarians or anarcho-capitalists, but proprietarians[214], or better still, *proprietary democrats.*

214 Merriam-Webster defines a proprietarian as 'an advocate of proprietary government'. See 'proprietarian' (Merriam-Webster Dictionary), in the reference section.

# AFTERWORD

The origins of this book lie somewhere in 2019 in a small student dorm room. In those days, I had many long, discursive phone calls with my best friend at the time, a gifted Indian immigrant from North London. It was the time of the SPAC (Special Purpose Acquisition Company) hype. A SPAC is a company without operations, in which shares are sold on the stock market for the sole purpose of acquiring or merging with another company. Our conversations were often very unserious, and when talking about SPACs I asked him what he thought would happen if someone tried to start one not to take over a company, but a country. In theory, a company could raise capital on the public markets to assemble a private army and use this army to conquer a country. That country would then be made more productive, such that the investors could be rewarded out of tax revenue. A country like Cuba, for example, could thereby be made much more prosperous. There was actually a good argument for it – The people, made more productive by better governance, could thereby be made better off and contribute more in taxes. A win-win for both the people and their new government. Later, my friend asked hedge fund manager Bill Ackman what he thought of this idea. Ackman jokingly replied that it would be the greatest corporate raid of all time.

This was of course only a jocular thought experiment, but it made me ask myself an important question. That is, why are governments not shareholder corporations pursuing profit? If for-profit proprietary companies are more efficient in all other markets, why not in the market for governance? A quite obvious answer was that subordination is not necessarily voluntary. Other entrepreneurs usually cannot force people to be their customers, but a government can keep its subjects captive. However, if the rule of law can prevent representative governments from doing so, it could in theory also prevent a proprietary government from doing so. The more I thought about this question, the more obvious it seemed to me that the role of government could well be fulfilled by proprietary corporations. In important ways, the interests of a proprietary government align with those of its subjects. But do they always? If not, can their interests be aligned? And how?

After asking myself these questions, I came to a number of insights. At their core is the idea of consumer sovereignty. An important criterion for proprietary governance is the extent to which there is consumer sovereignty over a proprietary government, i.e. the extent to which it maximises profits by maximising the value it creates for its subjects. Since the economic system under consumer sovereignty can be described as a democracy in which the consumer is in control, we could call consumer sovereignty over proprietary governments proprietary democracy. This term would be appropriate in the context of government and points to the fact that proprietary governance can be democratic in another way.

Based on these thoughts, I then wrote an article, called 'Proprietary Democracy: A Better Form of Government', which was published on the website of what was then called the Free Private Cities Foundation. Later, after I saw its flaws and withdrew it from their website, I continued to improve and expand it. When a coherent theory had formed in my mind, I decided to turn it into a book.

## FROM THEORY TO THEORY

My first intention for this book was to find out under what conditions there would be consumer sovereignty over governments. Unsatisfied with my initial answers, this led me to reconsider some foundational ideas in economics, or rather praxeology. Crucially, the focus of praxeology should not be on exchange or trade, but on cooperation. Starting from the definition of cooperation, I derived a theory that explains the nature and necessity of contract, rights, enforcement and the state. This new foundational theory also points to the nature and importance of private property as alienable property, the possibility of a proprietary government and its distinguishing features, and has resulted in a theory of entrepreneurship and consumer sovereignty that differs in important ways from common doctrine in the Austrian School. I have also addressed the theory of Heath and Heath MacCallum, and hope to have contributed to the field of public choice by explaining that the problems of public choice stem from the cooperative nature of an organisation. Crucially, therefore, these problems do not exist in the proprietary system and are not inherent in governments, but in cooperative organisations under certain circumstances.

This book therefore covers a wide range of areas. I hope to have made valuable contributions to all of them. I have challenged some of the most accepted ideas in economics by introducing new points of view, including the following.

First, I believe that knowledge in the field of economics, or in fact praxeology, can be improved by framing things in terms of cooperation. Cooperation is a broader and more definite category of actions than trade or exchange. Studying the intrinsic characteristics of cooperation will therefore yield knowledge about a much wider range of actions. In this book, it has provided insights into the nature of contract, rights, enforcement, and governments, why they exist and why they are absolutely necessary for a prosperous society. It has also provided important insights into entrepreneurship and consumer sovereignty. As explained in Chapter 7, consumer sovereignty is limited and can be enhanced by governments. I encourage others to extend my work and use the cooperative framework to gain further insights.

Second, the Coase Theorem is flawed because there are more conditions that must be satisfied for contracting to eliminate problems of externalities. The absence of transaction costs is necessary but not sufficient. It must also be possible to contract flawlessly and to enforce rights perfectly. Moreover, instead of costless contracting, there may also be complete information. And if these conditions are satisfied, not only can problems of externalities be eliminated, but all Pareto inefficient courses of action.

Third, the role of a government is not to ensure 'voluntary transactions'. Voluntariness, while widely supported, is not important. What matters is that actions are congruous with the rights that have been granted, and that rearrangements of rights are consensual.

Fourth, the problems of public choice have been explained to stem from the cooperative nature of organisations. There is nothing inherent in a government that creates public choice problems. Private property has in this book been explained to be distinguished by its alienability, and public choice problems stem from the absence of private property in organisations, under certain conditions.

Fifth, the now increasingly popular theory of Heath and Heath MacCallum is critically flawed. However, pointing out the critical flaw in their theory supports the idea of the proprietary government. By solving the diseconomies of scale in Heathian proprietary administration, we arrive at a proprietary government.

## THE IMPORTANCE AND SHORTCOMINGS OF PROPRIETARY DEMOCRACY

At its core, this book explains that privatising jurisdictions can bring great benefits, but only if it is done properly. It can also be done poorly, which could lead to grave abuses. In the unlikely case that a proprietary government ruthlessly maximises profit, is unrestricted in the rights it can claim and that the terms it can get from subjects are completely independent of the terms it gives in return, it will not treat its subjects like customers, but like cattle. The logical, material consequences of this could be rather grim. One could imagine that such a government would turn the unproductive into biodiesel[215] and force the rest to work as much as they can bear. Its jurisdiction would look less like Dubai and more like George Orwell's Animal Farm.

But this seems to be a very unlikely outcome. There will probably always be some degree of proprietary democracy, under which a proprietary government provides many benefits that other types of government do not. Exceptions to proprietary democracy are likely, however, and allow a government to benefit at the expense of its subjects. It is the responsibility of those involved in the privatisation of jurisdictions to ensure that measures are taken in favour of proprietary democracy.

Even if there were no exceptions to proprietary democracy, and a government therefore could not benefit in ways that come at the expense of its subjects, it would still have relative weaknesses. In a utilitarian sense, non-proprietary systems have benefits that proprietary systems do not. For these systems to still provide their unique benefits, proprietary governments must be embedded in hybrid sys-

215 An idea once thought of by Mencius Moldbug. See Chapter 2 of Mencius Moldbug (2008).

tems. In this way, the benefits of non-proprietary systems, such as the welfare state, can be preserved.

## THE TIME IS RIPE

We can expect strong opposition to proprietary governance, but given the benefits explained in this book, the case for it is strong. The time is ripe to start privatising jurisdictions. Not only can it bring great benefits, it can also help us deal with the problems of today, such as uncontrolled immigration. Importantly, privatising jurisdictions can especially benefit poor countries. The more desperate the country, the greater the willingness to experiment with new institutions. They have more to gain from privatising jurisdictions and have less to lose. Their institutions also lend themselves better for privatisation. The ZEDEs in Honduras attest to the growing interest in this field. If these projects succeed, they can set an example for other countries to follow. Regions like Central America, historically plagued by weak governments and corrupt institutions, could become as prosperous as the developed world.

Proprietary governance could lift millions, if not billions, out of poverty. Those who are practically involved in this field should ensure that it maximises human prosperity. To inspire more countries to facilitate proprietary governance, it is important to take measures that promote proprietary democracy and to recognise its shortcomings, such that government systems are created in which proprietary governments deliver their unique benefits while other kinds of governments do as well.

## A CALL TO ACTION

For decades, libertarians have tried to liberalise governance, but to no avail. As Peter Thiel once observed, the goals of libertarians cannot be achieved in a democratic system.[216] Libertarians are currently

216 '...I no longer believe that freedom and democracy are compatible' Thiel (2009).

fighting a battle they cannot win. As this book explains, they are in some ways wrong about the government and its role in society, partly because they mistakenly attribute many problems to the government as such, rather than to the representative system. The proprietary state, however, provides an answer to these problems. It is viable and will have an appropriate role in society as opposed to the representative state. I thus hope to have converted many libertarians, as well as anarcho-capitalists, to proprietarianism.

Proprietarianism is not only correct, it also stands a chance. And not merely a small one. Whereas representative jurisdictions are difficult to liberalise, they are much easier to privatise. Proprietarians do not need to win any elections to succeed[217], they only need to align powerful interests with the privatisation of jurisdictions. Incumbent politicians and elites have strong political and economic interests in privatising parts of their jurisdictions and can be given such interests if necessary. Powerful individuals can thus be mobilised to support our cause. Competing *within* the representative system is a dead end, but we have the advantage if we choose to compete *with* it. Opposing political movements, from social democrats to nationalists and socialists, can only lose in this competition. They may have the advantage in democratic politics, but will be fighting an uphill battle against the proprietarians. Libertarians will be happy with the result as well.

To deal with the exceptions to and shortcomings of proprietary democracy, proprietary governments may have to be submerged in hybrid systems. As a result, some of the benefits of proprietary governance may be difficult to realise. Libertarians should still support it, however, because institutions can thereby still be improved at the margin. Moreover, once jurisdictions are to some extent privatised and a proprietary government sector has emerged, forces will have been set in motion to expand their policy discretion and perhaps

[217] Nor do proprietarians need to settle on the seas, such as the seasteading movement tries to do, or on unclaimed territory as the Liberlanders (after many other groups in modern history) try to do. Proprietarians do not need to find a way to build an advanced society on floating platforms, nor do they need to fend off any country's border police.

even to give them sovereignty in some places. This, in turn, will give the most lucrative taxpayers more low-tax jurisdictions to move to, forcing legacy systems consider privatising their jurisdictions as well. Through this positive feedback loop, the privatisation of jurisdictions in desperate countries can lead to the privatisation of jurisdictions in the developed world. It is clear, then, where we should begin our efforts.

While the libertarian project has failed thus far, the proprietarian project has all the potential to succeed. Libertarians who have not become proprietarians will also be pleased with the results.

We have found a new route to liberty. We can leave the old world behind and create a new one, like the first proprietarians did centuries ago. Board the ship and hoist the sails, the wind is favourable!

# REFERENCES


*'Government.'.* (n.d.). Retrieved November 9, 2022., from Merriam-Webster.com Dictionary: https://www.merriam-webster.com/dictionary/government

*'Proprietarian.'.* (n.d.). Retrieved September 21, 2023, from Merriam-Webster.com Dictionary: https://www.merriam-webster.com/dictionary/proprietarian

*'Proprietarianism.'.* (n.d.). Retrieved September 30, 2023, from Wiktionary.org: https://en.wiktionary.org/wiki/proprietarianism

*'Proprietary.'.* (n.d.). Retrieved November 9, 2022, from Merriam-Webster.com Dictionary: https://www.merriam-webster.com/dictionary/proprietary

(1965). In *Restatement (Second) of Torts.* St. Paul, Minnesota, U.S.A.: American Law Institute Publishers.

Acosta-Ormaechea, S., Sola, S., & Yoo, J. (2019). Tax Composition and Growth: A Broad Cross-country Perspective. *German Econ Rev*, 20: e70-e106. Retrieved from https://doi.org/10.1111/geer.12156

Alchian, A. A. (1965). SOME ECONOMICS OF PROPERTY RIGHTS. *Il Politico, 30*(4), 816–829. Retrieved from http://www.jstor.org/stable/43206327

Allen, D. W. (1991). What Are Transaction Costs? *Research in Law and Economics, 14*, 1-18. Retrieved from https://ssrn.com/abstract=3882114

American assembly's address to the governor on 8 December 1759. (1775). In I. Pemberton, & J. Pemberton, *Votes and proceedings of the House of Representatives of the Province of Pennsylvania* (Vols. 5. Oct. 14, 1758-Sept. 26, 1767). Philadephia, United States: Printed and sold by Henry Miller in Race-Street.

An Anthology of Henry George's Thought: Volume I of the Henry George Centennial Trilogy. (1997). In K. C. Wenzer (Ed.), *Volume 1 of the Henry George Centennial Trilogy.* University of Rochester Press.

*An Introduction to Charter Cities.* (n.d.). Retrieved March 18, 2023, from Charter Cities Institute: https://www.chartercitiesinstitute.org/intro

*Archive.org: zede.hn.* (n.d.). Retrieved August 19, 2023, from Internet Archive: https://web.archive.org/web/20200803154114/https://www.zede.hn/

Arnold, J. M., Brys, B., Heady, C., Johansson, Å., Schwellnus, C., & Vartia, L. (2011). Tax Policy for Economic Recovery and Growth. *The Economic Journal*, 121: F59-F80. Retrieved from https://doi.org/10.1111/j.1468-0297.2010.02415.x

Augeron, M., & Vidal, L. (2007). "Chapter One. Creating Colonial Brazil: The First Donatary Captaincies, Or The System Of Private Exclusivity (1534–1549)". In L. H. Roper, & B. Van Ruymbeke (Eds.), *Constructing Early Modern Empires: Proprietary Ventures in the Atlantic World, 1500-1750.* Leiden, The Netherlands: Brill. Retrieved from https://doi.org/10.1163/ej.9789004156760.i-425.6

Banks, K. J. (2007). "Chapter Three. Financiers, Factors, And French Proprietary Companies In West Africa, 1673–1713". In L. H. Roper, & B. Van Ruymbeke (Eds.), *Constructing Early Modern Empires: Proprietary Ventures in the Atlantic World, 1500-1750.* Leiden, The Netherlands: Brill. Retrieved from https://doi.org/10.1163/ej.9789004156760.i-425.17

Bastiat, F. (1848, September 25). L'État. *Journal des Débats*, p. 1, col. 5. Retrieved August 11, 2023, from https://gallica.bnf.fr/ark:/12148/bpt6k448145j/f2.item.zoom

Basu, K. (2018). Methodological individualism. In G. e. Jones, *The new Palgrave dictionary of economics, 3rd ed., vol. 13* (pp. 8715-8720). London: Palgrave Macmillan.

Bell, T. W. (2011, September 1). Graduated Consent in Contract and Tort Law: Toward a Theory of Justification. *Case Western Reserve Law Review, 61*(1). Retrieved from https://ssrn.com/abstract=2011428

Bell, T. W. (2017). *Your Next Government?: From Nation States to Stateless Nations.* Cambridge: Cambridge University Press. doi:10.1017/9781316676387.017

Bergson, A., Wellisz, S., & Baumol, W. J. (1962). Discussion. *The American Economic Review, 52*(2), 284-290. Retrieved from http://www.jstor.org/stable/1910893

Boucher, P. (2007). "Chapter Six. French Proprietary Colonies In The Greater Caribbean, 1620s–1670s". In L. H. Roper, & B. Van Ruymbeke (Eds.), *Constructing Early Modern Empires: Proprietary Ventures in the Atlantic World, 1500-1750.* Leiden, The Netherlands: Brill. Retrieved from https://doi.org/10.1163/ej.9789004156760.i-425.20

Brodhead, J. R. (1856). *Documents Relative to the Colonial History of New-York.* Albany: Weed, Parsons and Company, printers. Retrieved March 15, 2023, from https://archive.org/details/documentsrelativ01brod/page/n9/mode/2up?view=theater

Brown, S. R. (2009). *Merchant Kings: When Companies Ruled the World, 1600-1900.* Madeira Park, Canada: D & M Publishers.

Burke, W., Eidous, M., & Burke, E. (1767). *Histoire des colonies européennes dans l'Amérique.* France: Merlin.

Calvin Duke. (2020). *Entrepreneurial Communities: An Alternative to the State.* self-published through Book Villages Publishers.

Caplan, B. (2001). Rational Ignorance versus Rational Irrationality. *Kyklos, 54*, 3-26. Retrieved from https://doi.org/10.1111/1467-6435.00138

Caplan, B. (2003). The Logic of Collective Belief. *Rationality and Society, 15*(2), pp. 218-242. Retrieved from https://doi.org/10.1177/1043463103015002003

Castle-Miller, M. (2018). The Law and Policy of Refugee Cities: Special Economic Zones for Migrants. *Chapman Law Review, 21*(2), 313-315. Retrieved from https://ssrn.com/abstract=3212930

Choquette, L. (2007). "Chapter Four. Proprietorships In French North America". In L. H. Roper, & B. Van Ruymbeke (Eds.), *Constructing Early Modern Empires: Proprietary Ventures in the Atlantic World, 1500-1750.* Leiden, The Netherlands: Brill. Retrieved from https://doi.org/10.1163/ej.9789004156760.i-425.18

Churchill, W. S. (1909, July 17). *The Mother of All Monopolies (from a speech delivered at the King's Theatre in Edinburgh on 17 July 1909).* Retrieved January 24, 2023, from cooperative-individualism.org: https://www.cooperative-individualism.org/churchill-winston_mother-of-all-monopolies-1909.htm

Clemens, M., Montenegro, C. E., & Pritchett, L. (2016, June 28). *Bounding the Price Equivalent of Migration Barriers - Working Paper 428.* Retrieved from Center for Global Development: https://www.cgdev.org/publication/bounding-price-equivalent

Clemens, M., Montenegro, C., & Pritchett, L. (2008). *The Place Premium: Wage Differences for Identical Workers across the U.S. Border.* Retrieved from Center for Global Development: http://www.cgdev.org/content/publications/detail/16352

Cleppe, P. (2016, July 28). "Startup cities" for refugees: a long-term solution to the migration crisis? *CAPX.* Retrieved from https://capx.co/start-up-cities-for-refugees-a-long-term-solution-to-the-refugee-crisis/

Coase, R. H. (1960). The Problem of Social Cost. *The Journal of Law & Economics, 3,* 1–44. Retrieved from http://www.jstor.org/stable/724810

*coercion.* (n.d.). Retrieved December 13, 2022, from Cambridge Dictionary: https://dictionary.cambridge.org/dictionary/english/coercion

*Democratic Peace Theory.* (n.d.). Retrieved February 28, 2023, from Wikipedia.org: https://en.wikipedia.org/wiki/Democratic_peace_theory

Doucet, L. (2021a, December 9). Does Georgism Work? Part 1: Is Land A Really Big Deal? *Astral Codex Ten.* Retrieved February 24, 2023, from https://astralcodexten.substack.com/p/does-georgism-work-is-land-really

Doucet, L. (2021b, December 11). Does Georgism Work, Part 3: Can Unimproved Land Value be Accurately Assessed Separately From Buildings? *Astral Codex Ten*. Retrieved January 24, 2023, from https://astralcodexten.substack.com/p/does-georgism-work-part-3-can-unimproved?utm_source=url

*East India Company and Raj 1785-1858.* (n.d.). Retrieved August 18, 2023, from UK Parliament: https://www.parliament.uk/

*Economy of Dubai.* (n.d.). Retrieved from Wikipedia.org: https://en.wikipedia.org/wiki/Economy_of_Dubai

Fabius, G. J. (1915). HET LEENSTELSEL VAN DE WESTINDISCHE COMPAGNIE. *Bijdragen Tot de Taal-, Land- En Volkenkunde van Nederlandsch-Indië, 70*(3/4), 555–594. Retrieved from http://www.jstor.org/stable/20769789

Ferrari, F. (2021, January 19). *Understanding the Action Axiom.* Retrieved August 8, 2023, from mises.org: https://mises.org/power-market/understanding-action-axiom

Fetter, F. A. (1905). *The Principles of Economics with Applications to Practical Problems.* New York: The Century Co.

Foldvary, F. (2014). Reply to the Caplan and Gochenour critique of Georgism. *The Review of Austrian Economics, 27*(4), 451-461. Retrieved from https://ideas.repec.org/a/kap/revaec/v27y2014i4p451-461.html

Franklin, B. (1779 [originally published as a pamphlet on 11 August 1764]). Preface to Mr. Galloway's Speech. In B. Franklin, & B. Vaughan, *Political, Miscellaneous, and Philosophical Pieces* (pp. 418-464). United Kingdom: J. Johnson.

Friedman, D. D. (1979). Private Creation and Enforcement of Law: A Historical Case. *The Journal of Legal Studies, 8*(2), 399–415. Retrieved from http://www.jstor.org/stable/724116

Friedman, D. D. (2023, January 4). A Problem With Georgism. *Ideas*. Retrieved January 24, 2023, from http://daviddfriedman.blogspot.com/2023/01/a-problem-with-georgism.html

Frost, J. (1800). *The Pictorial History of America: From the Discovery by the Northmen in the Tenth Century.* United Kingdom: Willoughby.

Gebel, T. (2018). *Free Private Cities: Making Governments Compete For You.* self-published.

Gebel, T. (2023, January). Free Private Cities Whitepaper. Retrieved March 26, 2023, from https://free-cities.org/free-private-cities-whitepaper/

Gochenour, Z., & Caplan, B. D. (2012, February 14). A Search-Theoretic Critique of Georgism. Retrieved from https://ssrn.com/abstract=1999105

Grossman, S. J., & Hart, O. D. (1986). The Costs and Benefits of Ownership: A Theory of Vertical and Lateral Integration. *Journal of Political Economy, 94*(4), 691-719.

Hansmann, H. (1996). *The Ownership of Enterprise.* Harvard University Press. Retrieved from https://doi.org/10.2307/j.ctv1pncrw1

Hardoon, D., & Heinrich, F. (2011). *Bribe Payers Index 2011.* Berlin: Transparency International Secretariat. Retrieved February 24, 2023, from https://issuu.com/transparencyinternational/docs/bribe_payers_index_2011

Hayek, F. A. (1958 [1948]). *Individualism and Economic Order.* Chicago, Illinois, U.S.A.: The University of Chicago Press.

Hayek, F. A. (1960). *The Constitution of Liberty.* Chicago: University of Chicago Press.

Hayek, F. A. (1961). The Non Sequitur of the 'Dependence Effect'. *The Non Sequitur of the 'Dependence Effect', Southern Economic Journal, 27*(4), 346-348. Retrieved from https://www.jstor.org/stable/1055533

Hayes, A. (n.d.). *Organization of the Petroleum Exporting Countries (OPEC).* Retrieved August 18, 2023, from Investopedia.com: https://www.investopedia.com/terms/o/opec.asp

Heath, S. (1933). *Politics Versus Proprietorship.*

Heath, S. (2021 [1957]). *Citadel, Market and Altar: Scholar's Edition.* (F. Litvay, J. Brand, & C. Boehr, Eds.)

Hooper, C. (1993). Henry George. In D. R. Henderson (Ed.), *The Fortune Encyclopedea in Economics* (pp. 789-790). New York: Warner.

Hoover Institution: Friedman, Milton. "Is Tax Reform Possible?" Milton Friedman Speaks. Address given at the Americanism Educational League 51st Anniversary Dinner, Pasadena, CA. (1978, February 6).

Hutt, W. H. (1940). The Concept of Consumers' Sovereignty. *The Economic Journal, 50*(197), 66-77. Retrieved from https://doi.org/10.2307/2225739

Jacobs, J. (2007). "Chapter Ten. Dutch Proprietary Manors In America: The Patroonships In New Netherland". In L. H. Roper, & B. Van Ruymbeke (Eds.), *Constructing Early Modern Empires: Proprietary Ventures in the Atlantic World, 1500-1750.* Leiden, The Netherlands: Brill. Retrieved from https://doi.org/10.1163/ej.9789004156

Janse, A. (n.d.). 'Een in zichzelf verdeeld rijk'. In *Geschiedenis van Holland (Deel 1: tot 1572).*

Johansson, Å., Heady, C., Arnold, J. M., Brys, B., & Vartia, L. (2008). Taxation and Economic Growth. *OECD Economics Department Working Papers, No. 620.* Retrieved from https://doi.org/10.1787/241216205486

John Smoke. (2021). The Charity-Industrial Complex. Retrieved August 13, 2023, from https://im1776.com/2021/11/16/lets-be-uncharitable/

*Jurisdiction.* (n.d.). Retrieved March 28, 2023, from Cambridge Dictionary: https://dictionary.cambridge.org/dictionary/english/jurisdiction

Kerpestein, G. A. (2022, February 14). Architecture and Evolution: VIII. The Value of Beauty and How to Profit From It. *Casual Realism.* Retrieved January 24, 2023, from https://casualrealism.substack.com/p/architecture-and-evolution-viii-the?utm_source=profile&utm_medium=reader2

Kirzner, I. M. (1973). *Competition and Entrepreneurship.* Chicago, U.S.A.: University of Chicago Press.

Kirzner, I. M. (2011 [1963]). *Market Theory and the Price System.* Indianapolis, Indiana, U.S.A.: Liberty Fund Inc.

Klein, B., Crawford, R. G., & Alchian, A. A. (1978). Vertical Integration, Appropriable Rents, and the Competitive Contracting Process. *The Journal of Law & Economics, 21*(2), 297–326. Retrieved from http://www.jstor.org/stable/725234

Knight, F. H. (1924). Some Fallacies in the Interpretation of Social Cost. *The Quarterly Journal of Economics, 38*(4), 582-606.

Knight, F. H. (1933). Review of The Philosophy of Henry George, by George R. Geiger. *Journal of Political Economy, 41.*

Knight, F. H. (1948 [1921]). *Risk, Uncertainty, and Profit.* London: Lund Humphries.

Knight, F. H. (1953, August 10). The Fallacies in the Single Tax. *Freeman.*

Leeson, P. T. (2007). Efficient Anarchy. *Public Choice, 130,* 41-53. Retrieved from https://doi.org/10.1007/s11127-006-9071-7

Leeson, P. T. (2014). *Anarchy Unbound: Why Self-Governance Works Better Than You Think.* Cambridge: Cambridge University Press. Retrieved from https://doi.org/10.1017/CBO9781139198813

Long, R. T. (2008). Wittgenstein, Austrian Economics and the Logic of Action: Praxeological Investigations. *Psychology Press,* p. 3 footnote 5. Retrieved August 8, 2023, from https://praxeology.net/wiggy-draft.pdf

*Lord of the Manor – Lordship Rights in Law.* (n.d.). Retrieved April 24, 2024, from Manorial Counsel: https://manorialcounselltd.co.uk/lord-of-the-manor-lordship-rights-in-law/

Lukes, S. M. (n.d.). *Individualism.* Retrieved February 11, 2023, from britannica.com: https://www.britannica.com/topic/individualism

MacCallum, S. (1970). *The Art of Community.* Menlo Park, California: Institute for Humane Studies.

MacCallum, S. (1997). The Quickening of Social Evolution: Perspectives on Proprietary (Entrepreneurial) Communities. *The Independent Review, 2*(2), 287–302. Retrieved from http://www.jstor.org/stable/24560772

MacCallum, S. (2003). 12. The Entrepreneurial Community in Light of Advancing Business Practices and Technologies. In F. Foldvary, & D. Klein (Eds.), *The Half-Life of Policy Rationales: How New Technology Affects Old Policy Issues* (pp. ccxxxviii-ccliii). New York, USA: New York University Press. Retrieved from https://doi.org/10.18574/nyu/9780814729243.003.0016

Mencius Moldbug. (2008, November 13). Patchwork: A Political System for the 21st Century. *Unqualified Reservations.* Retrieved March 5, 2023, from https://www.unqualified-reservations.org/2008/11/patchwork-positive-vision-part-1/

Menger, C. (1985 [1883]). *Investigations into the Method of the Social Sciences with special reference to Economics.* (F J. Nock, Trans.) New York: New York University Press.

Merriam-Webster (Ed.). (n.d.). *Coerce.* Retrieved September 30, 2023, from Merriam-Webster.com Dictionary: https://www.merriam-webster.com/dictionary/coerce

Merriam-Webster (Ed.). (n.d.). *Voluntary.* Retrieved September 30, 2023, from Merriam-Webster.com Dictionary: https://www.merriam-webster.com/dictionary/voluntary

Mill, J. S. (1844). On the Definition of Political Economy; and on the Method of Investigation Proper To It. In J. S. Mill, *Essays on Some Unsettled Questions of Political Economy.* London: John W. Parker.

Moberg, L. (2017). *The Political Economy of Special Economic Zones: Concentrating Economic Development* (1 ed.). Routledge. Retrieved from https://doi.org/10.4324/9781315298955

Moore, M. S. (2017, May 3). This Land is Your Land. *Pacific Standard.* Retrieved February 24, 2023, from https://psmag.com/news/this-land-is-your-land-3392

North, D. C. (1991). Institutions. *The Journal of Economic Perspectives, 5*(1), 97-112. Retrieved from http://www.jstor.org/stable/1942704

North, D. C. (2003, June 30). The Effect of Institutions on Market Performance (lecture given at the United States Federal Communications Commission).

North, D. C., & Weingast, B. R. (1989). Constitutions and Commitment: The Evolution of Institutions Governing Public Choice in Seventeenth-Century England. *The Journal of Economic History, 49*(4), 803-832. doi:10.1017/S0022050700009451

Olson, M. (1993). Dictatorship, Democracy, and Development. *The American Political Science Review, 87*(3), 567–576. Retrieved from https://doi.org/10.2307/2938736

Olson, M. (2000). *Power and Prosperity: Outgrowing Communist and Capitalist Dictatorships.* New York, U.S.A.: Basic Books.

Osgood, H. L. (1896a). The Corporation as a Form of Colonial Government. I. *Political Science Quarterly, 11*(2), 259–277. Retrieved from https://doi.org/10.2307/2139807

Osgood, H. L. (1896b). The Corporation as a Form of Colonial Government. II. *Political Science Quarterly, 11*(3), 502–533. Retrieved from https://doi.org/10.2307/2139935

Osgood, H. L. (1896c). The Corporation as a Form of Colonial Government. III. *Political Science Quarterly, 11*(4), 694–715. Retrieved from https://doi.org/10.2307/2139624

Osgood, H. L. (1897). The Proprietary Province as a Form of Colonial Government. *The American Historical Review, 2*(4), 644–664. Retrieved from https://doi.org/10.2307/1833981

Osgood, H. L. (1904). *The American Colonies in the Seventeenth Century, Volume I: The Chartered Colonies, Beginnings of Self-Government.* New York: The Macmillan Company.

Ostrom, V., Tiebout, C. M., & Warren, R. (1961). The Organization of Government in Metropolitan Areas: A Theoretical Inquiry. *The American Political Science Review, 55*(4), 831–842. Retrieved from https://doi.org/10.2307/1952530

Petit, E. (1771). *Droit public, ou, Gouvernement des colonies françoises: d'après les loix faites pour ces pays.* Canada: Chez Delalain, libraire.

Phillips, A., & Sharman, J. C. (2015). *International Order in Diversity: War, Trade and Rule in the Indian Ocean.* New York: Cambridge University Press.

Pritchett, L. (2018, March). *Alleviating Global Poverty: Labor Mobility, Direct Assistance, and Economic Growth - working paper 479.* Retrieved from Center for Global Development: https://www.cgdev.org/publication/alleviating-global-poverty-labormobility-direct-assistance-and-economic-growth

*Próspera Charter.* (n.d.). Retrieved August 19, 2023, from pac.hn: http://pac.hn/wp-content/uploads/2020/10/Prospera-Legal-Code-TOC-v11.10-Compressed-Protected.pdf

*Rational Ignorance.* (n.d.). Retrieved from Wikipedia: https://en.wikipedia.org/wiki/Rational_ignorance

Reuters. (2022, April 21). Honduras: President announced repeal of the ZEDE Law and classifies it as a violation of national sovereignty. Retrieved from https://www.business-humanrights.org/en/latest-news/honduras-president-announces-repeal-of-the-zede-law-and-classifies-it-as-a-violation-of-national-sovereignty/

Richwine, J. (2023). Savings behavior among immigrants and their U.S.-born children: A test of the culture-transplant model. *Economics Letters*. Retrieved from https://doi.org/10.1016/j.econlet.2023.111279

Robinet, J. B. (1778). *Dictionnaire universel des sciences morale, économique, politique et diplomatique; ou Bibliotheque de l'homme-d'état et du citoyen*. United Kingdom: Chez les libraires associés.

Roper, L. H., & Van Ruymbeke, B. (Eds.). (2007). *Constructing Early Modern Empires: Proprietary Ventures in the Atlantic World, 1500-1750*. Leiden, The Netherlands: Brill. Retrieved from https://doi.org/10.1163/ej.9789004156760.i-425

Salmon, T. (1767). *A New Geographical and Historical Grammar*. United Kingdom: Sands, Murray, and Cochran.

Scott Alexander. (n.d.). 'The Anti-Reactionary FAQ', chapter 2. *Slate Star Codex*.

Scott Alexander. (2021, April 14). Prospectus On Próspera. *Astral Codex Ten*. Retrieved August 19, 2023, from https://astralcodexten.substack.com/p/prospectus-on-prospera

*Seignory*. (n.d.). Retrieved October 7, 2023, from Wikipedia.org: https://en.wikipedia.org/wiki/Seignory

Şen, H., & Kaya, A. (2023). Do revenue-neutral tax swaps boost growth? *Journal of Economic Policy Reform*. doi:10.1080/17487870.2023.2238107

Smith, N., & Cleppe, P. (2015, April 29). Free Havens for Refugees (mostly by Pieter Cleppe). *openborders.info*. Retrieved from https://openborders.info/blog/free-havens-refugees-pieter-cleppe/

Spruyt, H. (1994). *The Sovereign State and Its Competitors: An Analysis of Systems Change*. Princeton, New Jersey, U.S.A.: Princeton University Press. Retrieved from https://doi.org/10.2307/j.ctvzxx91t

Srinivasan, B. (2022). *The Network State: How to Start a New Country*. self-published.

Stringham, E. P. (2015). *Private Governance: Creating Order in Economic and Social Life*. Oxford: Oxford University Press. Retrieved from https://doi.org/10.1093/acprof:oso/9780199365166.001.0001

Thiel, P. (2009, April 13). The Education of a Libertarian. *Cato Unbound.* Retrieved October 2, 2023, from https://www.cato-unbound.org/2009/04/13/peter-thiel/education-libertarian/

Tideman, N. (1994). The Economics of Efficient Taxation on Land. In N. Tideman (Ed.), *Land and Taxation.* London: Shepheard-Walwyn in association with Centre for Incentive Taxation.

van Boven, M. W. (2006). Memory of the World - Archives of the Dutch East India Company: Nomination Form - VOC Archives Appendix 2. Retrieved May 25, 2024, from https://media.unesco.org/sites/default/files/webform/mow001/netherlands_voc_archives.pdf

Vidal, C. (2007). "Chapter Five. French Louisiana In The Age Of The Companies, 1712–1731". In L. H. Roper, & B. Van Ruymbeke (Eds.), *Constructing Early Modern Empires: Proprietary Ventures in the Atlantic World, 1500-1750.* Leiden, The Netherlands: Brill.

von Mises, L. H. (1920). Economic Calculation in the Socialist Commonwealth. In F. A. Hayek (Ed.), *Collectivist Economic Planning* (pp. 87-130). London: George Routledge & Sons, 1935. Retrieved August 18, 2023, from https://mises.org/library/economic-calculation-socialist-commonwealth

von Mises, L. H. (1981, September 1). *Praxeology.* Retrieved from Foundation for Economic Education: https://fee.org/articles/praxeology/

von Mises, L. H. (2007 [1949]). *Human Action: A Treatise on Economics* (4th ed., Vol. Three: Economic Calculation). (B. B. Greaves, Ed.) Indianapolis: Liberty Fund.

Weber, M. (1947). *Theory of Social and Economic Organization.* New York: Oxford University Press.

Wen, H., Zhang, Y., & Zhang, L. (2014). Do educational facilities affect housing price? An empirical study in Hangzhou, China. *Habitat International, 42*, 155-163. Retrieved from https://doi.org/10.1016/j.habitatint.2013.12.004

Wilson, W. (1917, Aprl 2). Address to Congress on April 2, 1917. Sixty-Fifth Congress, 1 Session, Senate Document No. 5.

*ZEDE Organic Law.* (n.d.). Retrieved August 19, 2023, from pzgps.hn: https://pzgps.hn/wp-content/uploads/2019/05/ZEDE-Organic-Law.pdf

*Zone for Employment and Economic Development*. (n.d.). Retrieved August 19, 2023, from Wikipedia.org: https://en.wikipedia.org/wiki/Zone_for_Employment_and_Economic_Development.

# ABOUT THE AUTHOR

Andries Kerpestein is an economist with a special interest in improving institutions. Apart from his work in the special jurisdiction sector, he works to improve institutions in the higher education sector, driven by the conviction that private institutions should play a larger role in these fields. Kerpestein believes that institutions have the power to make or break societies and that reform is urgent.

*book design by chico_maciel*

Printed in Poland
by Amazon Fulfillment
Poland Sp. z o.o., Wrocław

56777676R00193